YOUR STARRY FUTURE!

Sydney Omarr, America's most accurate astrologer, will help you make 1990 the year you turn all your dreams into realities. Whatever aspect of your future intrigues you—romance, health, career opportunities, finances—his sound advice will counsel you through a year of heavenly possibilities.

This expert astrologer's time-tested wisdom shows you how all you desire can be yours if you look to the stars for guidance. You'll learn all about the key numbers in your life, the days that are most favorable to your goals, and all the other important information you need to chart your way to happiness in 1990—the very first year of the 20th-century's last decade!

SYDNEY OMARR'S

DAY-BY-DAY ASTROLOGICAL GUIDE FOR

LIBRA

SEPTEMBER 23—OCTOBER 22

1990

A SIGNET BOOK

NEW AMERICAN LIBRARY

A DIVISION OF PENGUIN BOOKS USA INC.

NAL BOOKS ARE AVAILABLE AT QUANTITY DISCOUNTS
WHEN USED TO PROMOTE PRODUCTS OR SERVICES.
FOR INFORMATION PLEASE WRITE TO PREMIUM MARKETING DIVISION,
NEW AMERICAN LIBRARY, 1633 BROADWAY,
NEW YORK, NEW YORK 10019.

Sydney Omarr is syndicated worldwide by Los Angeles Times Syndicate.

SIGNET TRADEMARK REG. U.S. PAT. OFF. AND FOREIGN COUNTRIES
REGISTERED TRADEMARK—MARCA REGISTRADA
HECHO EN DRESDEN, TN

SIGNET, SIGNET CLASSIC, MENTOR, ONYX, PLUME, MERIDIAN AND NAL BOOKS are published by New American Library, a division of Penguin Books USA Inc., 1633 Broadway, New York, New York 10019

First Printing, July, 1989

1 2 3 4 5 6 7 8 9

PRINTED IN THE UNITED STATES OF AMERICA

Contents

	Introduction: Astrology from the Dark Ages to the New Age	*7*
1	**How Much Do You Really Know About Astrology?**	*10*
2	**Eight Planets That Color Your Horoscope**	*21*
3	**Learning About *Your* Personal Universe** *Reading the mysterious language of astrology*	*69*
4	**The Celebrity Astro-Quiz** *Do you know the stars' signs?*	*79*
5	**Using Astrology Every Day** *How to cope with the stressful times in 1990*	*85*
6	**Your Star-Guide for Choosing the Best Partner**	*96*
7	**What and Why You Need to Know About the Moon**	*101*
8	**The Great Debates: Astrology vs. Science and Religion**	*111*
9	**Loving Every Sign in the Zodiac** *All the possible pairs!*	*116*
10	**All About Libra**	*137*
11	**Libra's Rising Signs** *How the moment you were born influences your horoscope*	*141*

12	**Libra Positives and Negatives**	*149*
13	**Your Libra Success Strategy**	*151*
14	**Libra's Place in the Family**	*153*
15	**What Suits Libra Best**	*156*
16	**Libra Astro-Outlook for 1990**	*159*
17	**Fifteen Months of Day-by-Day Predictions**	*161*

Introduction:

Astrology From the Dark Ages to the New Age

As we enter the decade of the 1990s we can look at astrology and say, "What a long way this ancient study has come!" In this century alone, it has emerged from the darkness of disrepute into the light with new respect and more popularity than ever.

Once accessible only to a privileged few, astrology can now be studied by anyone. Astrological textbooks and self-help books like this one are readily available, where once only a small priestly class of intellectuals were given the kind of knowledge you'll find on these pages. Precise tables to help you locate the exact position of your planets and moon sign changes to help you plan your activites according to the current moon sign eliminate hours of pouring through books or doing long complicated calculations. Very often we take for granted the descriptions of each of the sun signs and planets, forgetting that centuries of observation went into the development of the horoscope that we know today.

Astrology has entered the high-tech era with computer programs and nationwide networks of astrologers. Each year, there are astrological conventions, astrology seminars, and lectures attended by thousands of astrology fans. Such a distance from the time in 1914 when astrologers were outlawed as disorderly persons in New York State, thrown into the same category as men who desert their wives, acrobats, and fortunetellers!

Astrology in the nineties has become accessible astrology, ready to apply to many areas of life and studied from many points of view. You could use it every day to help you time routine matters such as planning a vacation or asking for a loan. Or, on a deeper level, you can gain insight into your special place in the cosmos. That is why this ancient art is more popular, relevant, and dynamic today than it was many thousands of years ago.

Astrology has become very much a part of the New Age consciousness, giving each of us practical tools to create our own reality and a real vision of the links between man and the universe. We've learned that through the study of the planets, we can study ourselves, and bring into balance the inner and outer universe.

This puts each of us more in control over our life's events than we may have thought possible, as we learn to recognize the guideposts, warning signals, green lights and stop signs clearly visible in the heavens. And that is the purpose of our 1990 guide, to help put *you* clearly at the helm.

This year's edition aims to get you up and running with astrology. It's for people who want to learn more about themselves and the world at large by applying astrological principles to their lives. You'll actually learn how to do your own estimated chart, what those mysterious symbols mean and how your sun sign evolved its meaning. You'll learn that nothing in astrology happened by accident or hocus-pocus.

"To everything there is a season, and a time to every purpose unto Heaven," goes the familiar Biblical saying. We go even further to help you pinpoint the perfect time and prepare in advance for problems. For instance, if you must make a business trip during a time when you know Mercury will be going retrograde, you'll be prepared for delays or possible mechanical and communications breakdowns. You'll learn why it's better to ask for a raise when the moon is passing through Leo, rather than put it off until the next day when the moon is in Virgo. And when it comes to choosing a partner in business or in love, astrology gives you guidelines for compatibility that have held true for centuries.

You'll not only learn all about your sun sign, but also about the nine other planets in your horoscope. And our easy-to-follow quiz format is a fun way to test your basic knowledge and answer those puzzling questions. You can then sharpen your powers of observation with the celebrity astro-types quiz.

Let this guide help you make this a year of growth and prosperity by reading the message in the stars for you in 1990!

1

How Much Do You Really Know About Astrology?

Here's a chance to test your knowledge of the fundamentals of astrology and clear up a few misunderstandings. For those who are just beginning to study astrology or who are curious about the whys behind some of the astrological principles, let the answers become your introductory lessons.

1. True or false: To do an accurate horoscope, all an astrologer needs to know about you is the day you were born.

2. True or false: An astrologer should have psychic abilities.

3. True or false: Your rising sign is directly overhead.

4. What does the word "Zodiac" mean?

5. What is the difference between a sign, a constellation, and a "house"?

6. An astrology chart most resembles . . . a checkerboard, a bar graph, or a pizza pie?

7. True or false: An Aquarius is someone who was born when the sun was in the constellation of Aquarius.

8. True or false: Men like Newton, Galileo, Thomas Jefferson, and Ben Franklin knew nothing about astrology.

9. Where in astrology would you look to learn about a person's emotional life?

10. Identify the *elements* of the following signs: Sagittarius, Virgo, Cancer, Aquarius.

11. What do we mean by the element, quality, and polarity, of a sign?

12. What is the difference between a sun sign and an air sign?

13. How are the elements, qualities, and polarities of the signs placed in sequence?

14. Fill in the blanks for each astrological sign as in the Aries and Taurus examples.

	Element	**Quality**	**Polarity**
ARIES	Fire	Cardinal	Masculine
TAURUS	Earth	Fixed	Feminine
GEMINI	_____	_____	_____
CANCER	_____	_____	_____
LEO	_____	_____	_____
VIRGO	_____	_____	_____
LIBRA	_____	_____	_____
SCORPIO	_____	_____	_____
SAGITTARIUS	_____	_____	_____
CAPRICORN	_____	_____	_____
AQUARIUS	_____	_____	_____
PISCES	_____	_____	_____

15. Mercury, Venus, and Mars are the planets closest to the earth and are those which most affect your personality and daily happenings. Fill in the following sentences which explain how each planet works in your life.

a.______shows your outgoing energy and drive.
b.______shows how you think and communicate.
c.______shows your tastes, what you respond to.

16. When you miss important messages and forget your keys, look to the planet______.

17. When you are especially attractive to others, the planet______is favorable.

18. When you have energy to burn, your sun sign is influenced by______.

19. A lottery win, a weight gain, a raise in salary could come when the planet______is in your sun sign.

20. To learn about a person's sense of duty and responsibility, you would look to the planet ______.

21. Name the three outer planets.

22. True or false: Astrologers have known about the planets Uranus, Neptune, and Pluto for many hundreds of years.

23. Before the discovery of Neptune, the ruling planet of Pisces was______.

24. Uranus remains in a sign for______years.

25. Which is the most distant planet?

Answers:

1. *False.* An astrologer also needs to know the time (as close to the minute as possible) and place of your birth as well as the date to do a truly accurate and complete horoscope.

   If you missed this question, perhaps you are confused about what a horoscope really is. This is common to many readers whose knowledge of astrology is limited to reading their daily forecast in newspapers. A horoscope is a *total* picture of a moment in time and space, a happening at a specific place. This event could be not only the birth of a person, but a meeting, or the signing of a contract or constitution marking the birth of a company or a country. You can have a horoscope done about something very personal such as the date of the purchase of your new beach house or the time of your wedding. Virtually anything that has a time and place can have an accurate horoscope.

   Now, you may well ask, what if I don't know the exact moment of my birth? Or what if I want the horoscope of a historical figure or of someone who can only give me the date. Would the reading then be invalid?

The reading would not be as precise, but you could still get much valuable information from the placement of the planets on that specific day and their interrelationships. The sun, moon, and planets in a horoscope all represent energy forces which affect each other according to their place in the sky at a given time. For instance, if there was a full moon, if two or more planets were orbiting in the same section of the sky, if two planets were on opposite sides of the sky . . . these affect the happenings on that day. Now, a truly accurate horoscope will pinpoint where the planets will affect the activities of the subject, but you cannot do this unless you know the exact time.

If you knew a few more facts about the subject, you could make a good educated guess about the time of the horoscope. If the subject is a person, the physical appearance, emotional milestones, career interests—all give clues which could help an astrologer estimate the time of the chart. Astrologers often do a "rectified" chart on subjects, which approximates the time of the chart when it is not available.

2. *False.* An astrologer is drawing conclusions from specific information about a moment in time. However, each astrologer will interpret a chart according to his or her own frame of reference. Some will be more intuitive, others more scientific, and still others will focus on a certain aspect of the chart. But it is not necessary to have psychic talent or any other kind of parapsychological background to be a good astrologer. And an astrologer who also advertises psychic services is not necessarily a better astrologer.

In fact, an astrologer who, in a personal consultation, gives you a reading based *only* on your sun sign, without drawing up a detailed chart, is one to avoid.

Then what about the validity of the daily

newspaper horoscopes or the daily forecasts such as the ones in the back of this book? Astrologers who do newspaper forecasts are looking at the outlook on that day for your sun sign in general. Depending on the astrologer, many factors are considered in relation to the overall sign, such as the position of the moon to gauge the mood of the day and the relationships between the planets at that time. Sometimes the numerical cycle of that sign is also considered. The horoscopes will be most accurate for those who have the strongest "sun" influence and were probably born early in the morning. If you had many other strong factors in your horoscope, for instance if there were many planets grouped together in anther sign at the time you were born, then the horoscope might seem less accurate.

3. *False.* Your rising sign, or ascendant, is the sign on the eastern horizon when you were born. Rising signs change every two hours as the earth rotates. The position directly overhead is known as the midheaven. The western horizon is the descendant and the midpoint opposite the midheaven is called the nadir. Each is a very important point in the chart.
4. *"Zodiac"* comes from the Greek word meaning "circle of animals." It refers to an imaginary circle in the sky around which the moon and planets appear to travel. The ancient astrologers noted the planets' positions by certain constellations along this belt of sky, and named these groups of stars after mythical creatures. Only the stars which fall on the zodiac were used by astrologers. Constellations such as the Big Dipper and Orion are not of interest to western astrologers because they do not fall within the zodiac.
5. *Both houses and signs are divisions of the sky.* A *sign* is a 30-degree segment of the zodiac circle. A constellation can be any group of stars, not only those in the zodiac. The constellations that are located on the zodiac were originally used to mark the signs. But over the centuries these constella-

tions have actually moved from the earth's point of view, so the stellar signposts are no longer valid. The 30-degree segments, however, remain.

A *house* is used in interpreting a horoscope. It too is one of 12 segments of the sky, each of which delineates a specific area of your total life experience. Most astrologers agree on the meanings of each of the 12 houses and their order of appearance, but there are many different systems of calculating the size of the houses, which are, in most systems, greater or lesser than 30 degrees in size.

In general, the territory of each house in the total scheme of the horoscope is described by the characteristics of a specific sign but the house will be strongly affected by energies of the planets traveling through that segment and by the sign passing over the beginning of the house (house cusp) at the time. For instance, the first house, or the Aries house, has to do with the outward projection of the subject. Now, if, at a certain time of day, the sign of Sagittarius was passing over the beginning of the first house, the subject's outward projection would take on Sagittarian overtones. If Mars and Jupiter were passing through that part of the sky, then these two powerful planets would intensify that subject's outward projection, adding their own unique combination of forces.

6. *A pizza pie,* sliced in twelve segments (the houses). You might also visualize a wagon wheel, with the spokes being the cusps of each of the 12 houses.
7. *False.* As we mentioned before, a sign is not necessarily the same as a constellation.
8. *False.* There is evidence that all had deep knowledge of astrology. Bear in mind that astrology was really the father of astronomy. The ancient scientists were the first to believe that there was an inner universe which corresponded to the outer. "As above, so below" is a saying which has been passed down through occult traditions through the centuries. Many of our founding fathers were steeped in masonic and occult traditions. It is even said that Jefferson used astrol-

ogy to set the timing of the signing of the Declaration of Independence.

9. *To the moon.* The position and the sign of the moon reveals your inner feelings and needs.
10. *Fire, earth, water, and air, respectively.*
11. *These three terms are used in combination* to define a sign, for instance Aries is a fire (element) sign, of cardinal (quality) and masculine (polarity).

Element refers to one of the four building blocks of astrology: earth, air, fire, and water. The ancients believed that all things were made of a combination of these four elements. That includes man's character, which could be fiery-choleric, earthy-melancholy, watery-phlegmatic or airy-sanguine. The elements also refer to our emotional (water), mental (air), spiritual (fire), and physical (earth) natures. These four energies were also observed to relate to a time of year when the sun was passing through a certain constellation. Therefore, the fiery energy of Aries corresponded to the first beginnings of spring, earthy Taurus to the planting season, and so on. Fire signs (Aries, Leo, Sagittarius) embody the characteristics of that element: energy, warmth, enthusiasm, confidence, spirit. Air signs (Gemini, Libra, Aquarius) are more mental: communicators, game players, thinkers. Water signs (Cancer, Scorpio, and Pisces) are feelers: intuitive, emotional, creative. Earth signs (Taurus, Virgo, Capricorn) are involved with the here and now: the builders and organizers.

The *quality* of a sign defines how each sign behaves. Cardinal signs (Aries, Cancer, Capricorn, and Libra) are high-energy doers. These signs, which begin each of the four seasons, are initiators, who get things going. Fixed signs (Taurus, Leo, Scorpio, Aquarius) are the central stabilizers; here are the steady builders, noted for stamina and stubbornness. Mutable signs (Gemini, Pisces, Virgo, and Sagittarius) break things up, get ready for a transition; these are the most flexible, adaptable catalysts.

The sign's polarity refers to its masculine, positive or feminine, negative charge of energy. Like a battery, these forces alternate in the parade of signs to generate and propel energy around the zodiac, from sign to sign. As it lines up, the fire and air sign energy is masculine, extroverted and active. These signs are open in character, expanding outward. The earth and water signs are feminine, fertile, receptive. These signs allow the energy to develop structure and form. They are the nurturing signs.

12. *The sun sign* is the sign the sun was traveling through when the subject was born (or happened, if an event). *An air sign* (or an earth, fire, or water sign) describes one aspect of the sign itself. For instance, Pisces is a water sign. When you say you are a "Pisces," you mean that the sun was traveling through that particular water sign.

    Bear in mind that we have parts of every sign included in our total horoscope, to a greater or lesser degree. Each sign will influence a house and perhaps one more planet. So, though your sun sign is very important, it is by no means all of the picture.

13. *The four elements, three qualities, and two polarities* all divide into the 12 signs of the zodiac, in a beautiful mathematical design. No combination is repeated and each factor is given a complete range of expression, so the zodiac becomes a balanced expression of energy, with everything fitting perfectly in its plan.

    Each sequence of fire, earth, air, and water alternates around the zodiac, in that order, making three signs of each element.

    The three qualities cardinal, fixed, and mutable also alternate with four signs of each quality.

    Then comes the masculine/feminine energy force, again alternating with six signs of each polarity.

14. Aries begins the zodiac propelled by the masculine charge, plus cardinal energy, plus the force

of fire. All these work together to give Aries its unique personality. After this dynamic start, Taurus, the earth sign, becomes the builder, the stabilizer, the fertile ground. Air sign Gemini reaches out to others, again with the positive masculine charge, making new contacts. Water sign Cancer is the active cardinal force that bears fruit from the contacts, and nurtures the energy. Then Leo expresses the energy outwardly again with the confidence of fixed fire. Mutable earthy Virgo makes sure all is functioning. In the cardinal air sign Libra, the energy goes out into the world, meets and greets, finds its equilibrium. Fixed water sign Scorpio gains inner control and power. Sagittarius, the mutable masculine fire sign, expands again traveling mentally and physically. To organize, consolidate, and achieve requires the cardinal feminine earth sign of Capricorn. Fixed air sign Aquarius again broadens and reaches out with concentrated mental energy. Finally, mutable feminine Pisces gathers and reflects on all the knowledge gained from this trip around the zodiac and prepares for the rebirth of Aries.

Correct Sequence

ARIES	Fire	Cardinal	Masculine
TAURUS	Earth	Fixed	Feminine
GEMINI	Air	Mutable	Masculine
CANCER	Water	Cardinal	Feminine
LEO	Fire	Fixed	Masculine
VIRGO	Earth	Mutable	Feminine
LIBRA	Air	Cardinal	Masculine
SCORPIO	Water	Fixed	Feminine
SAGITTARIUS	Fire	Mutable	Masculine
CAPRICORN	Earth	Cardinal	Feminine
AQUARIUS	Air	Fixed	Masculine
PISCES	Water	Mutable	Feminine

Note: Can you see how the description of each sign grew from the interrelationships of these three components plus one other factor: the place in order of the sign on the zodiac?

15. *a. Mars, b. Mercury, c. Venus*
16. *Mercury.* At times like this, there may be a mercury retrograde, when the planet appears to be moving backwards in the sky, relative to earth. When this happens, mercury related incidents seem to go haywire. There is potential for confusion, misunderstandings, slipups and communications breakdowns.
17. *Venus*
18. *Mars*
19. *Jupiter* is where you grow and expand. This planet is the Santa Claus of the zodiac, a jolly giant made of swirling gases, full of promises, bringing opportunity and luck. Things seems to come easily to you if you have a powerful Jupiter in your chart, or at those times when Jupiter is most favorable to your sun sign. However, there is a catch—the easygoing vibrations of this planet can make you lazy or overindulgent. Jupiter has no restraints—you can pile on the pounds (forget dieting under a strong Jupiter influence), or throw caution to the winds and blow the budget completely. You may promise more than you can realistically deliver or go overboard in other ways—one recent Wall Street mogul went too far in his Jupiter year, and his excesses landed him in jail. Jupiter makes you think you won't get "caught."
20. *Saturn.* Jupiter's next door neighbor is the taskmaster of the zodiac. With Saturn, you get what you earn, no more, no less. Think of the beautiful rings of Saturn as testing, measuring marks. When Saturn affects your horoscope, you have one of life's testing times, out of which you emerge more sober, strong, and responsible!
21. *Uranus, Neptune, and Pluto.*
22. *False.* These three planets are called the "modern planets" because of their comparatively recent discovery—Uranus in 1781, Neptune in 1846, and Pluto in 1930. Since their discovery, many astrologers feel that their influence has increased and their nature has become more relevant to

our time. Pluto is often rated to the rise of atomic power, Uranus to electricity, Neptune to the petroleum industry.

23. *Jupiter.* On the basis of of accumulated experience about the modern planets, astrologers have assigned Neptune to Pisces, replacing Jupiter; Pluto to Scorpio, replacing Mars; and Uranus to Aquarius, replacing Saturn. It is thought that these planets relate most to the energies of the signs they now rule. But some traditional astrologers still relate the original planets to the signs, and consider the modern planets to be co-rulers.
24. *Approximately seven years.* The lengthy stay of each of the modern planets in a particular sign influences the whole generation born during that period. Neptune stays in a sign about 13 years while Pluto can reside from 11 to 31 years in a sign.
25. *This is a tricky question to answer,* because the planet Pluto has a highly irregular elliptical orbit which sometimes comes inside the orbit of Neptune. So the most distant planet could be either Neptune or Pluto.

2

Eight Planets That Color Your Horoscope

Besides the sun and moon, there are eight planets in your horoscope which make up the composite energy picture that is uniquely *you.* Each has a special personality of its own that also picks up the influence of the sign the planet is passing through at the time the horoscope is cast. In some signs the planetary energies are very much at home and can easily express themselves. In others, the planet is ill at ease, slightly out of sorts. The signs which most correspond to the energies of the planet are said to be ruled by that planet.

Here are the signs and the planets they rule:

ARIES—MARS
TAURUS—VENUS, in its most sensual form.
GEMINI—MERCURY, in its communicative role
CANCER—THE MOON
LEO—THE SUN
VIRGO—ALSO MERCURY, this time in its critical capacity
LIBRA—ALSO VENUS, in its aesthetic form
SCORPIO—PLUTO, replacing the original ruler, Mars
SAGITTARIUS—JUPITER
CAPRICORN—SATURN
AQUARIUS—URANUS, replacing Saturn
PISCES—NEPTUNE, replacing Jupiter

The Close Neighbors: Mercury, Venus, and Mars These are the planets that work in your immediate, personal life. Mercury affects how you communicate and how your mental processes work. Are you a quick study who grasps information rapidly or do you learn more slowly and thoroughly? How is your concentration? Can you express yourself easily? Are you a good writer? All these questions can be answered by your Mercury placement.

Venus shows what you react to. What turns you on? What appeals to you aesthetically? Are you charming to others? Are you attractive to look at? Your taste, your refinement and sense of balance and proportion are all Venus-ruled.

Mars is your outgoing energy, your drive and ambition. Do you reach out for new adventures? Are you assertive? Are you motivated? Self-confident? Hot-tempered? How you channel your energy and drive is revealed by your Mars placement.

The Mercury in You

Since Mercury never travels far from the sun, look at Mercury in your sun sign and the sign preceding and following it. Then decide which most reflects the way your mind works.

Mercury in Aries: Your mind is active and assertive. You never hesitate to say exactly what you think or shy away from a battle. In fact, you may relish a verbal confrontation.

Mercury in Taurus: You may be a slow learner, but you have good concentration and mental stamina. You want to make your ideas really happen. You'll attack a problem methodically and consider every angle thoroughly, never jumping to conclusions. You'll stick with a subject until you master it.

Mercury in Gemini: You are a wonderful communicator, with a great facility for expressing yourself verbally and in writing. Though you learn fast, you may lack focus and discipline. Watch a tendency to jump from subject to subject.

Mercury in Cancer: You are intuitive, rather than logical. Your mental processes are usually colored by your emotions. This gives you the advantage of great imagination and empathy for others.

Mercury in Leo: You are enthusiastic and quite dramatic in the way you express yourself. You like to hold the attention of groups, and could be a great public speaker. Your mind thinks big and likes to deal with the overall picture rather than details.

Mercury in Virgo: One of the best places for Mercury. This gives you critical ability, attention to details, and thorough analysis. Your mind focuses on the practical side of things. You are an excellent teacher and editor.

Mercury in Libra: You are a born diplomat who smoothes over ruffled feathers; you may be a talented debater or lawyer. However, you vacillate when it comes to taking a stand or making decisions; you're forever weighing the pros and cons.

Mercury in Scorpio: This is the investigative mind, which stops at nothing to get the answer. You may have a sarcastic, stinging wit—a gift for the cutting remark. There is always a grain of truth to your verbal sallies, thanks to your penetrating insight.

Mercury in Sagittarius: You are a supersalesman, with a tendency to expound. You are very broad-minded, but you could be dogmatic when it comes to telling others what's good for them. You won't hesitate to tell the truth as you see it, so watch a tendency toward tactlessness. On the plus side, you have a great sense of humor.

Mercury in Capricorn: This placement endows good mental discipline. You have a love of learning and an orderly approach to your subjects. You will patiently plod through facts and figures until you master your tasks. You grasp structured situations easily, but may be short on creativity.

Mercury in Aquarius: You are an independent thinker, who won't hesitate to break the rules to find the most original, innovative approach to problems. But once your mind is made up, it is difficult to change.

Mercury in Pisces: You have the psychic, intuitive mind of a natural poet. You should learn to make use of your creative imagination. You also think in terms of helping others. But check a tendency to be vague and forgetful of details.

The Venus in You

Venus tells how you relate to others and to your environment—where you receive pleasure, what you *love* to do. It is never more than two or three signs away from the sun.

Find your Venus placement on the chart in this book by looking for the year of your birth in the left-hand column. Then follow the line of that year across the page until you reach the time period of your birthday. The sign heading that column will be your Venus. If you were born on a day when Venus was changing signs, check the signs preceding or following that day to determine if that feels more like your Venus nature.

Venus in Aries: Oh, do you love excitement! You can't stand to be bored, confined, or ordered around. But a good challenge, maybe even a rousing row turns you on. Confess: Don't you pick a fight now and then just to get everyone moving? You're attracted by the chase, not the catch, which could create problems in your love life if the object of your affection becomes too attainable. You like to wear the color red and to be first with the very latest fashion. You'll spot a trend before anyone else.

Venus in Taurus: All your senses work in high gear. You love to be surrounded by glorious tastes, smells, textures, sounds, visuals. Austerity is not for you; neither is being rushed. You like time to enjoy your pleasures. Soothing surroundings with no stinting on creature comforts are your cup of tea. You like to feel secure in your nest—with no sudden jolts or surprises.

Venus in Gemini: You have a lively, sparkling personality that thrives in a situation where there is constant variety and a frequent change of scenes. A varied social life is important to you with plenty of stimulation and a chance to engage in some light flirtation. Commitment may be difficult for you; playing the field is so much more fun.

Venus in Cancer: An atmosphere where you feel protected, coddled, and mothered is best for you. You love to be surrounded by children, in a cozy homelike situation. You are attracted to those who are tender and nurturing, who make you feel secure, well provided for. You may also be quite secretive about your emotional life or be attracted to clandestine relationships.

Venus in Leo: First-class attention in large doses turns you on. And so does the glitter of real gold and the flash of mirrors. You like to feel like the star at all times, surrounded by your admiring audience. The side effect is that you may be attracted to flatterers and tinsel while the real gold requires some digging.

Venus in Virgo: Everything neatly in its place? On the surface, you are attracted to an atmosphere where everything is in perfect order. But underneath are some basic earthy urges. You are attracted to those who appeal to your need to teach or to play out a

Pygmalion fantasy. You're at your best when you are busy doing something useful.

Venus in Libra: "Elegance" and "harmony" are your key words. You can't abide an atmosphere of contention. Your taste tends toward the classic with light harmonies of color, nothing clashing, too trendy, or outrageous. You love doing things with a partner, but should be careful to pick one who is decisive but patient enough to let you weigh the pros and cons. And steer clear of argumentative types.

Venus in Scorpio: Hidden mysteries intrigue you—in fact anything that is too open and aboveboard is a bit of a bore. You surely have a stack of whodunits by the bed (along with an erotic magazine or two). You may also be fascinated with the occult, crime, or scientific research. Intense all-or-nothing situations add spice to life, but you could get burned by your flair for living dangerously. The color black, spicy food, dark wood furniture, and heady perfume all get you in the right mood.

Venus in Sagittarius: If you are not actually a world traveler, your surroundings are sure to reflect your love of faraway places. You like a casual outdoor atmosphere and a dog or two to pet. You should have plenty of room for athletic equipment and suitcases. You're attracted to kindred souls who love to travel and who share your freedom-loving philosophy of life. Athletics, spiritual, or New Age pursuits are your other interests.

Venus in Capricorn: No fly-by-night relationships for you! You want substance in life. You are attracted to whatever will help you get where you are going. Status objects turn you on. So do those who have a serious, responsible businesslike approach or who remind you of a beloved parent. It is characteristic of this placement to be attracted to someone of a different generation. Antiques, traditional clothing, and dignified behavior favor you.

Venus in Aquarius: This Venus wants to make friends more than to make love. You like to be in a group, particularly one pushing a worthy cause. You feel quite at home surrounded by people, remaining detached from any intense commitment. Original ideas and unpredictable people fascinate you. You don't like everything to be planned out in advance. You prefer spontaneity and delightful surprises.

Venus in Pisces: This Venus is attracted to being of service. You love to give of yourself, and find plenty of takers. Stray animals and people appeal to your heart and your pocketbook. Be careful to look at their motives realistically once in a while. Fantasy, theater, and psychic or spiritual activities also speak to you.

The Mars in You

Mars is the mover and shaker in your life. It shows how you pursue your goals, whether you have energy to burn or proceed in a slow, steady pace. Or are you nervous, restless, and unable to sit still? It will also show how you get angry: Do you explode or do a slow burn or hold everything inside and get revenge.

To find your Mars, turn to the chart in Chapter 2. Find your birth year in the left-hand column and trace the line across horizontally until you come to the column headed by the month of your birth. There you will find an abbreviation of your Mars sign. If the description of your Mars sign doesn't ring true, read the descriptions of the sign preceding and following it. You may have been born on a day when Mars was changing signs, so your Mars would be in the adjacent sign.

Mars in Aries: In the sign it rules, Mars shows its brilliant fiery nature. You have an explosive temper, can be quite impatient, but on the other hand have tremendous courage, energy, and drive. You'll let

VENUS SIGN 1910–1990

	Aries	Taurus	Gemini	Cancer	Leo	Virgo
1910	5/7-6/3	6/4-6/29	6/30-7/24	7/25-8/18	8/19-9/12	9/13-10/6
1911	2/28-3/23	3/24-4/17	4/18-5/12	5/13-6/8	6/9-7/7	7/8-11/8
1912	4/13-5/6	5/7-5/31	6/1-6/24	6/24-7/18	7/19-8/12	8/13-9/5
1913	2/3-3/6	3/7-5/1	7/8-8/5	8/6-8/31	9/1-9/26	9/27-10/20
	5/2-5/30	5/31-7/7				
1914	3/14-4/6	4/7-5/1	5/2-5/25	5/26-6/19	6/20-7/15	7/16-8/10
1915	4/27-5/21	5/22-6/15	6/16-7/10	7/11-8/3	8/4-8/28	8/29-9/21
1916	2/14-3/9	3/10-4/5	4/6-5/5	5/6-9/8	9/9-10/7	10/8-11/2
1917	3/29-4/21	4/22-5/15	5/16-6/9	6/10-7/3	7/4-7/28	7/29-8/21
1918	5/7-6/2	6/3-6/28	6/29-7/24	7/25-8/18	8/19-9/11	9/12-10/5
1919	2/27-3/22	3/23-4/16	4/17-5/12	5/13-6/7	6/8-7/7	7/8-11/8
1920	4/12-5/6	5/7-5/30	5/31-6/23	6/24-7/18	7/19-8/11	8/12-9/4
1921	2/3-3/6	3/7-4/25	7/8-8/5	8/6-8/31	9/1-9/25	9/26-10/20
	4/26-6/1	6/2-7/7				
1922	3/13-4/6	4/7-4/30	5/1-5/25	5/26-6/19	6/20-7/14	7/15-8/9
1923	4/27-5/21	5/22-6/14	6/15-7/9	7/10-8/3	8/4-8/27	8/28-9/20
1924	2/13-3/8	3/9-4/4	4/5-5/5	5/6-9/8	9/9-10/7	10/8-11/12
1925	3/28-4/20	4/21-5/15	5/16-6/8	6/9-7/3	7/4-7/27	7/28-8/21
1926	5/7-6/2	6/3-6/28	6/29-7/23	7/24-8/17	8/18-9/11	9/12-10/5
1927	2/27-3/22	3/23-4/16	4/17-5/11	5/12-6/7	6/8-7/7	7/8-11/9
1928	4/12-5/5	5/6-5/29	5/30-6/23	6/24-7/17	7/18-8/11	8/12-9/4
1929	2/3-3/7	3/8-4/19	7/8-8/4	8/5-8/30	8/31-9/25	9/26-10/19
	4/20-6/2	6/3-7/7				
1930	3/13-4/5	4/6-4/30	5/1-5/24	5/25-6/18	6/19-7/14	7/15-8/9
1931	4/26-5/20	5/21-6/13	6/14-7/8	7/9-8/2	8/3-8/26	8/27-9/19

VENUS SIGN 1910–1990

Libra	Scorpio	Sagittarius	Capricorn	Aquarius	Pisces
10/7-10/30	10/31-11/23	11/24-12/17	12/18-12/31	1/1-1/15	1/16-1/28
				1/29-4/4	4/5-5/6
11/19-12/8	12/9-12/31		1/1-1/10	1/11-2/2	2/3-2/27
9/6-9/30	1/1-1/4	1/5-1/29	1/30-2/23	2/24-3/18	3/19-4/12
	10/1-10/24	10/25-11/17	11/18-12/12	12/13-12/31	
10/21-11/13	11/14-12/7	12/8-12/31		1/1-1/6	1/7-2/2
8/11-9/6	9/7-10/9	10/10-12/5	1/1-1/24	1/25-2/17	2/18-3/13
	12-6/12-30	12/31			
9/22-10/15	10/16-11/8	1/1-2/6	2/7-3/6	3/7-4/1	4/2-4/26
		11/9-12/2	12/3-12/26	12/27-12/31	
11/3-11/27	11/28-12/21	12/22-12/31		1/1-1/19	1/20-2/13
8/22-9/16	9/17-10/11	1/1-1/14	1/15-2/7	2/8-3/4	3/5-3/28
		10/12-11/6	11/7-12/5	12/6-12/31	
10/6-10/29	10/30-11/22	11/23-12/16	12/17-12/31	1/1-4/5	4/6-5/6
11/9-12/8	12/9-12/31		1/1-1/9	1/10-2/2	2/3-2/26
9/5-9/30	1/1-1/3	1/4-1/28	1/29-2/22	2/23-3/18	3/19-4/11
	9/31-10/23	10/24-11/17	11/18-12/11	12/12-12/31	
10/21-11/13	11/14-12/7	12/8-12/31		1/1-1/6	1/7-2/2
8/10-9/6	9/7-10/10	10/11-11/28	1/1-1/24	1/25-2/16	2/17-3/12
	11/29-12/31				
9/21-10/14	1/1	1/2-2/6	2/7-3/5	3/6-3/31	4/1-4/26
	10/15-11/7	11/8-12/1	12/2-12/25	12/26-12/31	
11/3-11/26	11/27-12/21	12/22-12/31		1/1-1/19	1/20-2/12
8/22-9/15	9/16-10/11	1/1-1/14	1/15-2/7	2/8-3/3	3/4-3/27
		10-12/11-6	11/7-12/5	12/6-12/31	
10/6-10/29	10/30-11/22	11/23-12/16	12/17-12/31	1/1-4/5	4/6-5/6
11/10-12/8	12/9-12/31	1/1-1/7	1/8	1/9-2/1	2/2-2/26
9/5-9/28	1/1-1/3	1/4-1/28	1/29-2/22	2/23-3/17	3/18-4/11
	9/29-10/23	10/24-11/16	11/17-12/11	12/12-12/31	
10/20-11/12	11/13-12/6	12/7-12/30	12/31	1/1-1/5	1/6-2/2
8/10-9/6	9/7-10/11	10/12-11/21	1/1-1/23	1/24-2/16	2/17-3/12
	11/22-12/31				
9/20-10/13	1/1-1/3	1/4-2/6	2/7-3/4	3/5-3/31	4/1-4/25
	10/14-11/6	11/7-11/30	12/1-12/24	12/25-12/31	

VENUS SIGN 1910–1990

	Aries	Taurus	Gemini	Cancer	Leo	Virgo
1932	2/12-3/8	3/9-4/3	4/4-5/5	5/6-7/12	9/9-10/6	10/7-11/1
			7/13-7/27	7/28-9/8		
1933	3/27-4/19	4/20-5/28	5/29-6/8	6/9-7/2	7/3-7/26	7/27-8/20
1934	5/6-6/1	6/2-6/27	6/28-7/22	7/23-8/16	8/17-9/10	9/11-10/4
1935	2/26-3/21	3/22-4/15	4/16-5/10	5/11-6/6	6/7-7/6	7/7-11/8
1936	4/11-5/4	5/5-5/28	5/29-6/22	6/23-7/16	7/17-8/10	8/11-9/4
1937	2/2-3/8	3/9-4/17	7/7-8/3	8/4-8/29	8/30-9/24	9/25-10/18
	4/14-6/3	6/4-7/6				
1938	3/12-4/4	4/5-4/28	4/29-5/23	5/24-6/18	6/19-7/13	7/14-8/8
1939	4-25/5/19	5/20-6/13	6/14-7/8	7/9-8/1	8/2-8/25	8/26-9/19
1940	2/12-3/7	3/8-4/3	4/4-5/5	5/6-7/4	9/9-10/5	10/6-10/31
			7/5-7/31	8/1-9/8		
1941	3/27-4/19	4/20-5/13	5/14-6/6	6/7-6/1	7/2-7/26	7/27-8/20
1942	5/6-6/1	6/2-6/26	6/27-7/22	7/23-8/16	8/17-9/9	9/10-10/3
1943	2/25-3/20	3/21-4/14	4/15-5/10	5/11-6/6	6/7-7/6	7/7-11/8
1944	4-10/5-3	5/4-5/28	5/29-6/21	6/22-7/16	7/17-8/9	8/10-9/2
1945	2/2-3/10	3/11-4/6	7/7-8/3	8/4-8/29	8/30-9/23	9/24-10/18
	4/7-6/3	6/4-7/6				
1946	3/11-4/4	4/5-4/28	4/29-5/23	5/24-6/17	6/18-7/12	7/13-8/8
1947	4/25-5/19	5/20-6/12	6/13-7/7	7/8-8/1	8/2-8/25	8/26-9/18
1948	2/11-3/7	3/8-4/3	4/4-5/6	5/7-6/28	9/8-10/5	10/6-10/31
			6/29-8/2	8/3-9/7		
1949	3/26-4/19	4/20-5/13	5/14-6/6	6/7-6/30	7/1-7/25	7/26-8/19
1950	5/5-5/31	6/1-6/26	6/27-7/21	7/22-8/15	8/16-9/9	9/10-10/3
1951	2/25-3/21	3/22-4/15	4/16-5/10	5/11-6/6	6/7-7/7	7/8-11/9
1952	4/10-5/4	5/5-5/28	5/29-6/21	6/22-7/16	7/17-8/9	8/10-9/3
1953	2/2-3/13	3/4-3/31	7/8-8/3	8/4-8/29	8/30-9/24	9/25-10/18
	4/1-6/5	6/6-7/7				

VENUS SIGN 1910–1990

Libra	Scorpio	Sagittarius	Capricorn	Aquarius	Pisces
11/2-11/25	11/26-12/20	12/21-12/31		1/1-1/18	1/19-2/11
8/21-9/14	9/15-10/10	1/1-1/13	1/14-2/6	2/7-3/2	3/3-3/26
		10/11-11/5	11/6-12/4	12/5-12/31	
10/5-10/28	10/29-11/21	11/22-12/15	12/16-12/31	1/1-4/5	4/6-5/5
11/9-12/7	12/8-12/31		1/1-1/7	1/8-1/31	2/1-2/25
9/5-9/27	1/1-1/2	1/3-1/27	1/28-2/21	2/22-3/16	3/17-4/10
	9/28-10/22	10/23-11/15	11/16-12/10	12/11-12/31	
10/19-11/11	11/12-12/5	12/6-12/29	12/30-12/31	1/1-1/5	1/6-2/1
8/9-9/6	9/7-10/13	10/14-11/14	1/1-1/22	1/23-2/15	2/16-3/11
	11/15-12/31				
9/20-10/13	1/1-1/3	1/4-2/5	2/6-3/4	3/5-3/30	3/31-4/24
	10/14-11/6	11/7-11/30	12/1-12/24	12/25-12/31	
11/1-11/25	11/26-12/19	12/20-12/31		1/1-1/18	1/19-2/11
8/21-9/14	9/15-10/9	1/1-1/12	1/13-2/5	2/6-3/1	3/2-3/26
		10/10-11/5	11/6-12/4	12/5-12/31	
10/4-10/27	10/28-11/20	11/21-12/14	12/15-12/31	1/1-4/4	4/6-5/5
11/9-12/7	12/8-12/31		1/1-1/7	1/8-1/31	2/1-2/24
9/3-9/27	1/1-1/2	1/3-1/27	1/28-2/20	2/21-3/16	3/17-4/9
	9/28-10/21	10/22-11/15	11/16-12/10	12/11-12/31	
10/19-11/11	11/12-12/5	12/6-12/29	12/30-12/31	1/1-1/4	1/5-2/1
8/9-9/6	9/7-10/15	10/16-11/7	1/1-1/21	1/22-2/14	2/15-3/10
	11/8-12/31				
9/19-10/12	1/1-1/4	1/5-2/5	2/6-3/4	3/5-3/29	3/30-4/24
	10/13-11/5	11/6-11/29	11/30-12/23	12/24-12/31	
11/1-1/25	11/26-12/19	12/20-12/31		1/1-1/17	1/18-2/10
8/20-9/14	9/15-10/9	1/1-1/12	1/13-2/5	2/6-3/1	3/2-3/25
		10/10-11/5	11/6-12/5	12/6-12/31	
10/4-10/27	10/28-11/20	11/21-12/13	12/14-12/31	1/1-4/5	4/6-5/4
11/10-12/7	12/8-12/31		1/1-1/7	1/8-1/31	2/1-2/24
9/4-9/27	1/1-1/2	1/3-1/27	1/28-2/20	2/21-3/16	3/17-4/9
	9/28-10/21	10/22-11/15	11/16-12/10	12/11-12/31	
10/19-11/11	11/12-12/5	12/6-12/29	12/30-12/31	1/1-1/5	1/6-2/1

VENUS SIGN 1910–1990

	Aries	Taurus	Gemini	Cancer	Leo	Virgo
1954	3/12-4/4	4/5-4/28	4/29-5/23	5/24-6/17	6/18-7/13	7/14-8/8
1955	4/25-5/19	5/20-6/13	6/14-7/7	7/8-8/1	8/2-8/25	8/26-9/18
1956	2/12-3/7	3/8-4/4	4/5-5/7	5/8-6/23	9/9-10/5	10/6-10/31
			6:24-8/4	8/5-9/8		
1957	3-26/4-19	4/20-5/13	5/14-6/6	6/7-7/1	7/2-7/26	7/27-8/19
1958	5-6/5-31	6/1-6/26	6/27-7/22	7/23-8/15	8/16-9/9	9/10-10/3
1959	2-25/3-20	3/21-4/14	4/15-5/10	5/11-6/6	6/7-7/8	7/9-9/20
					9/21-9/24	9/25-11/9
1960	4-10/5-3	5/4-5/28	5/29-6/21	6/22-7/15	7/16-8/9	8/10-9/2
1961	2-3/6-5	6/6-7/7	7/8-8/3	8/4-8/29	8/30-9/23	9/24-10/17
1962	3/11-4/3	4/4-4/28	4/29-5/22	5/23-6/17	6/18-7/12	7/13-8/8
1963	4/24-5/18	5/19-6/12	6/13-7/7	7/8-7/31	8/1-8/25	8/26-9/18
1964	2/11-3/7	3/8-4/4	4/5-5/9	5/10-6/17	9/9-10/5	10/6-10/31
			6/18-8/5	8/6-9/8		
1965	3/26-4/18	4/19-5/12	5/13-6/6	6/7-6/30	7/1-7/25	7/26-8/19
1966	5/6-6/31	6/1-6/26	6/27-7/21	7/22-8/15	8/16-9/8	9/9-10/2
1967	2/24-3/20	3/21-4/14	4/15-5/10	5/11-6/6	6/7-7/8	7/9-9/9
					9/10-10/1	10/2-11/9
1968	4/9-5/3	5/4-5/27	5/28-6/20	6/21-7/15	7/16-8/8	8/9-9/2
1969	2/3-6/6	6/7-7/6	7/7-8/3	8/4-8/28	8/29-9/22	9/23-10/17
1970	3/11-4/3	4/4-4/27	4/28-5/22	5/23-6/16	6/17-7/12	7/13-8/8
1971	4/24-5/18	5/19-6/12	6/13-7/6	7/7-7/31	8/1-8/24	8/25-9/17
1972	2/11-3/7	3/8-4/3	4/4-5/10	5/11-6/11		
			6/12-8/6	8/7-9/8	9/9-10/5	10/6-10/30
1973	3/25-4/18	4/18-5/12	5/13-6/5	6/6-6/29	7/1-7/25	7/26-8/19
1974						
	5/5-5/31	6/1-6/25	6/26-7/21	7/22-8/14	8/15-9/8	9/9-10/2
1975	2/24-3/20	3/21-4/13	4/14-5/9	5/10-6/6	6/7-7/9	7/10-9/2
					9/3-10/4	10/5-11/9

VENUS SIGN 1910–1990

Libra	Scorpio	Sagittarius	Capricorn	Aquarius	Pisces
8/9-9/6	9/7-10/22	10/23-10/27	1/1-1/22	1/23-2/15	2/16-3/11
	10/28-12/31				
9/19-10/13	1/1-1/6	1/7-2/5	2/6-3/4	3/5-3/30	3/31-4/24
	10/14-11/5	11/6-11/30	12/1-12/24	12/25-12/31	
11/1-11/25	11/26-12/19	12/20-12/31		1/1-1/17	1/18-2/11
8/20-9/14	9/15-10/9	1/1-1/12	1/13-2/5	2/6-3/1	3/2-3/25
		10/10-11/5	11/6-12/16	12/7-12/31	
10/4-10/27	10/28-11/20	11/21-12/14	12/15-12/31	1/1-4/6	4/7-5/5
11/10-12/7	12/8-12/31		1/1-1/7	1/8-1/31	2/1-2/24
9/3-9/26	1/1-1/2	1/3-1/27	1/28-2/20	2/21-3/15	3/16-4/9
	9/27-10/21	10/22-11/15	11/16-12/10	12/11-12/31	
10/18-11/11	11/12-12/4	12/5-12/28	12/29-12/31	1/1-1/5	1/6-2/2
8/9-9/6	9/7-12/31		1/1-1/21	1/22-2/14	2/15-3/10
9/19-10/12	1/1-1/6	1/7-2/5	2/6-3/4	3/5-3/29	3/30-4/23
	10/13-11/5	11/6-11/29	11/30-12/23	12/24-12/31	
11/1-11/24	11/25-12/19	12/20-12/31		1/1-1/16	1/17-2/10
8/20-9/13	9/14-10/9	1/1-1/12	1/13-2/5	2/6-3/1	3/2-3/25
		10/10-11/5	11/6-12/7	12/8-12/31	
10/3-10/26	10/27-11/19	11/20-12/13	2/7-2/25	1/1-2/6	4/7-5/5
			12/14-12/31	2/26-4/6	
11/10-12/7	12/8-12/23		1/1-1/6	1/7-1/30	1/31-2/23
9/3-9/26	1/1	1/2-1/26	1/27-2/20	2/21-3/15	3/16-4/8
	9/27-10/21	10/22-11/14	11/15-12/9	12/10-12/31	
10/18-11/10	11/11-12/4	12/5-12/28	12/29-12/31	1/1-1/4	1/5-2/2
8/9-9/7	9/8-12/31		1/1-1/21	1/22-2/14	2/15-3/10
9/18-10/11	1/1-1/7	1/8-2/5	2/6-3/4	3/5-3/29	3/30-4/23
	10/12-11/5	11/6-11/29	11/30-12/23	12/24-12/31	
	11/25-12/18	12/19-12/31		1/1-1/16	1/17-2/10
10/31-11/24					
8/20-9/13		1/1-1/12	1/13-2/4	2/5-2/28	3/1-3/24
		10/9-11/5	11/6-12/7	12/8-12/31	
			1/30-2/28	1/1-1/29	
10/3-10/26	10/27-11/19	11/20-12/13	12/14-12/31	3/1-4/6	4/7-5/4
			1/1-1/6	1/7-1/30	1/31-2/23
11/10-12/7	12/8-12/31				

VENUS SIGN 1910–1990

	Aries	Taurus	Gemini	Cancer	Leo	Virgo
1976	4/8–5/2	5/2–5/27	5/27–6/20	6/20–7/14	7/14–8/8	8/8–9/1
1977	2/2–6/6	6/6–7/6	7/6–8/2	8/2–8/28	8/28–9/22	9/22–10/17
1978	3/9–4/2	4/2–4/27	4/27–5/22	5/22–6/16	6/16–7/12	7/12–8/6
1979	4/23–5/18	5/18–6/11	6/11–7/6	7/6–7/30	7/30–8/24	8/24–9/17
1980	2/9–3/6	3/6–4/3	4/3–5/12	5/12–6/5	9/7–10/4	10/4–10/30
			6/5–8/6	8/6–9/7		
1981	3/24–4/17	4/17–5/11	5/11–6/5	6/5–6/29	6/29–7/24	7/24–8/18
1982	5/4–5/30	5/30–6/25	6/25–7/20	7/20–8/14	8/14–9/7	9/7–10/2
1983	2/22–3/19	3/19–4/13	4/13–5/9	5/9–6/6	6/6–7/10	7/10–8/27
					8/27–10/5	10/5–11/9
1984	4/7–5/2	5/2–5/26	5/26–6/20	6/20–7/14	7/14–8/7	8/7–9/1
1985	2/2–6/6	6/6–7/6	7/6–8/2	8/2–8/28	8/28–9/22	9/22–10/16
1986	3/9–4/2	4/2–4/26	4/26–5/21	5/21–6/15	6/15–7/11	7/11–8/7
1987	4/22–5/17	5/17–6/11	6/11–7/5	7/5–7/30	7/30–8/23	8/23–9/16
1988	2/9–3/6	3/6–4/3	4/3–5/17	5/17–5/27	9/7–10/4	10/4–10/29
			5/27–8/6	8/6–9/7		
1989	3/23–4/16	4/16–5/11	5/11–6/4	6/4–6/29	6/29–7/24	7/24–8/18
1990	5/4–5/30	5/30–6/25	6/25–7/20	7/20–8/13	8/13–9/7	9/7–10/1

VENUS SIGN 1910–1990

Libra	Scorpio	Sagittarius	Capricorn	Aquarius	Pisces
9/1–9/26	9/26–10/20	1/1–1/26	1/26–2/19	2/19–3/15	3/15–4/8
		10/20–11/14	11/14–12/6	12/9–1/4	
10/17–11/10	11/10–12/4	12/4–12/27	12/27–1/20		1/4–2/2
8/6–9/7	9/7–1/7			1/20–2/13	2/13–3/9
9/17–10/11	10/11–11/4	1/7–2/5	2/5–3/3	3/3–3/29	3/29–4/23
		11/4–11/28	11/28–12/22	12/22–1/16	
10/30–11/24	11/24–12/18	12/18–1/11			1/16–2/9
8/18–9/12	9/12–10/9	10/9–11/5	1/11–2/4	2/4–2/28	2/28–3/24
			11/5–12/8	12/8–1/23	
10/2–10/26	10/26–11/18	11/18–12/12	1/23–3/2	3/2–4/6	4/6–5/4
			12/12–1/5		
11/9–12/6	12/6–1/1			1/5–1/29	1/29–2/22
9/1–9/25	9/25–10/20	1/1–1/25	1/25–2/19	2/19–3/14	3/14–4/7
		10/20–11/13	11/13–12/9		
10/16–11/9	11/9–12/3	12/3–12/27			1/4–2/2
8/7–9/7	9/7–1/7			1/20–3/13	2/13–3/9
9/16–10/10	10/10–11/3	1/7–2/5	2/5–3/3	3/3–3/28	2/38–4/22
		11/3–11/28	11/28–12/22	12/22–1/15	
10/29–11/23	11/23–12/17	12/17–1/10			1/15–2/9
8/18–9/12	9/12–18/8	10/8–11/5	1/10–2/3	2/3–2/27	2/27–3/23
			11/5–12/10	12/10–1/16	
10/1–10/25	10/25–11/18	11/18–12/12	1/16–3/3	3/3–4/6	4/6–5/4
			12/12–1/5		

nothing stand in your way as you race to be first! Obstacles are met head on and broken through by force. However, those that require patience and persistence can have you exploding in rage. You're a great starter but not necessarily around for the finish.

Mars in Taurus: Slow, steady, concentrated energy gives you the power. You have great stamina and you won't give up. Your tactic is to wear away obstacles and stick to it. Often you come out a winner because you have had the patience to hang in there. When angered, you do a slow burn.

Mars in Gemini: You can't sit still for long. This Mars craves variety. You often have two or more things going on at once. It's all an amusing game to you. Your life can get very complicated, but, to you, that only ads spice and stimulation. What drives you into a nervous, hyper state? Boredom. Sameness. Routine. And confinement. You can do wonderful things with your hands and you have a way with words.

Mars in Cancer: You rarely attack head on—instead, you'll keep things to yourself, make plans in secret, and always cover your actions. This might be interpreted by some as pretty sneaky and manipulative, but you are only being self-protective. You get furious when anyone knows too much about you. But you do like to know all about them. Your mothering and feeding instincts can be put to good use in your work in food, hotel, or child care businesses. You may have to overcome your fragile sense of security, which prompts you not to take risks and to get physically upset when criticized. Don't take things so personally!

Mars in Leo: You have a very dominant personality that takes over center stage. Modesty is not one of your traits. Nor is taking a back seat. You prefer giving the orders and have been known to make a dramatic scene if they are not obeyed. Properly used, this Mars confers good leadership ability, endurance, and courage.

Mars in Virgo: You are the faultfinder of the zodiac, who notices every detail. Mistakes of any kind make you very nervous. You may worry even if everything is going smoothly. You may not express your anger directly, but you sure can nag. You have definite likes and dislikes and you are sure you can do the job better than anyone else. You are certainly more industrious than most other signs. Why don't you express your Mars energy by teaching instead of criticizing?

Mars in Libra: This Mars will have a passion for beauty, justice, and art. But you will generally avoid confrontations at all costs. You prefer to spend your energy finding a diplomatic solution or weighing pros and cons. Your other techniques are passive aggression, or you exercise your well-known charm to get people to do what you want.

Mars in Scorpio: This is a powerful placement, so intense that it demands careful channeling into worthwhile activities. Otherwise you could be obsessed with your sexuality or may use your need for power and control to manipulate others emotionally. You are strong-willed, shrewd, and very private about your affairs and usually have a secret agenda behind your actions. Your great stamina, focus, and discipline are excellent assets for careers in the military or medical field especially in research or surgery. When angry, you don't get mad, you get even!

Mars in Sagittarius: This expansive Mars often propells people into sales, travel, athletics, or philosophy. Your energies function well when you are on the move. You have a hot temper and are inclined to say what you think before you consider the consequences. You shoot for high goals—and talk endlessly about them—but you may be weak on groundwork. This Mars needs a solid foundation. Watch a tendency to take unnecessary risks.

Mars in Capricorn: This is an ambitious Mars with an excellent sense of timing. You have an eye for those who can be of use to you. And may dismiss people ruthlessly when angry. But you drive yourself hard and deliver full value. This is a good placement for an executive. You'll aim for status and a high material position in life and keep climbing despite the odds.

Mars in Aquarius: This is the most rebellious Mars. You seem to have a drive to assert yourself against the status quo. You may enjoy provoking people, shocking them out of traditional views. Or this placement could express itself in an offbeat sex life. Others could find you a bit eccentric; somehow, you often find yourself in unconventional situations. You enjoy being a leader of an active group, which pursues forward-looking studies or goals.

Mars in Pisces: This Mars is a good actor who knows just how to appeal to the sympathies of others. You can create and project wonderful fantasies or use your sensitive antennae to crusade for those less fortunate. You get what you want through creating a veil of illusion and glamor. This is a good Mars for a dancer, performer, photographer, or someone in motion pictures. Many famous film stars such as Jane Fonda have this placement. Watch a tendency to manipulate by making others feel sorry for you.

The Jupiter in You

Jupiter is the planet in your horoscope that makes you want more. This big bright swirling mass of gases is associated with abundance, prosperity—the kind of windfall you get without too much hard work. You're optimistic under Jupiter's influence—anything seems possible. You'll travel, expand your mind with higher education, publish to share your knowledge widely. But a strong Jupiter has its down side, too. Jupiter's influence is neither discriminating nor disciplined. It represents the principle of growth without judgment—and could result in extravagance, weight gain, laziness, and carelessness.

Be sure to look up your Jupiter in the tables in this book. When the current position of Jupiter is favorable, you may get that lucky break. At any rate, it's a great time to try new things, take risks, travel, or get more education. Opportunities seem to open up at this time, so take advantage of them.

Once a year, Jupiter changes signs. That means you are due for an expansive time, once every twelve years when Jupiter travels through your sun sign. You'll also have up periods every four years when Jupiter is in the same *element* as your sun sign.

Jupiter in Aries: You are the soul of enthusiasm and optimism. Your luckiest times are when you are getting started on an exciting project or selling an idea that you really believe in. You may have to watch a tendency to be arrogant with those who do not share your enthusiasm. You follow your impulse often ignoring budget or other common-sense limitations. To produce real solid benefits, you'll need patience and follow-through wherever this Jupiter falls in your horoscope.

Jupiter in Taurus: You may be especially lucky in matters of real estate. You'll spend on beautiful material things—especially those that come from nature. Minerals or precious gems, for instance. You can't have too much comfort, or sensual pleasures. Watch a tendency to overindulge in good food, or to pamper yourself too much with "nothing but the best." Spartan living is not for you!

Jupiter in Gemini: You are the great talker of the zodiac. You may be a great writer, too. But restlessness could be your weak point. You jump around, talk too much, and could be a jack-of-all-trades. You also have to watch a tendency to spill the beans. Keeping a secret is especially difficult. Since you love to be in the center of a beehive of activity, you'll have a vibrant social life. Your best opportunities will come through your talent for language: speaking, writing, communicating, selling.

Jupiter in Cancer: You are luckiest in situations where you can find emotional closeness or deal with basic security needs such as food, nurturing, shelter. You may be a great collector or you may simply love to accumulate things. You are the one who stashes things away for a rainy day. You probably have a very good memory and love children. In fact, you may have many children to care for. The food, hotel, child care, or shipping businesses hold good opportunities for you.

Jupiter in Leo: You are a natural showman who loves to live in a larger-than-life way. Yours is a personality full of color, which always finds its way into the limelight. You can't have too much attention or applause. Show biz is a natural place for you. Any area where you can exercise your flair for drama, your natural playfulness, and your romantic nature brings you good fortune. But watch a tendency to be overly extravagant or to monopolize center stage.

Jupiter in Virgo: You actually love those minute details others find boring. To you, they make all the difference between the perfect and the ordinary. You are the fine craftsman who spots every flaw. You expand your awareness by finding the most practical methods and by being of service to others. A great teacher, you'll have luck in education, nutrition, publishing, crafts, health-promotion. Watch a tendency to overwork.

Jupiter in Libra: This is an other-directed Jupiter which develops best with a partner. You seem to need the stimulation of others in order to grow. You are also most comfortable in harmonious, beautiful situations and work well with artistic people. You have a great sense of fair play and an ability to evaluate the pros and cons of a situation. You usually prefer to play the role of diplomat rather than adversary.

Jupiter in Scorpio: You love the feeling of power and control, of taking things to their limit. You can't resist a mystery. Your shrewd penetrating minds sees right through to the heart of most situations and people. You have luck in work that probes for solutions to matters of life and death. You may be drawn to undercover work, behind-the-scenes intrigue, psychotherapy, the occult, and sex-related ventures. Your challenge will be to develop a sense of moderation and tolerance for others' beliefs. This Jupiter can be fanatical. You may have luck in handling others' money—insurance, taxes, and an inheritance can bring you a windfall.

Jupiter in Sagittarius: Independent, outgoing, and idealistic, you'll shoot for the stars. This Jupiter compels you to travel far and wide, both physically and mentally via higher education. You may have luck while traveling in an exotic place. You also have luck with outdoor ventures, exercise and animals (particularly horses). You tend to be very open about your opinions; watch a tendency toward tactlessness and exaggeration. Instead, use your wonderful sense of humor to make your point.

Jupiter in Capricorn: Jupiter is much more restrained in Capricorn. Here, Jupiter can make you overwork and heighten any ambition or sense of duty you may have. You'll expand in areas that advance your position, put you farther up the social or corporate ladder. You are lucky working within the establishment, in a very structured situation, where you can show off your ability to organize and which will provide rewards for your hard work.

Jupiter in Aquarius: This is another freedom-loving Jupiter with great tolerance and originality. You are at your best when you are working for a humanitarian cause and in the company of many supporters.

This is a good Jupiter for a political career. You'll relate to all kinds of people on all social levels. You have an abundance of original ideas. However, you are best off away from routine and any situation that imposes rigid rules. You need mental stimulation!

Jupiter in Pisces: You are a "giver" whose feelings and pocketbook are easily touched by others; so choose your companions with care. You could be the original sucker for a hard luck story. Better find a worthy hospital or charity to appreciate your selfless support. You have a great creative imagination and may attract good fortune in fields related to perfume, pharmaceuticals, petroleum, dance, footwear, and alcohol. But beware of overindulgence in drugs or alcohol. Focus on a creative outlet instead.

The Saturn In You

Jupiter speeds you up with lucky breaks, then along comes Saturn to slow you down with the disciplinary brakes. Saturn has unfairly been called a malefic planet, one of the bad guys of the zodiac. On the contrary, Saturn is one of our best friends, the kind that tells you what's wrong with you for your own good. Under a Saturn transit, we grow up, take responsibility for our lives, and emerge from whatever test this planet has in store far wiser and more capable and mature.

When Saturn hits a critical point in your horoscope, you can count on an experience that will make you slow up, pull back, and reexamine your life. It is a call to eliminate what is not working—in other words, to shape up. In its twenty-eight-year trip around the zodiac, Saturn will have tested you in all areas of your life. The major tests usually happen in seven-year cycles, when Saturn passes over your rising sign, midheaven, descendant, and nadir. This is when the real life-changing experiences happen. But you are also in for a testing period whenever Saturn passes a planet in your chart or stresses that planet from a distance. It is useful to check your planetary positions with the travel schedule of Saturn to be prepared in advance, or at least to brace yourself.

When Saturn returns to its location at the time of your birth, at approximately age twenty-eight, you will have your first "Saturn return." At this time, a person usually takes stock or settles down to find his mission in life and assume full adult duties and responsibilities.

Another way Saturn helps us is to reveal the karmic lessons from previous lives—and give us the chance to overcome them. So look at Saturn's challenges as much-needed opportunities for self-improvement. Under a Jupiter influence you'll have more fun, but Saturn gives you solid, long-lasting results.

Look up your natal Saturn in the tables in this book for clues on where you need work.

Saturn in Aries: Saturn here gives you great ambition and independence. You don't let anyone push you around. And you know what's best for you. Following orders is not your strong point. Neither is diplomacy. Because no one quite lives up to your standards, you often wind up doing everything yourself. You are best off running your own business, though you may be quite lonely at times.

Saturn in Taurus: A big issue with you is getting control of the cash flow. There will be lean periods which can be frightening, but you have the patience and endurance to stick them out and the methodical drive to prosper in the end. Learn to take a philosophical attitude like Ben Franklin, who also had this placement.

Saturn in Gemini: You are a rather cold, detached, serious student. You may not be inclined to communicate or share your knowledge. You dwell in the realms of science, theory, or abstract analysis, even when you are dealing with the emotions, like Sigmund Freud, who had this placement.

Saturn in Cancer: Your tests come with establishing a secure emotional base. In doing so, you may have to deal with some very basic fears centering on your early home environment. Most of your Saturn tests will have emotional roots in those early childhood experiences. You may have difficulty remaining objective in terms of what you try to achieve. So it will be especially important for you to deal with negative feelings such as guilt, paranoia, jealousy, resentment, and suspicion. Galileo and Michelangelo also navigated these murky waters.

Saturn in Leo: This is an authoritarian Saturn. A strict, demanding parent, you may deny the pleasure principle in your zeal to see that rules are followed. Though you may feel guilty about taking the spotlight, you are ambitious and loyal. You have to watch a tendency toward rigidity, also toward overwork and holding back affection. Joseph Kennedy and Billy Graham also have this placement.

Saturn in Virgo: This is a cautious exacting Saturn, intensely hard on yourself, most of all. You give yourself the roughest time with your constant worries about every little detail. You may often make yourself sick. Your tests will come in learning tolerance and understanding of others. Charles DeGaulle and Nathaniel Hawthorne had this meticulous Saturn.

Saturn in Libra: You'll choose very serious, older partners in life. Perhaps that stems from a fear of dependency. You need to learn to stand solidly on your own before you commit to another. You are extremely cautious as you deliberate every involvement, with good reason. It is best that you find an occupation that makes good use of your sense of duty and honor. Steer clear of fly-by-night situations. Khrushchev and Mao Tse-tung had this placement, too.

Saturn in Scorpio: You have great staying power. This Saturn tests you in matters of control and transformation. You may feel drawn to some kind of intrigue or undercover work, like J. Edgar Hoover. Or there may be an air of mystery surrounding your life and death like Marilyn Monroe and Robert Kennedy, who had this placement. There are lessons to be learned from your sexual involvements—often sex is used for manipulation here, or is somehow out of the ordinary. The mad Roman emperor Caligula and the well-known transvestite Christine Jorgenson are extreme cases.

Saturn in Sagittarius: Your challenges and lessons will come from tests of your spiritual and philosophical values, as happened to Martin Luther King Jr., and Gandhi. You are high-minded and sincere, with this reflective, moral placement. Uncompromising in your ethical standards, you could be benevolent despot.

Saturn in Capricorn: With the help of Saturn at maximum strength, your judgment will improve with age. And, like Spencer Tracy's screen image, you'll be the gray-haired hero with a strong sense of responsibility. You advance in life slowly but steadily, always with a strong hand at the helm and an eye for the advantageous situation. Negatively, you may be a loner, prone to periods of melancholy.

Saturn in Aquarius: Your tests come from your relationships with groups. Do you care too much about what others think? You may fear being different from others, and therefore slight your own unique, forward-looking gifts or, like Lord Byron and Howard Hughes, take the opposite tack and rebel in the extreme. You can apply discipline to accomplish great humanitarian goals, like Albert Schweitzer.

Saturn in Pisces: Your fear of the unknown and the irrational may lead you to a secluded solitary life-style. You may go on the run like Jesse James, who had this placement, to avoid looking too deeply inside. Or you may take refuge in institutions, espe-

MARS SIGN 1901–2000

1901	MAR	1	Leo
	May	11	Vir
	JUL	13	Lib
	AUG	31	Scp
	OCT	14	Sag
	NOV	24	Cap
1902	JAN	1	Aqu
	FEB	8	Pic
	MAR	19	Ari
	APR	27	Tau
	JUN	7	Gem
	JUL	20	Can
	SEP	4	Leo
	OCT	23	Vir
	DEC	20	Lib
1903	APR	19	Vir
	MAY	30	Lib
	AUG	6	Scp
	SEP	22	Sag
	NOV	3	Cap
	DEC	12	Aqu
1904	JAN	19	Pic
	FEB	27	Ari
	APR	6	Tau
	MAY	18	Gem
	JUN	30	Can
	AUG	15	Leo
	OCT	1	Vir
	NOV	20	Lib
1905	JAN	13	Scp
	AUG	21	Sag
	OCT	8	Cap
	NOV	18	Aqu
	DEC	27	Pic
1906	FEB	4	Ari
	MAR	17	Tau
	APR	28	Gem
	JUN	11	Can
	JUL	27	Leo
	SEP	12	Vir
	OCT	30	Lib
	DEC	17	Scp
1907	FEB	5	Sag
	APR	1	Cap
	OCT	13	Aqu
	NOV	29	Pic
1908	JAN	11	Ari
	FEB	23	Tau
	APR	7	Gem
	MAY	22	Can
	JUL	8	Leo
	AUG	24	Vir
	OCT	10	Lib
	NOV	25	Scp
1909	JAN	10	Sag
	FEB	24	Cap
	APR	9	Aqu
	MAY	25	Pic
	JUL	21	Ari
	SEP	26	Pic
	NOV	20	Ari
1910	JAN	23	Tau
	MAR	14	Gem
	MAY	1	Can
	JUN	19	Leo
	AUG	6	Vir
	SEP	22	Lib
	NOV	6	Scp
	DEC	20	Sag
1911	JAN	31	Cap
	MAR	14	Aqu
	APR	23	Pic

	JUN	2	Ari
	JUL	15	Tau
	SEP	5	Gem
	NOV	30	Tau
1912	JAN	30	Gem
	APR	5	Can
	MAY	28	Leo
	JUL	17	Vir
	SEP	2	Lib
	OCT	18	Scp
	NOV	30	Sag
1913	JAN	10	Cap
	FEB	19	Aqu
	MAR	30	Pic
	MAY	8	Ari
	JUN	17	Tau
	JUL	29	Gem
	SEP	15	Can
1914	MAY	1	Leo
	JUN	26	Vir
	AUG	14	Lib
	SEP	29	Scp
	NOV	11	Sag
	DEC	22	Cap
1915	JAN	30	Aqu
	MAR	9	Pic
	APR	16	Ari
	MAY	26	Tau
	JUL	6	Gem
	AUG	19	Can
	OCT	7	Leo
1916	MAY	28	Vir
	JUL	23	Lib
	SEP	8	Scp
	OCT	22	Sag
	DEC	1	Cap
1917	JAN	9	Aqu
	FEB	16	Pic
	MAR	26	Ari
	MAY	4	Tau
	JUN	14	Gem
	JUL	28	Can
	SEP	12	Leo
	NOV	2	Vir
1918	JAN	11	Lib
	FEB	25	Vir
	JUN	23	Lib
	AUG	17	Scp
	OCT	1	Sag
	NOV	11	Cap
	DEC	20	Aqu
1919	JAN	27	Pic
	MAR	6	Ari
	APR	15	Tau
	MAY	26	Gem
	JUL	8	Can
	AUG	23	Leo
	OCT	10	Vir
	NOV	30	Lib
1920	JAN	31	Scp
	APR	23	Lib
	JUL	10	Scp
	SEP	4	Sag
	OCT	18	Cap
	NOV	27	Aqu
1921	JAN	5	Pic
	FEB	13	Ari
	MAR	25	Tau
	MAY	6	Gem
	JUN	18	Can
	AUG	3	Leo
	SEP	19	Vir
	NOV	6	Lib
	DEC	26	Scp
1922	FEB	18	Sag
	SEP	13	Cap
	OCT	30	Aqu
	DEC	11	Pic

1923 JAN 21 Ari
MAR 4 Tau
APR 16 Gem
MAY 30 Can
JUL 16 Leo
SEP 1 Vir
OCT 18 Lib
DEC 4 Scp
1924 JAN 19 Sag
MAR 6 Cap
APR 24 Aqu
JUN 24 Pic
AUG 24 Aqu
OCT 19 Pic
DEC 19 Ari
1925 FEB 5 Tau
MAR 24 Gem
MAY 9 Can
JUN 26 Leo
AUG 12 Vir
SEP 28 Lib
NOV 13 Scp
DEC 28 Sag
1926 FEB 9 Cap
MAR 23 Aqu
MAY 3 Pic
JUN 15 Ari
AUG 1 Tau
1927 FEB 22 Gem
APR 17 Can
JUN 6 Leo
JUL 25 Vir
SEP 10 Lib
OCT 26 Scp
DEC 8 Sag
1928 JAN 19 Cap
FEB 28 Aqu
APR 7 Pic
MAY 16 Ari
JUN 26 Tau
AUG 9 Gem
OCT 3 Can
DEC 20 Gem
1929 MAR 10 Can
MAY 13 Leo
JUL 4 Vir
AUG 21 Lib
OCT 6 Scp
NOV 18 Sag
DEC 29 Cap
1930 FEB 6 Aqu
MAR 17 Pic
APR 24 Ari
JUN 3Tau
JUL 14 Gem
AUG 28 Can
OCT 20 Leo
1931 FEB 16 Can
MAR 30 Leo
JUN 10 Vir
AUG 1 Lib
SEP 17 Scp
OCT 30 Sag
DEC 10 Cap
1932 JAN 18 Aqu
FEB 25 Pic
APR 3 Ari
MAY 12 Tau
JUN 22 Gem
AUG 4 Can
SEP 20 Leo
NOV 13 Vir
1933 JUL 6 Lib
AUG 26 Scp
OCT 9 Sag
NOV 19 Cap
DEC 28 Aqu
1934 FEB 4 Pic

	MAR	14	Ari
	APR	22	Tau
	JUN	2	Gem
	JUL	15	Can
	AUG	30	Leo
	OCT	18	Vir
	DEC	11	Lib
1935	JUL	29	Scp
	SEP	16	Sag
	OCT	28	Cap
	DEC	7	Aqu
1936	JAN	14	Pic
	FEB	22	Ari
	APR	1	Tau
	MAY	13	Gem
	JUN	25	Can
	AUG	10	Leo
	SEP	26	Vir
	NOV	14	Lib
1937	JAN	5	Scp
	MAR	13	Sag
	MAY	14	Scp
	AUG	8	Sag
	SEP	30	Cap
	NOV	11	Aqu
	DEC	21	Pic
1938	JAN	30	Ari
	MAR	12	Tau
	APR	23	Gem
	JUN	7	Can
	JUL	22	Leo
	SEP	7	Vir
	OCT	25	Lib
	DEC	11	Scp
1939	JAN	29	Sag
	MAR	21	Cap
	MAY	25	Aqu
	JUL	21	Cap
	SEP	24	Aqu
	NOV	19	Pic
1940	JAN	4	Ari
	FEB	17	Tau
	APR	1	Gem
	MAY	17	Can
	JUL	3	Leo
	AUG	19	Vir
	OCT	5	Lib
	NOV	20	Scp
1941	JAN	4	Sag
	FEB	17	Cap
	APR	2	Aqu
	MAY	16	Pic
	JUL	2	Ari
1942	JAN	11	Tau
	MAR	7	Gem
	APR	26	Can
	JUN	14	Leo
	AUG	1	Vir
	SEP	17	Lib
	NOV	1	Scp
	DEC	15	Sag
1943	JAN	26	Cap
	MAR	8	Aqu
	APR	17	Pic
	MAY	27	Ari
	JUL	7	Tau
	AUG	23	Gem
1944	MAR	28	Can
	MAY	22	Leo
	JUL	12	Vir
	AUG	29	Lib
	OCT	13	Scp
	NOV	25	Sag
1945	JAN	5	Cap
	FEB	14	Aqu
	MAR	25	Pic
	MAY	2	Ari
	JUN	11	Tau

	JUL	23	Gem
	SEP	7	Can
	NOV	11	Leo
	DEC	26	Can
1946	APR	22	Leo
	JUN	20	Vir
	AUG	9	Lib
	SEP	24	Scp
	NOV	6	Sag
	DEC	17	Cap
1947	JAN	25	Aqu
	MAR	4	Pic
	APR	11	Ari
	MAY	21	Tau
	JUL	1	Gem
	AUG	13	Can
	OCT	1	Leo
	DEC	1	Vir
1948	FEB	12	Leo
	MAY	18	Vir
	JUL	17	Lib
	SEP	3	Scp
	OCT	17	Sag
	NOV	26	Cap
1949	JAN	4	Aqu
	FEB	11	Pic
	MAR	21	Ari
	APR	30	Tau
	JUN	10	Gem
	JUL	23	Can
	SEP	7	Leo
	OCT	27	Vir
	DEC	26	Lib
1950	MAR	28	Vir
	JUN	11	Lib
	AUG	10	Scp
	SEP	25	Sag
	NOV	6	Cap
	DEC	15	Aqu
1951	JAN	22	Pic
	MAR	1	Ari
	APR	10	Tau
	MAY	21	Gem
	JUL	3	Can
	AUG	18	Leo
	OCT	5	Vir
	NOV	24	Lib
1952	JAN	20	Scp
	AUG	27	Sag
	OCT	12	Cap
	NOV	21	Aqu
	DEC	30	Pic
1953	FEB	8	Ari
	MAR	20	Tau
	MAY	1	Gem
	JUN	14	Can
	JUL	29	Leo
	SEP	14	Vir
	NOV	1	Lib
	DEC	20	Scp
1954	FEB	9	Sag
	APR	12	Cap
	JUL	3	Sag
	AUG	24	Cap
	OCT	21	Aqu
	DEC	4	Pic
1955	JAN	15	Ari
	FEB	26	Tau
	APR	10	Gem
	MAY	26	Can
	JUL	11	Leo
	AUG	27	Vir
	OCT	13	Lib
	NOV	29	Scp
1956	JAN	14	Sag
	FEB	28	Cap
	APR	14	Aqu
	JUN	3	Pic

	DEC	6	Ari
1957	JAN	28	Tau
	MAR	17	Gem
	MAY	4	Can
	JUN	21	Leo
	AUG	8	Vir
	SEP	24	Lib
	NOV	8	Scp
	DEC	23	Sag
1958	FEB	3	Cap
	MAR	17	Aqu
	APR	27	Pic
	JUN	7	Ari
	JUL	21	Tau
	SEP	21	Gem
	OCT	29	Tau
1959	FEB	10	Gem
	APR	10	Can
	JUN	1	Leo
	JUL	20	Vir
	SEP	5	Lib
	OCT	21	Scp
	DEC	3	Sag
1960	JAN	14	Cap
	FEB	23	Aqu
	APR	2	Pic
	MAY	11	Ari
	JUN	20	Tau
	AUG	2	Gem
	SEP	21	Can
1961	FEB	5	Gem
	FEB	7	Can
	MAY	6	Leo
	JUN	28	Vir
	AUG	17	Lib
	OCT	1	Scp
	NOV	13	Sag
	DEC	24	Cap
1962	FEB	1	Aqu
	MAR	12	Pic
	APR	19	Ari
	MAY	28	Tau
	JUL	9	Gem
	AUG	22	Can
	OCT	11	Leo
1963	JUN	3	Vir
	JUL	27	Lib
	SEP	12	Scp
	OCT	25	Sag
	DEC	5	Cap
1964	JAN	13	Aqu
	FEB	20	Pic
	MAR	29	Ari
	MAY	7	Tau
	JUN	17	Gem
	JUL	30	Can
	SEP	15	Leo
	NOV	6	Vir
1965	JUN	29	Lib
	AUG	20	Scp
	OCT	4	Sag
	NOV	14	Cap
	DEC	23	Aqu
1966	JAN	30	Pic
	MAR	9	Ari
	APR	17	Tau
	MAY	28	Gem
	JUL	11	Can
	AUG	25	Leo
	OCT	12	Vir
	DEC	4	Lib
1967	FEB	12	Scp
	MAR	31	Lib
	JUL	19	Scp
	SEP	10	Sag
	OCT	23	Cap
	DEC	1	Aqu
1968	JAN	9	Pic

	FEB	17	Ari
	MAR	27	Tau
	MAY	8	Gem
	JUN	21	Can
	AUG	5	Leo
	SEP	21	Vir
	NOV	9	Lib
	DEC	29	Scp
1969	FEB	25	Sag
	SEP	21	Cap
	NOV	4	Aqu
	DEC	15	Pic
1970	JAN	24	Ari
	MAR	7	Tau
	APR	18	Gem
	JUN	2	Can
	JUL	18	Leo
	SEP	3	Vir
	OCT	20	Lib
	DEC	6	Scp
1971	JAN	23	Sag
	MAR	12	Cap
	MAY	3	Aqu
	NOV	6	Pic
	DEC	26	Ari
1972	FEB	10	Tau
	MAR	27	Gem
	MAY	12	Can
	JUN	28	Leo
	AUG	15	Vir
	SEP	30	Lib
	NOV	15	Scp
	DEC	30	Sag
1973	FEB	12	Cap
	MAR	26	Aqu
	MAY	8	Pic
	JUN	20	Ari
	AUG	12	Tau
	OCT	29	Ari
	DEC	24	Tau
1974	FEB	27	Gem
	APR	20	Can
	JUN	9	Leo
	JUL	27	Vir
	SEP	12	Lib
	OCT	28	Scp
	DEC	10	Sag
1975	JAN	21	Cap
	MAR	3	Aqu
	APR	11	Pic
	MAY	21	Ari
	JUL	1	Tau
	AUG	14	Gem
	OCT	17	Can
	NOV	25	Gem
1976	MAR	18	Can
	MAY	16	Leo
	JUL	6	Vir
	AUG	24	Lib
	OCT	8	Scp
	NOV	20	Sag
1977	JAN	1	Cap
	FEB	9	Aqu
	MAR	20	Pic
	APR	27	Ari
	JUN	6	Tau
	JUL	17	Gem
	SEP	1	Can
	OCT	26	Leo
1978	JAN	26	Can
	APR	10	Leo
	JUN	14	Vir
	AUG	4	Lib
	SEP	19	Scp
	NOV	2	Sag
	DEC	12	Cap
1979	JAN	20	Aqu
	FEB	27	Pic

	APR	7	Ari
	MAY	16	Tau
	JUN	26	Gem
	AUG	8	Can
	SEP	24	Leo
	NOV	19	Vir
1980	MAR	11	Leo
	MAY	4	Vir
	JUL	10	Lib
	AUG	29	Scp
	OCT	12	Sag
	NOV	22	Cap
	DEC	30	Aqu
1981	FEB	6	Pic
	MAR	17	Ari
	APR	25	Tau
	JUN	5	Gem
	JUL	18	Can
	SEP	2	Leo
	OCT	21	Vir
	DEC	16	Lib
1982	AUG	3	Scp
	SEP	20	Sag
	OCT	31	Cap
	DEC	10	Aqu
1983	JAN	17	Pic
	FEB	25	Ari
	APR	5	Tau
	MAY	16	Gem
	JUN	29	Can
	AUG	13	Leo
	SEP	30	Vir
	NOV	18	Lib
1984	JAN	11	Scp
	AUG	17	Sag
	OCT	5	Cap
	NOV	15	Aqu
	DEC	25	Pic
1985	FEB	2	Ari
	MAR	15	Tau
	APR	26	Gem
	JUN	9	Can
	JUL	25	Leo
	SEP	10	Vir
	OCT	27	Lib
	DEC	14	Scp
1986	FEB	2	Sag
	MAR	28	Cap
	OCT	9	Aqu
	NOV	26	Pic
1987	JAN	8	Ari
	FEB	20	Tau
	APR	5	Gem
	MAY	21	Can
	JUL	6	Leo
	AUG	22	Vir
	OCT	8	Lib
	NOV	24	Scp
1988	JAN	8	Sag
	FEB	22	Cap
	APR	6	Aqu
	MAY	22	Pic
	JUL	13	Ari
	OCT	23	Pic
	NOV	1	Ari
1989	JAN	19	Tau
	MAR	11	Gem
	APR	29	Can
	JUN	16	Leo
	AUG	3	Vir
	SEP	19	Lib
	NOV	4	Scp
	DEC	18	Sag
1990	JAN	29	Cap
	MAR	11	Aqu
	APR	20	Pic
	MAY	31	Ari
	JUL	12	Tau

	AUG	31	Gem
	DEC	14	Tau
1991	JAN	21	Gem
	APR	3	Can
	MAY	26	Leo
	JUL	15	Vir
	SEP	1	Lib
	OCT	16	Scp
	NOV	29	Sag
1992	JAN	9	Cap
	FEB	18	Aqu
	MAR	28	Pic
	MAY	5	Ari
	JUN	14	Tau
	JUL	26	Gem
	SEP	12	Can
1993	APR	27	Leo
	JUN	23	Vir
	AUG	12	Lib
	SEP	27	Scp
	NOV	9	Sag
	DEC	20	Cap
1994	JAN	28	Aqu
	MAR	7	Pic
	APR	14	Ari
	MAY	23	Tau
	JUL	3	Gem
	AUG	16	Can
	OCT	4	Leo
	DEC	12	Vir
1995	JAN	22	Leo
	MAY	25	Vir
	JUL	21	Lib
	SEP	7	Scp
	OCT	20	Sag
	NOV	30	Cap
1996	JAN	8	Aqu
	FEB	15	Pic
	MAR	24	Ari
	MAY	2	Tau
	JUN	12	Gem
	JUL	25	Can
	SEP	9	Leo
	OCT	30	Vir
1997	JAN	3	Lib
	MAR	8	Vir
	JUN	19	Lib
	AUG	14	Scp
	SEP	28	Sag
	NOV	9	Cap
	DEC	18	Aqu
1998	JAN	25	Pic
	MAR	4	Ari
	APR	13	Tau
	MAY	24	Gem
	JUL	6	Can
	AUG	20	Leo
	OCT	7	Vir
	NOV	27	Lib
1999	JAN	26	Scp
	MAY	5	Lib
	JUL	5	Scp
	SEP	2	Sag
	OCT	17	Cap
	NOV	26	Aqu
2000	JAN	4	Pic
	FEB	12	Ari
	MAR	23	Tau
	MAY	3	Gem
	JUN	16	Can
	AUG	1	Leo
	SEP	17	Vir
	NOV	4	Lib
	DEC	23	Scp

JUPITER SIGN 1901–2000

1901	JAN	19	Cap
1902	FEB	6	Aqu
1903	FEB	20	Pic
1904	MAR	1	Ari
	AUG	8	Tau
	AUG	31	Ari
1905	MAR	7	Tau
	JUL	21	Gem
	DEC	4	Tau
1906	MAR	9	Gem
	JUL	30	Can
1907	AUG	18	Leo
1908	SEP	12	Vir
1909	OCT	11	Lib
1910	NOV	11	Scp
1911	DEC	10	Sag
1913	JAN	2	Cap
1914	JAN	21	Aqu
1915	FEB	4	Pic
1916	FEB	12	Ari
	JUN	26	Tau
	OCT	26	Ari
1917	FEB	12	Tau
	JUN	29	Gem
1918	JUL	13	Can
1919	AUG	2	Leo
1920	AUG	27	Vir
1921	SEP	25	Lib
1922	OCT	26	Scp
1923	NOV	24	Sag
1924	DEC	18	Cap
1926	JAN	6	Aqu
1927	JAN	18	Pic
	JUN	6	Ari
	SEP	11	Pic
1928	JAN	23	Ari
	JUN	4	Tau
1929	JUN	12	Gem
1930	JUN	26	Can
1931	JUL	17	Leo
1932	AUG	11	Vir
1933	SEP	10	Lib
1934	OCT	11	Scp
1935	NOV	9	Sag
1936	DEC	2	Cap
1937	DEC	20	Aqu
1938	MAY	14	Pic
	JUL	30	Aqu
	DEC	29	Pic
1939	MAY	11	Ari
	OCT	30	Pic
	DEC	20	Ari
1940	MAY	16	Tau
1941	MAY	26	Gem
1942	JUN	10	Can
1943	JUN	30	Leo
1944	JUL	26	Vir
1945	AUG	25	Lib
1946	SEP	25	Scp
1947	OCT	24	Sag
1948	NOV	15	Cap
1949	APR	12	Aqu
	JUN	27	Cap
	NOV	30	Aqu
1950	APR	15	Pic
	SEP	15	Aqu
	DEC	1	Pic
1951	APR	21	Ari
1952	APR	28	Tau
1953	MAY	9	Gem
1954	MAY	24	Can
1955	JUN	13	Leo
	NOV	17	Vir
1956	JAN	18	Leo
	JUL	7	Vir
	DEC	13	Lib

1957	FEB	19	Vir
	AUG	7	Lib
1958	JAN	13	Scp
	MAR	20	Lib
	SEP	7	Scp
1959	FEB	10	Sag
	APR	24	Scp
	OCT	5	Sag
1960	MAR	1	Cap
	JUN	10	Sag
	OCT	26	Cap
1961	MAR	15	Aqu
	AUG	12	Cap
	NOV	4	Aqu
1962	MAR	25	Pic
1963	APR	4	Ari
1964	APR	12	Tau
1965	APR	22	Gem
	SEP	21	Can
	NOV	17	Gem
1966	MAY	5	Can
	SEP	27	Leo
1967	JAN	16	Can
	MAY	23	Leo
	OCT	19	Vir
1968	FEB	27	Leo
	JUN	15	Vir
	NOV	15	Lib
1969	MAR	30	Vir
	JUL	15	Lib
	DEC	16	Scp
1970	APR	30	Lib
	AUG	15	Scp
1971	JAN	14	Sag
	JUN	5	Scp
	SEP	11	Sag
1972	FEB	6	Cap
	JUL	24	Sag
	SEP	25	Cap
1973	FEB	23	Aqu
1974	MAR	8	Pic
1975	MAR	18	Ari
1976	MAR	26	Tau
	AUG	23	Gem
	OCT	16	Tau
1977	APR	3	Gem
	AUG	20	Can
	DEC	30	Gem
1978	APR	12	Can
	SEP	5	Leo
1979	FEB	28	Can
	APR	20	Leo
	SEP	29	Vir
1980	OCT	27	Lib
1981	Nov	27	Scp
1982	DEC	26	Sag
1984	JAN	19	Cap
1985	FEB	6	Aqu
1986	FEB	20	Pic
1987	MAR	2	Ari
1988	MAR	8	Tau
	JUL	22	Gem
	NOV	30	Tau
1989	MAR	11	Gem
	JUL	30	Can
1990	AUG	18	Leo
1991	SEP	12	Vir
1992	OCT	10	Lib
1993	NOV	10	Scp
1994	DEC	9	Sag
1996	JAN	3	Cap
1997	JAN	21	Aqu
1998	FEB	4	Pic
1999	FEB	13	Ari
	JUN	28	Tau
	OCT	23	Ari
2000	FEB	14	Tau
	JUN	30	Gem

SATURN SIGN 1903–2000

1903	JAN	19	Aqu
1905	APR	13	Pic
	AUG	17	Aqu
1906	JAN	8	Pic
1908	MAR	19	Ari
1910	MAY	17	Tau
	DEC	14	Ari
1911	JAN	20	Tau
1912	JUL	7	Gem
	NOV	30	Tau
1913	MAR	26	Gem
1914	AUG	24	Can
	DEC	7	Gem
1915	MAY	11	Can
1916	OCT	17	Leo
	DEC	7	Can
1917	JUN	24	Leo
1919	AUG	12	Vir
1921	OCT	7	Lib
1923	DEC	20	Scp
1924	APR	6	Lib
	SEP	13	Scp
1926	DEC	2	Sag
1929	MAR	15	Cap
	MAY	5	Sag
	NOV	30	Cap
1932	FEB	24	Aqu
	AUG	13	Cap
	NOV	20	Aqu
1935	FEB	14	Pic
1937	APR	25	Ari
	OCT	18	Pic
1938	JAN	14	Ari
1939	JUL	6	Tau
	SEP	22	Ari
1940	MAR	20	Tau
1942	MAY	8	Gem
1944	JUN	20	Can
1946	AUG	2	Leo
1948	SEP	19	Vir
1949	APR	3	Leo
	MAY	29	Vir
1950	NOV	20	Lib
1951	MAR	7	Vir
	AUG	13	Lib
1953	OCT	22	Scp
1956	JAN	12	Sag
	MAY	14	Scp
	OCT	10	Sag
1959	JAN	5	Cap
1962	JAN	3	Aqu
1964	MAR	24	Pic
	SEP	16	Aqu
	DEC	16	Pic
1967	MAR	3	Ari
1969	APR	29	Tau
1971	JUN	18	Gem
1972	JAN	10	Tau
	FEB	21	Gem
1973	AUG	1	Can
1974	JAN	7	Gem
	APR	18	Can
1975	SEP	17	Leo
1976	JAN	14	Can
	JUN	5	Leo
1977	NOV	17	Vir
1978	JAN	5	Leo
	JUL	26	Vir
1980	SEP	21	Lib
1982	NOV	29	Scp
1983	MAY	6	Lib
	AUG	24	Scp

1985	NOV	17	Sag	1994	JAN	28	Pic
1988	FEB	13	Cap	1996	APR	7	Ari
	JUN	10	Sag	1998	JUN	9	Tau
	NOV	12	Cap		OCT	25	Ari
1991	FEB	6	Aqu	1999	MAR	1	Tau
1993	MAY	21	Pic	2000	AUG	10	Gem
	JUN	30	Aqu		OCT	16	Tau

cially hospital, charity or religious work. Queen Victoria, who also had this placement, symbolized an era in which institutions of all kinds were sustained. Discipline applied to artistic work, especially poetry and dance, or spiritual work such as yoga and meditation can help you.

Uranus, Neptune, and Pluto Affect Your Whole Generation

These three planets remain in signs such a long time that a whole generation is affected. Mass movements, great sweeping changes, fads that characterize a generation, even the issues of conflicts and wars of the time are influenced by the outer three. When one of these distant planets changes signs, there is a definite shift in the atmosphere, the feeling of the end of an era.

Since these planets are so far away from the sun, too far to be seen by the naked eye, they pick up signals from the universe at large. These planetary receivers literally link the sun with distant energies and they perform a similar function in your horoscope by linking your central character with intuitive, spiritual, transformative forces from the cosmos. Each planet has a special domain and will reflect this in the area of your life where it falls.

Uranus—The Aha-Planet!

There is nothing ordinary about this quirky green planet that seems to be traveling on its side, surrounded by a swarm of at least fifteen moons. Is it any wonder that astrologers assigned it to Aquarius, the most eccentric and gregarious sign? Uranus seems to wend its way around the sun, marching to its own tune.

Uranus energy is electrical, happening in sudden flashes. It is not influenced by karma or past events, nor does it regard tradition, sex, or sentiment. The Uranian keyword is surprise, awakening. Uranus wakes you up, jolts you out of your comfortable rut. Suddenly, there's that flash of inspiration, that bright idea, that totally new approach to revolutionize whatever scheme you were undertaking. The Uranus place in your life is where you awaken and become your own person. And it is probably the most unconventional place in your chart.

Look up the sign of Uranus at the time of your birth and see where you follow your own tune.

Uranus in Aries—A Fiery Shocker!

BIRTH DATE: March 31–November 4, 1927
January 13, 1928–June 6, 1934
October 10, 1934–March 28, 1935

Your generation is original, creative, pioneering—developing the computer, the airplane, the cyclotron. You let nothing hold you back from exploring the unknown and have a powerful mixture of fire and electricity behind you. You have a surprise in store for everyone; like Yoko Ono and Jacqueline Onassis, your life can be jolted by sudden and violent changes.

Uranus in Taurus—Sudden Shakeups!

BIRTH DATE: June 6, 1934–October 10, 1935
March 28, 1935–August 7, 1941
October 5, 1941–May 15, 1942

You are probably self-employed or would like to be. You have original ideas about making money and brace yourself for sudden changes of fortune. This Uranus can cause shake-ups, particularly in finances, but it can also make you a born entrepreneur, like Jane Fonda.

Uranus in Gemini—The Walking Talk Show

BIRTH DATE: August 7–October 5, 1941
May 15, 1942–August 30, 1948
November 12, 1948–June 10, 1949

You were the first children to be influenced by television. And in your adult years, your generation stocks up on answering machines, cordless phones, automobile phones, computers, and fax machines—any new way you can communicate. You have an inquiring mind, but your interests are rather short-lived. This Uranus can be easily fragmented if there is no structure and focus.

Uranus in Cancer—Domestic Disturbances
BIRTH DATE: August 30–November 12, 1948
June 10, 1949–August 24, 1955
January 28–June 10, 1956

This generation came at a time when divorce was becoming commonplace—so your home image is unconventional. You may have an unusual relationship with your parents, have come from a broken home or an unusual one. You'll have unorthodox ideas about parenting, intimacy, food, and shelter. "Mayflower Madam" Sydney Biddle Barrows was a rule breaker with this placement. You may also be interested in dreams, psychic phenomena, and memory work.

Uranus in Leo—A Flashy Performer
BIRTH DATE: August 24, 1955–January 28, 1956
June 10, 1956–November 1, 1961
January 10–August 10, 1962

This generation understood how to use electronic media to promote themselves. You, like Isadora Duncan, may have a very eccentric kind of charisma and a life that is sparked by unusual love affairs. Your children, too, may have traits that are out of the ordinary. Where this planet falls in your chart, you'll have a love of freedom, be a bit of an egomaniac, and show the full force of your personality in a unique way, like tennis great Martina Navratilova.

Uranus in Virgo—Eccentric Genius
BIRTH DATE: November 1, 1961–January 10, 1962
August 10, 1962–September 28, 1968
May 20, 1969–June 24, 1969

You'll have highly individual work methods. Like Einstein, who had this placement, you'll break the rules brilliantly. Your generation came at a time of student rebellions, the civil rights movement, and the general acceptance of health foods. Chances are, you are concerned about pollution and cleaning up the environment. You may also be involved with nontraditional healing methods. Heavyweight champ Mike Tyson has this placement.

Uranus in Libra—On-again, Off-again Partners
BIRTH DATE: September 28, 1968–May 20, 1969
June 24, 1969–November 21, 1974
May 1–September 8, 1975

Your generation will be always changing partners. Born during the time of Women's Lib, you may have come from a broken home and have no clear image of what a marriage entails. There will be many sudden splits and experiments before you settle down. Your generation will be much involved in legal and political reforms and in changing artistic and fashion looks.

Uranus in Scorpio—The New Age
BIRTH DATE: November 21, 1974–May 1, 1975
September 8, 1975–February 17, 1981
March 20–November 16, 1981

Interest in transformation, meditation and life after death signaled the beginning of New Age consciousness. Your generation recognizes no boundaries, no limits or external controls. You'll have new attitudes toward death and dying, psychic phenomena, and the occult. Like Mae West and Casanova, you'll shock 'em sexually, too.

Uranus in Sagittarius—Space Trippers
BIRTH DATE: February 17–March 20, 1981
November 16, 1981–February 15, 1988
May 27, 1988–Dec 2, 1988

Could this generation be the first to travel in outer space? The last generation with this placement included Charles Lindbergh. At that time, the first zeppelins and the Wright Brothers were conquering the skies. Uranus here forecasts great discoveries, mind expansion, and long-distance travel. Like Galileo and Martin Luther, those born in these years will generate new theories about the cosmos and man's relation to it.

Uranus in Capricorn—Movers and Shakers
BIRTH DATE: December 20, 1904–Jan 30, 1912
September 4–November 12, 1912
February 15–May 27, 1988
December 2, 1988—April 1, 1995
June 9, 1995—January 12, 1996

These year's babies will be out to challenge traditions with the help of electronic gadgets. In these years, we'll get organized with the help of technology put to practical use. Great leaders, who were movers and shakers of history, like Julius Caesar and Henry VIII, were born under this placement.

Uranus in Aquarius—The Innovators
BIRTH DATE: January 30–September 4, 1912
November 12, 1912–April 1, 1919
August 16, 1919–January 22, 1920

The last generation with this placement produced such great innovative minds as Leonard Bernstein and Orson Welles. The next, after the year 2000, will be another radical breakthrough generation, much concerned with global issues that involve all humanity. Intuition, innovation, and sudden changes will surprise everyone when Uranus is in its home sign. This will be a time of experimentation on every level.

Uranus in Pisces—That's Entertainment
BIRTH DATE: April 1–August 16, 1919
January 22, 1920–March 31, 1927
November 4, 1927–January 13, 1928

In this century, Uranus in Pisces focused attention on the rise of electrical entertainment—radio and the cinema—and the secretiveness of Prohibition. This produced a generation of idealists exemplified by Judy Garland's theme, "Over the Rainbow."

Neptune—Dreams and Illusions

Under Neptune's influence, you see what you want to see. But Neptune also encourages you to create, to let your fantasies and daydreams run free. Neptune is often maligned as the planet of illusions, drugs, and alcohol, where you can't bear to face reality. But it also embodies the energy of glamour, subtlety, mystery, and mysticism and governs anything that takes you out of the mundane world, including out-of-body experiences.

Neptune acts to break through your ordinary perceptions and take you to another level of reality, where you can experience either confusion or ecstasy. Neptune's force can pull you off course, as this planet affects its neighbor Uranus, but only if *you* allow this to happen. Those who use Neptune wisely can translate their daydreams into poetry, theater, design, or inspired moves in the business world, avoiding the tricky con artist side of this planet.

Find your Neptune listed here:

BIRTH DATE: July 19–Dec. 25 1901
May 21, 1902–September 23, 1914
Dec. 14, 1914–July 19, 1915
March 19–May 2, 1916

Neptune in Cancer
This age brought dreams of the homeland, idealistic patriotism, and glamorization of the nurturing assets of women.

BIRTH DATE: September 23–December 14, 1914
July 19, 1915–March 19, 1916
May 2, 1916–September 21, 1928
February 19, 1929–July 24, 1929

Neptune in Leo

Here was the glamor of the 1920s and the big spenders. Gambling, seduction, theater, and lavish entertaining distracted from the realities of the age.

BIRTH DATE: September 21, 1928–February 19, 1929
July 24, 1929–October 3, 1942
April 17–August 2, 1943

Neptune in Virgo

This combination encompassed the great depression and World War II. Those born at this time later spread the gospel of health and fitness. This generation's devotion to spending hours at the office inspired the term "workaholic."

BIRTH DATE: October 2, 1942–April 17, 1943
August 2, 1943–December 24, 1955
March 12–October 9, 1956
June 15–August 6, 1957

Neptune in Libra

This began the romantic generation who would later be concerned with "relating." As this generation matured there was a new trend toward marriage and commitment. Racial and sexual equality became an important issue, as they redesigned traditional roles to suit modern times.

BIRTH DATE: August 6, 1957–January 4, 1970
May 3–November 6, 1970

Neptune in Scorpio

This combination brought in a generation which would become interested in transformative power. Born in an era which glamorized sex, drugs, rock and roll, and eastern religion, these young people matured in a more sobering time of AIDS, cocaine abuse, and New Age spirituality. As they go on, they will become active in transforming the environment and healing the planet from the results of the abuse of power.

BIRTH DATE: January 4–May 3, 1970
November 6, 1970–January 19, 1984
June 23–November 21, 1984

Neptune in Sagittarius
That was when space and astronaut travel became a reality. The Neptune influence glamorized new approaches to mysticism, religion, and mind-expansion. This generation will take a new approach to spiritual life, with emphasis on visions, mysticism, and clairvoyance.

BIRTH DATE: January 19, 1984–June 23rd, 1984
November 21, 1984–January 29, 1998

Neptune in Capricorn
Beginning in 1984 and due to last until 1998, this period is when delusions about material power are glamorized and then dashed on the rocks of reality. It is also a time when the psychic world and the material world merge in the commercial marketplace. The occult gains an aura of respectability, while traditional values go topsy-turvey.

Pluto in Your Life

Pluto is a mysterious, far-out little planet with a strange elliptical orbit that occasionally runs inside the orbit of its neighbor Neptune. It has neither been seen nor photographed but we know it exists by its powerful magnetic force. It is actually thought to be quite a tiny planet, though its influence is great. When Pluto zaps a strategic point in your horoscope, your life changes dramatically.

This little planet is the power behind the scenes; it affects you at deep levels of consciousness, causing events to come to the surface that will transform you and your generation. The Pluto place in your horoscope is where you have invisible power (Mars governs the visible power), where you can transform, heal, and affect the unconscious needs of the masses. Pluto governs your need to control, your attitudes toward death and immortality. Much of the strength of Pluto will depend on its position in your chart and the aspects it makes with other planets. For instance, the position of Pluto falling on the ascendant in Michael Jackson's chart accounts for much of his charisma and power to sway the masses.

Pluto in Gemini: (late 1800s until May 28, 1914)
This was a time of mass suggestion and breakthroughs in communications, when many brilliant writers, such as Ernest Hemingway and F. Scott Fitzgerald, were born. Henry Miller, D. H. Lawrence, and James Joyce scandalized with explicit sex in their literature.

Pluto in Cancer: (May 28, 1914–June 16, 1939)
Dictators and mass media arose to weld emotional power over the masses. Women's rights was a popular issue. Deep sentimental feelings, acquisitiveness, and possessiveness characterized these times and people.

Pluto in Leo: (June 16, 1939–August 19, 1957)
The performing arts played on the emotions of the masses. Mick Jagger, John Lennon, and rock and roll were born at this time. Those born here were self-centered, powerful, and boisterous. This generation does its own thing, for better or for worse.

Pluto in Virgo: (August 19, 1957–October 5, 1971; April 17, 1972–July 30, 1972)
This is the yuppie generation that sparked a mass movement toward fitness, health, and career. During this time, machines were invented to process the detail work perfectly. Inventions took on a practical turn; answering machines, fax machines, car telephones, home office equipment all contributed to transform the workplace.

Pluto in Libra: (October 5, 1971–April 17, 1972; July 30, 1972–August 28, 1984)
People born at this time are concerned with partnerships, working together, and finding diplomatic so-

lutions to problems. Marriage is being redefined along more traditional, but equal partnership lines. This was a time of women's liberation, gay rights, ERA, and abortion legislation, all of which transformed our ideas about relationships.

Pluto in Scorpio: (August 28, 1984–January 17, 1995)
Pluto is in its ruling sign for a comparatively short period of time. In 1989, it was at its perihelion or closest point to the sun and earth. So by now we have felt the transforming power somewhere in our lives. This is a time of record achievements, destructive sexually transmitted diseases, nuclear power controversies, explosive political issues. Pluto destroys in order to create new understanding, the phoenix rising from the ashes, which should be some consolation for those of you who felt Pluto's force last year.

Pluto in Sagittarius: 1995
This union should herald a time of great mass expansion, perhaps space travel. Higher spiritual and philosophical goals will be sought by many—in general, this should be a time of great spiritual development, bringing the century to an optimistic finale.

3

Learning About *Your* Personal Universe

Reading the mysterious language of astrology

Part of the fascination of astrology through the ages is that it gives us each a special way to relate to the universe, our own personal place in the cosmos. The horoscope chart is like a fingerprint—intricate, unique, and yours alone. It is a portrait of your moment in time, the moment when you began your independent existence on earth.

The chart is a basic tool for examining and analyzing the forces at work at a specific time. This round map, scattered with numbers and symbols, is a representation of the zodiac at a given moment, as seen from a specific place on earth. To help you understand your own chart, let's construct an approximate model, following these steps:

First, draw a circle; the outer rim represents the path of the sun, moon, and planets. Now draw a line bisecting the circle horizontally. This line represents the horizon, looking south; therefore the left side would be the eastern horizon, where the sun rises (the rising sign). The right intersection would be the western or "sunset" point of the chart. Then draw a line vertically creating a cross. The top intersection is the "noon" point, the bottom is "midnight." The central point or crossroad is the earth.

These four points on the circle are considered the most critical. When a planet passes over either the horizons, the noon or midnight points, it will have a particularly important affect on your chart.

Now, divide each of the four quarters of the chart into three equal parts, making a pie shape with 12 divisions. These pie-shaped slices are the bones of the chart, the framework of the house system. In the houses, you will place the planets, depending on the time of day of the chart. For instance, if the chart was for early morning, you would put the sun symbol in one of the houses near the eastern, or left, side of the chart. If in the early afternoon, the sun would go in the house to the right of the top of the chart. Near midnight, the sun would go to the bottom of the chart.

The same goes for the other nine planets. You would write their symbols in the house where they were located at the time of the chart. In the morning, when the sun was in the second house, Jupiter might be near the western horizon, Saturn in the late evening portion, Venus close to the sun, and so on. So, around the chart you would write symbols for the planets in different "slices."

In some charts, several planets are located in the same house, making it a strong powerhouse force to be reckoned with in the life of the subject. (Children born in 1990 will have several planets grouped together in their charts.) Other charts have planets spread out around the wheel in a more balanced formation. Planets traveling alone, isolated in a section of the chart, become more important because of their standout position.

The point where the boundary of each house intersects the outer circle is called the house cusp. These cusp points are numbered consecutively around the chart running counterclockwise, starting with the cusp of the first house on the eastern horizon point (the rising sign). The midnight point at the bottom of the chart is the cusp of the fourth house, the western horizon (or descendant) would be the cusp of the sixth house and the noon point at the top of the chart would be the cusp of the tenth house. (Of course, the houses in between are numbered accordingly.)

The meanings of the houses never change. Each segment always has to do with these same specific areas of experience. And these areas are related to the signs of the zodiac and the order in which they appear. Note that the critical horizon and midheaven houses are related to the cardinal signs, the center or stabilizing houses are related to the fixed signs, and the last signs in each quarter of the chart are related to the mutables.

The First House
The Aries house, where the self is born, starts off the parade. This shows the first impression the subject of the chart makes on others, the personality, the physical appearance and body type, how concerned the subject is with outward appearances, vitality, charisma. Your first house tells how you come across to others.

The Second House
The Taurus house is where you relate to stability and security in the material world: your attitude toward possessions, your talents and value system, and your sense of self-worth. This is known as the money house.

The Third House
The Gemini house is involved with communication, how you relate to those who are close to you. Here are your brothers and sisters, your neighbors, the way you relate to your immediate environment. Here is where you develop mental ability, motor skills. This house reveals how your mind works on a day-to-day basis.

The Fourth House
The Cancer house relates to the home and emotional foundations. Here are your parents, your unconscious, your heredity, and your final resting place in death. This house tells a great deal about what nurtures the inner you, what kind of home surroundings you need.

The Fifth House
This is the Leo house of self-expression. Look here for artistic expression, love, romance, children, games, theater. This is a warm, outgoing, playful house, where you have love affairs and romantic attractions rather than marriage.

The Sixth House
The Virgo house is where you deal with matters of health and maintenance. This is the operations department, where utilities, diet, and chores are taken care of as well as where you do your filing and bookkeeping. It is also concerned with small pets.

Notice that the first six houses have to do with your identity, how you deal with your immediate surroundings and those close to you. The next six houses will show you how your handle the world at large.

The Seventh House
The Libra house is concerned with one-on-one partnerships. Here is where you look for marriage, for legal contracts, working relationships, and those adversaries who confront you openly (the sneaky secret enemies come later). Lawsuits also happen here. Look at this house to find out about your most compatible partner and your own attitudes toward partnership.

The Eighth House
The Scorpio house is where you encounter deep and powerful matters of life or death, sex, birth, rebirth (or reincarnation), healing, crisis. It is also the place where you deal with other people's money: inheritance, taxes, insurance. Recycling and renovation—activities that transform the old into the new—happen here.

The Ninth House
In the Sagittarius house, you expand your mind and life experiences with travel, higher education. Here is your philosophy of life, your search for wisdom, your spiritual development. This is where you look

at the overall picture, where you publish or teach others what you know. The ninth house is often called the house of the higher mind, while the third house shows how the mind actually works.

The Tenth House
Here is your public image, career, social position. This Capricorn house deals with authority (and paternal authority figures) responsibility, ambition, and aspiration. The tenth house shows what career to choose and where you will succeed in the world at large.

The Eleventh House
The Aquarius house relates to your dealings with people in groups such as political parties, clubs, or organizations, friends in general, and social activities. It also indicates your ideals, your plans for the future, your connection with humanity as a whole. You deal with groups rather than specific people in this area.

The Twelfth House
Finally, the Pisces house reflects on the accumulation and consequences of experience. This house shows what is going on in your spiritual life, what is happening behind the scenes, where you offer selfless service. It also deals with institutions such as churches, hospitals, prisons, or the retreat where you go to be alone, to heal yourself. Old karma, charity work, meditation, research, and hidden enemies also belong here.

The matters of each house are fixed, but the personality of the house (the way the subject of the chart deals with these matters) depends on the sign of the zodiac that was rotating clockwise over the cusp, or beginning of the house at that moment. For example, if the chart is cast for a time near dawn when the sun was passing the first house cusp, the first house will be very significant. If the sun was in the sign of Taurus, then those first house matters will be handled in an intensely Taurean way.

Note: the zodiac and the planets move clockwise in a chart; the houses, however, are numbered counterclockwise. So when you are working with a chart, you are dealing with two circles, the zodiac and the houses. Every two hours, more or less, a new sign comes up over the horizon, as the zodiac pathway, with its parade of planets, rotates around the central earthpoint.

Now you can understand why knowing your birthtime is so necessary when calculating a chart. If you were born at 8 A.M. rather than P.M., the position of the planets would be completely opposite on the chart wheel and influence the happenings of the houses accordingly. Even a few moments difference in time can affect the cusps and therefore the character of the houses.

You now have enough knowledge to make an approximate chart. Hopefully, you know the time of your birth or can make a close estimate. Look up your rising sign on the tables in Chapter 11, and put that sign on the first house cusp (ascendant). Then, working counterclockwise, place each sign in consecutive order on the house cusp.

Example:

If the first house cusp is Gemini, the second house cusp would be Cancer; third house, Leo; fourth house, Virgo; fifth house, Libra; sixth house, Scorpio; seventh house, Sagittarius; eighth house, Capricorn; ninth house, Aquarius; tenth house, Pisces; eleventh house, Aries; twelfth house, Taurus.

The next step is to add the planets. Look up their sign in the tables in Chapter 2 and write them in the corresponding section of your diagram. Because this is an approximate chart, you may be off by a house. But the general area of the chart should be correct. By checking the meaning of the house against the meaning of the planet in each sign, you should be able to adjust its position on the chart. The only planet whose sign you will have to guess is the moon, which moves so rapidly that its tables are too long to include in this book.

Professional astrologers use a large book of tables called an "ephemeris" to calculate the exact position of a planet. These tables show the position of all the planets on any given day. Another option is to use one of the many computer programs available to cast a chart speedily and accurately. As you become more advanced in your astrological studies, you may wish to buy one of these programs for your home computer, or have your chart cast by an astrological computing service.

On a professional astrological chart, you will see symbols used instead of words to indicate the planets and signs. These serve as a convenient, universally recognized shorthand for astrologers.

The symbols for the planets are variations and combinations of three geometric forms: the circle, which symbolizes eternity; the half circle, the soul; and the cross, matter. Some symbols, such as the glyphs for Mercury and Pluto, combine all three forms.

The glyphs for the signs have an ancient ancestry; some go back as far as ancient Egypt and Chaldea. Their forms give abstract clues to the signs they represent. You can visualize a ram's horns from the curving V-shaped Aries glyph, or a bull's head in the Taurus glyph, or the roman numeral two in the Gemini glyph. Cancer, a "horizontal sixty-nine" form, has been said to resemble two female breasts. The Leo lion is a circle with a long curling tail. Virgo's M-shape symbolizes virginal female genitalia. Libra is recognizable as the scales. The Scorpio glyph, an M-shape with an arrow attached, represents erect male genitalia. The Sagittarius arrow is very easy to recognize. Capricorn could be loosely imagined as a bent knee. Aquarius has the ancient parallel wave symbol and two curved lines joined at the center portray Pisces' fishes.

A Quick Introduction to Chart Interpretation

Once the house cusps are established and the planets are placed in their houses, the real work of chart interpretation begins. First the houses are analyzed according to the sign on the cusp and the planets residing in the house; then the astrologer considers the dynamic relationships between each of the planets for clues to the challenges and character of the chart.

These relationships, or "aspects," are determined by the distance in degrees of the planet in question from the other planet (or planets) with which it is interacting. On the zodiac circle, which is divided into 360 degrees, some distances create an easy flow of energy. Other distances create energy which pulls in opposite directions or squares off in a tense conflict of interests. Weighing and balancing these different variable forces within each chart is the craft work of astrology.

The most important aspects to look for are:

Conjunctions
When two planets are within 10 degrees of each other. The closer they travel together, the more each planet's energies will affect the other. Some planets are more compatible working partners; others are less harmonious. For instance, conjunctions involving Saturn often restrict the activity of the other planets involved. On the other hand, Mars will have an energizing effect and Venus will bring an aesthetic, beautifying force.

Oppositions
These occur when two or more planets are opposite each other in the chart, at approximately 180 degrees, give or take 10 degrees. The most obvious example is the time of the full moon, when the sun and moon are directly opposite each other. This can be an aspect of great tension—or great illumination. Much depends on other happenings in the chart and

how the subject deals with the two opposing forces. An opposition usually signals a need for balance and awareness; otherwise the person will tend to seesaw between the two extremes.

Squares

The 90-degree separation between two planets, a distance of approximately a quarter of the zodiac, is traditionally considered a very stressful aspect, because it involves signs of inharmonious elements which cause the subject to feel at cross-purposes with himself. Squares are usually interpreted as inner conflicts, but they can also be seen as energizers, if the subject can find an outlet in his or her life which deals with these conflicts successfully and profitably. Many lawyers, artists, police officers, athletes, people in competitive fields have prominent squares. The question here, as in all of astrology is, How is the person using this energy?

Trines

Planets separated by approximately one-third of the zodiac circle or 120 degrees, have the most harmonious aspect, where the energy flows smoothly between planetary forces of the same element. With trines, you don't have to work to make things happen. However, this aspect can also breed laziness, overoptimism, arrogance, and passivity. A person with too many trines may have problems getting motivated, may tend to coast along with life's easy circumstances.

These are the four major aspects. There are other less important aspects: the semisquare (45 degrees apart), the sextile (60 degrees apart), semisextile (30 degrees apart), and the quincunx (150 degrees apart) are the ones most often considered. Sextiles are harmonious aspects of planets in signs of the same polarity (positive or negative). Semisextiles are less potent but still harmonious contacts. The semisquare is a minor aspect that can cause tension. The quincunx, or contact of planets five signs apart, is another mildly stressful aspect of energies which may not be easy to integrate, because the signs involved are in elements that do not mix easily, such as fire sign Leo with water sign Pisces or airy Gemini with earthy Capricorn.

The minor aspects usually take on importance when specific problems are considered.

A Look Into the Future: Can You Predict How This Year's Celestial Events Affect Your Chart?

Using the rough chart you have now made, you can try your hand at astrological forecasting. Look up this year's planetary movements under each planet in Chapter 2 and apply them to your chart. Which house will they affect? Which of your planets will be affected? The major 1990 events in the sign of Capricorn are sure to activate the Capricorn section of your chart. Jupiter in Cancer and Leo will expand those houses. Mercury retrogrades, lunar and solar eclipses . . . all will stimulate the houses in your chart where they occur.

Look ahead to these planetary movements in the plans you are developing. *Though you cannot change the course of events, you can prepare and modify your activities to take advantage of the best options available.* And remember, though astrology can provide a road map, you are in command of your own vehicle.

To become an expert at astrological prediction and analysis requires much study and practice in weighing and balancing the different aspects. The brief overview in this chapter has just barely scratched the surface, but perhaps this exercise in doing your own rough chart will whet your appetite to expand your knowledge of this fascinating craft.

4

The Celebrity Astro-Quiz
Do you know the stars' signs?

Can you recognize each of these celebrities from their sun sign hints? Their identities are revealed on pages 83–84.

1. A pair of battling lions, this superstar couple first wed, then shed the bonds of matrimony to roam free. He's the Leo bully, who roars and charges when anyone invades his territory or makes even a friendly move on his mate. She's the Golden Girl Leo who can't stay out of the limelight. Neither can share center stage—or costar—so this romantic show is always about to close. (However, at this writing, they are still legally tied.)

2. Here's a megawatt Virgo singer whose name is household word, yet, like his sign-mate, Greta Garbo, he guards his privacy. An extreme perfectionist, he revamped his looks with plastic surgery. Some say he went too far. This health and diet fanatic even transports his own water on international tours.

3. He's a Sagittarian TV heartthrob, known for fast action on and off screen and a love 'em and leave 'em philosophy. A trendsetter in men's fashion, he's part of the New Image of one of our Southern Cities.

4. The Aries man can be one of the zodiac's most elusive bachelors. Here's another Don Juan of renown, whose affairs include a long line of the world's

most beautiful and famous women. His heart lies where the real excitement is (for him, anyway)—in his work as director/actor/producer.

5. Both these Aquarians are good-guy hunks, whose screen image combines adventure with a touch of humor. Their moustaches and the twinkle in their eyes might remind you of another Aquarian star, "the King" Clark Gable. In private life, both were gun-shy of marriage, but finally settled in with long-term loves.

6. The not-so-gentle screen image of this Cancer man really depicts his hard-driving Capricorn ascendant—which gives him the discipline to overcome great obstacles. But real-life would-be romantic partners should look to his dynamo mother for clues to what makes this guy tick.

7. This talk show hostess capitalized on her Piscean ability to empathize with her guests and target the feelings of the audience to become a hit on both radio and TV, after many different careers, including owning a wine bar, mothering several natural and foster children, and writing a book of advice.

8. At first glance you might think she's an eccentric Aquarius, but this talented Capricorn actress, known for her innovative and highly individual personal style, is also a winner as a director and photographer. In her personal life, she remains a lone wolf, despite meaningful relationships with two famous actor/directors.

9. These two Oscar-winning female Taurean superstars are both known for their unusual unforgettable looks, their singing and acting talent, unpredictable love lives, iron self-discipline, and longevity after many ups and downs in show business.

10. Pisces men and women have amazing resilience. They often hit bottom and rise again, wiser and better! Here are three Pisces (one male, two female) who made it, lost it, and made it again! Two have the same last name!!!

11. Aquarians love helping people in groups—and living in unconventional ways: This Aquarian actress has many natural and adopted children, yet she prefers an unconventional relationship with her director/costar/lover, who is father of her youngest son. Both continue to live separately, have no plans to wed.

12. These two dynamic Aries stars, born within days of each other, costarred on TV's most successful sci-fi series. As explorers in outer space, their characters epitomized both sides of the Aries ego—the adventurous pioneer leader and the uncompromising idealist.

13. Two partners of the same sign often compete instead of collaborate. The exception to the rule is Scorpio, which has produced some long-lasting and legendary lovers. This couple were King and Queen of western movies for many years.

14. These two Aquarian sisters are noted for their glamor and flair for making the unconventional remark, as well as their many marriages. They love the electric flash of diamonds.

15. This former child model and actress earned fame and fortune at a young age, and could have coasted on her beauty for life. But being a Gemini, she placed equal importance on developing her mind and earned a degree at Princeton.

16. The Cancer and Scorpio sun sign positions of this couple, could portend royal bliss; however, their much publicized marriage occurred in the ominous "shadow of the eclipse" which guarantees treacherous twists and turns on the marital road.

17. Capricorn is the sign that "ages" well. Can you name at least three Capricorn film legends who remained stars well into their later years.

18. Libra produces some of the world's most beautiful stars. These two prototypes of the Libran love goddess and the classic blonde have, at different times, been called the "most beautiful woman in France."

19. Virgos believe in working one's way to the top—and have a great fondness for the "class act." This Virgo TV host has made his fortune by showing how the rich and famous live.

20. Sagittarians often achieve fame far from the country of their birth. This megastar's outspoken notoriety in the Far East and in Europe made her famous and infamous at home.

21. Oprah Winfrey is the epitome of the female of her sign—independent, outspoken, yet able to be detached and objective with controversial talk show guests, eager to help those less fortunate, a good friend to many. Can you guess her sign?

22. His Libra sun sign, ruled by Venus, the planet of love, may have inspired this international singing star's hit dedicated "To All the Girls I Loved Before."

23. An ageless sexpot, this steamy actress has an equally successful career as a best-selling authoress. True to her Gemini sun sign, she's good at two things. She fills her books with tantalizing gossip and stays remarkably youthful in looks and attitude.

24. A sharp tongue and a quick wit are shared by these Sagittarians: She's a singer/comedian who came a long way from her childhood in Hawaii. He's an erudite debater and writer, who crusades for conservative causes.

25. From his super-powerful physique to his marriage to an "American princess," this Leo does things in a big way. He's not a cat you'd be tempted to tease.

26. Virgo is the sign of the Virgin, but neither of these two bodacious Virgo beauties of Latin ancestry will ever play that role. Both have outgrown their sexpot image but not their allure.

27. Cancer women are known to be self-protective and to keep an eye on where the cash is flowing. This very tall blonde gained fame as a gunslinger on screen and a manhunter off screen.

28. Virgo men have a rarified mental appeal that can be quite erotic—as in these two stellar examples. One is a talented English film star, best known for his unforgettable portrayal of a student, which earned him the title of "the thinking woman's sex symbol." And our other Virgo hero was a different type of ladykiller on a long-running TV evening soap opera. Tough and demanding, he played with heads as well as hearts.

29. Water signs can be quite secretive, especially Scorpios, like this famous artist who claimed to be a Leo, but his birth certificate revealed otherwise. His preference for wearing black, his hidden fortune, and his mysterious death might help you identify him. He managed to be famous yet keep everyone guessing about his private life. The late Ambassadror Claire Booth Luce liked to tell people she was an Aries, but her fragile beauty, luminous eyes, and love of scuba diving will reveal her true sign.

30. These two Aries never costarred, though they were born on the same day, near the same place! Both reflect opposite sides of the Aries character. He became famous as an arrogant fiery rebel, who has always bucked the system. She was the symbol of the sunny energetic all-American girl with a secret love.

Answers:
If you scored 20–30, you should be able to spot most sun sign types.

1. Madonna and Sean Penn
2. Michael Jackson
3. Don Johnson
4. Warren Beatty
5. Burt Reynolds and Tom Selleck
6. "Rocky"—Sylvester Stallone
7. Sally Jessy Raphael
8. Diane Keaton
9. Cher and Barbra Streisand
10. James Taylor, Elizabeth Taylor, and Liza Minelli.
11. Mia Farrow

12. William Shatner and Leonard Nimoy
13. Roy Rogers and Dale Evans
14. Eva and Zsa Zsa Gabor
15. Brooke Shields
16. Scorpio Prince Charles and Cancer Lady Diana
17. Cary Grant, Marlene Dietrich, Loretta Young, Ava Gardner
18. Brigitte Bardot and Catherine Deneuve
19. Robin Leach of "Lifestyles of the Rich and Famous"
20. Jane Fonda
21. Aquarius
22. Julio Iglésias
23. Joan Collins
24. Bette Midler and William F. Buckley
25. Arnold Schwarzenegger
26. Raquel Welch and Sophia Loren
27. Brigitte Nielson
28. Jeremy Irons and Larry Hagman—J.R. Ewing of "Dallas"
29. Scorpio Andy Warhol and Pisces Claire Booth Luce
30. Marlon Brando and Doris Day

5

Using Astrology Every Day
How to cope with the stressful times in 1990

The great financier J. P. Morgan, a firm believer in astrology, was once asked if astrology made millionaires. "No, it makes billionaires," he replied. Morgan followed the advice of one of the most famous astrologers of all time, Evangeline Adams (a descendent of President John Quincy Adams), and it is no secret that presidents, celebrities, kings, and military leaders as well as tycoons keep their eye on the stars. But you may wonder if they have access to privileged information. The fact is that, if astrology worked for them, it can work for you, too. Anyone can follow the planetary movements, and once you know how to interpret them, you won't need the advice of an expert to grasp the overall trends and make profitable use of them.

Over the centuries it has been observed that certain kinds of activities go more or less smoothly depending on the position of corresponding planets. Some tides in the affairs of men change with the moon; communications flow with Mercury, love affairs with Venus, and so on. Why not put astrology to work in your life, just like political leaders and business tycoons by marking the favorable times on your calendar and circling in red those times when it's best to slow down and play it cool.

When Your Ruling Planet Changes Signs, You'll Change, Too

You are particularly sensitive to the movements of the planet that rules your sun sign and the sign it is currently passing through. In fact, you may temporarily take on some of the characteristics of that "new" sign. And when a planet is traveling through its native sign, as Pluto in Scorpio and Saturn in Capricorn are doing this year, it will have a supportive influence on those born under that sign. The sign of Cancer, known for its frequent mood swings, is ruled by the fastest-moving planet, the moon, so Cancerian moods change every two to two-and-a-half days. Mercury, another fast-moving planet, especially affects restless Gemini and Virgo, who should take special note of the dates listed below when Mercury changes signs.

You'll find your ruling planet listed in Chapter 2. The sun and moon (considered planets in astrology), Mars, Venus, and Mercury change signs frequently. Other planets may stay in the same sign all year long. Those of you who are especially affected by a certain planet other than your ruling planet will experience a change in your lives in some way when that planet changes signs.

Mercury Sign Changes

February 11—to Aquarius
March 3—to Pisces
March 20—to Aries
April 4—to Taurus
June 12—to Gemini
June 27—to Cancer
July 11—to Leo
July 29—to Virgo
October 5—to Libra
October 23—to Scorpio
November 11—to Sagittarius
December 2—to Capricorn
December 25—to Sagittarius (retrograde)

This year's focus will be on the sign of Capricorn, where Uranus (ruler of Aquarius), Neptune (ruler of Pisces) and Saturn (ruler of Capricorn) will stay together in Capricorn all year long. These signs will take on Capricornian traits, meaning Pisces and Aquarius will get down to business, get organized. (More about the Capricorn area of *your* life, later.)

Jupiter (ruler of Sagittarius) in Cancer will bring protection and a period of expansion to Cancerians, and will make Sagittarians stay closer to hearth and home. In mid-August, when this big planet moves into Leo, Sagittarians will become more outgoing, and Leos will burst into the spotlight again. Make a special note of August 18, when Jupiter changes signs—everyone should feel a lift, a new optimism then. You may be tempted to celebrate or splurge on an extravagant treat.

Some Full Moons Will Be Trickier Than Others—Here Are the Ones To Watch

This monthly event should be considered when you have important plans or meetings on your agenda, especially those that might cause emotional stress or tension. If pressure has been building up over the past two weeks, it will somehow come to light or be released at the full moon. This is the time to bring matters out into the open. People will be demanding a confrontation. You could make an excellent positive presentation now or go public in some way with your plans. In your emotional life, this is a passionate time, perfect for romance or a wedding, if all goes well. If there have been clandestine goings on, secretive behavior, jealousy or emotional turbulence, remember that this is the traditional time for crimes of passion, heavy drinking, and open quarrels.

You will feel the intense effects of some full moons more than others, particularly the full moon that falls in the same sign as your sun sign. Mark these full moon days on your calendar. Also potentially stressful times: when the full moon is a sign which is the same *quality* as your sign. For instance, Aries should also be particularly careful on the full moons which fall in other cardinal signs: Cancer, Libra, and Capricorn. Fixed signs (Taurus, Leo, Scorpio, Aquarius) should watch full moons in other fixed signs and the same goes for the mutable signs (Gemini, Virgo, Sagittarius, Pisces). These full moons fall at a stressful angle to your sun and are often times of emotional tension or challenge.

Mark the appropriate full moons on your calendar:

Full Moon in Cancer—January 11 and December 31
Full Moon in Leo—February 9 (Eclipse)
Full Moon in Virgo—March 11
Full Moon in Libra—April 10
Full Moon in Scorpio—May 9
Full Moon in Sagittarius—June 8
Full Moon in Capricorn—July 8
Full Moon in Aquarius—August 6 (Eclipse)
Full Moon in Pisces—September 4
Full Moon in Aries—October 4
Full Moon in Taurus—November 2
Full Moon in Gemini—December 2

You can also time your activities to take advantage of the phases of the moon. The new moon is the best time to start projects, when you have the two major planetary forces, the sun and moon, pulling together in the same sign. Anything new in your life gets an extra push during this time of spontaneous, instinctive action. But don't consider breaking off at this time—your instincts are in control and energy is high. Wait till you are more controlled, deliberate and reasonable, at the last quarter.

During the first quarter, up until the full moon, get your project off and running, lay the groundwork, focus, and set positive patterns.

The full moon, when emotions are out into the open, is the best time to face the public. This is the time to shine, but it is also the time when pressures are being released, people are letting off steam. Tensions that have been building up over a period of time are likely to burst at the full moon. This can happen literally as well as emotionally—recently, under a full moon in Taurus, a weak wall in a New York building gave way, causing the entire building to collapse. So try to avoid confrontations or arguments while the sun and moon oppose each other. And check those weak points in your physical surroundings and your own physical body. This is not a good time for surgical operations, which may produce heavier bleeding.

From the last quarter to the new moon, you should wind down, reevaluate, or break off. This is a better time for serious thinking, more inward-directed activities. You can accomplish some serious conscious creative work or correct any errors in strategy. Now, you can leave a job or get a divorce. Clean out your closets. Clear up any unfinished business. And the best time to get some rest, spend some time alone.

Eclipses—Count to Ten Before and Three After

When either the sun or the moon is blocked out, our natural rhythms are upset. Events which happen now may be off balance or shook up in some way and can have unpredictable results. So it is better to wait until the entire eclipse period has settled down before undertaking any important activities. To play it safe, wait out the shadow of the eclipse from ten days before until three days after the eclipse.

As with the full moons, those with planets in signs of the same *quality* as the sign of the eclipse will be most affected.

Eclipses in 1990

January 26—Solar Eclipse in Aquarius
February 9—Lunar Eclipse in Leo
July 22—Solar Eclipse in Leo
August 6—Lunar Eclipse in Aquarius

Take special note: Aquarius, Leo, Scorpio, Taurus

The Void of Course Moon: Resting Time

Approximately every two days, before the moon changes signs, a period called the Void of Course Moon occurs. This is the time between the last major aspect of the moon and its entrance into a new sign. It's a time when we, like the moon, might feel unconnected, in need of centering. This can last for a few minutes to as long as a day or two. The Void of Course is not a time for major purchases, contracts, important meetings, or presentations. Under this aspect, you may have to make changes later; plans and purchases don't work out as you envision.

Rest, relaxation, and concentration on nonmaterial matters such as introspection, prayer, spiritual activities, and sleep are favored. When the Void of Course happens at night or on the weekends it is more convenient. However, sometimes it happens during a hardworking day full of activities. Advance planning can be extremely helpful—better to take a break than to force matters at this time. The key is: Don't push during a Void of Course!

You can estimate the void of course period by looking in the daily forecasts in this book for the time when the moon changes signs. Then schedule a few hours of rest and relaxation, or low-priority chores, immediately beforehand. Or you can buy one of the several astrological calendars available which chart the exact void of course period.

Mercury Retrograde—Play for Time

One of the trickiest astrological happenings is the mercury retrograde. It happens three times a year and lasts about three weeks—a period of time when nothing seems to happen on schedule. There are waves of small irritations. Even the most organized person becomes forgetful. Trains and busses are delayed. That check you are waiting anxiously for gets held up or lost. People misunderstand or just don't hear what you say. These are all symptoms of a period of time when the planet Mercury is traveling backward relative to the earth's orbit. And those Mercury-ruled areas go off-kilter.

What can you do about it? Very little when it comes to train, planes, and telephones. Your best strategy is to be prepared. Carry along some work or a good book when you travel, to use the time most productively. Check schedules in advance. Try to avoid rushing and take care of critical matters before the retrograde period. It is a very good idea to postpone signing contracts, making serious commitments or major purchases until the three-week period is over. Be sure to make a note of this year's mercury retrogrades and plan accordingly.

Mercury Retrograde Periods in 1990

December 30, 1989–January 19, 1990 in Capricorn
  Take special note: cardinal signs
April 23–May 16 in Taurus
  Take special note: fixed signs
August 25–September 17 in Virgo
  Take Special Note: mutable signs

The Planetary Pile-up in Capricorn—When Will It Affect You?

Capricorn is the center of action this year, especially in January and February, when eight planets pass through. (The only ones who do not are Jupiter and Pluto.) Needless to say, Capricorns will have an exceptionally eventful year, perhaps the most important in their lives. Neptune, Uranus, and Saturn will be there all year. After a Mercury retrograde until January 19, Mars will be making mischief in Capricorn throughout late January and February, especially when it opposes Jupiter in Cancer on January 31.

On February 9, the same day as a lunar eclipse, Mars will be passing over Uranus in Capricorn—two very important happenings on the same day! It's a day for unpredictable shake-ups and emotionally charged events, so mark it in red on your calendar. Cardinal and fixed signs will be most affected, but anyone with placements in Capricorn should be on red alert. Go slow and be super cautious!

Mars next hits Neptune on February 17 and Saturn on March 1 and 2, first activating dreams and illusions, then putting them to the test. The Mars and Saturn combination has been compared to stepping on the gas with the brakes still on.

Saturn in 1990—Who Will Be Tested?

In 1990, Saturn is traveling through Capricorn. Since this is the sign it rules, Capricorn is most powerful here, and will be affecting you strongly in the Capricorn area of your horoscope. Everyone will be facing reality and scrutinizing the working operations in some part of their lives. We'll be more aware of our responsibilities and duties, and many of us will be turning to more traditional values and institutions for support.

Those of you born with sun in Capricorn will feel this transit strongly. So will Aries, Cancer, and Libra. If you have any planets in Capricorn, the moon in Capricorn or Capricorn rising, you're going to feel it, too.

Those of you who were born in 1931 and late 1960–1961 are experiencing a Saturn return this year, when Saturn revisits the sign where it was located at your birth, one of life's sobering-up periods, when you settle down and face your future realistically. Bear in mind that Saturn gives you what you've worked for. It's very fair. It finishes things off, takes away whatever isn't workable, or has finished its function in your life, whether it's a job, a relationship, a person. You get serious about your work, or about raising a family. You make important commitments. Many people get married, settle down to work, and deal with lingering health problems at this time.

Jupiter Holds Its Own in Cancer

Until mid-August, Cancer, the sign of the United States, is holding its own opposite Capricorn with the help and protection of Jupiter. This planet of luck and expansion will be opposed by a parade of fast-moving planets in January (sun, moon, Venus, Mars, and Mercury). Then after a brief respite, it will feel the opposition of the slow-moving Uranus on May 13, Neptune on June 6, and Saturn on July 13.

This means that sun sign Cancers, Aries, Capricorns, and Libras and those of you with other important planets in those signs will be affected. On the other hand, Pisces and Scorpio, who have an easier aspect, should do well. Everyone will breathe easier when Jupiter rolls into fun-loving Leo on August 18. But Leos had better watch their diet and budgets; many Leos will be expanding their family at this time.

Your Uranus Outlook for 1990

Uranus, joined by two other slow-movers, Saturn and Neptune, in Capricorn will have many of you on a roller coaster this year, especially in December and January when the sun, moon, Mercury, Mars, and Venus make contact.

You will be getting many mixed messages and often wondering what hit you. However, in Capricorn, this intuitive planet can be used to find new solutions to practical problems. Many of our established systems and traditions will be reevaluated and adapted for the future. This is a time when all of the systems our society has depended on will be questioned.

This is not a good time to cling to the past. You'll work best with this aspect if you stay open to new experiences and enlightening inspiration. With Saturn, the rule-maker, and Uranus, the rule-breaker in the same sign, we can find some completely new and innovative solutions to age-old problems.

What To Do About Neptune

Also traveling through Capricorn is Neptune, the planet of dreams, illusions, and creativity. In the most realistic sign, which emphasizes organization, structure and tradition, this glamorous planet might seem ill at ease. But working positively here, Neptune can crystallize those daydreams and add creativity and fantasy to the material marketplace. We have already seen the negative side of Neptune in Capricorn, in the insider trading scandals of the financial world. Positive results should be new products that tap today's real needs.

Those with a strong Capricorn influence may seem a bit confused and out of character, now. Under a strong Neptune aspect, you should beware of falling for schemes; be sure to check the facts; go for substance rather than a sales pitch; and don't be tempted to take the easy way out.

Pluto, the Transformer

Last spring, Pluto in its ruling sign of Scorpio, reached its perihelion, the point closest to the sun, where it still exerts its most powerful transformative force. Historically, Pluto's perihelion has coincided with ages of renaissance, enlightenment, and extremely gifted seers, philosophers, reformers, artists, and explorers. Since it is in excellent relationship to Neptune and Saturn in Capricorn, this could be a dramatic and prophetic time of great global spiritual development.

Pluto works on a grand scale to change the shape of events. In Scorpio, it will act directly and potently, with no compromises. It spends from 11 to 31 years in a sign, with only 11.2 years to make its mark in Scorpio.

In the Scorpio section of your chart, Pluto will urge you to overreact. In a positive sense, this is where you'll be making long-term changes in your life, even a complete transformation in that area.

Scorpios born between the 7th and 12th of November will be most affected this year. Suggestion to Scorpios: Concentrate on the healing aspect of your work. You can do wonderful things in that area. And those born between the 7th and 12th of May (Taurus), August (Leo), and February (Aquarius) will feel strong Pluto power this year. Taurus will feel it in their relationships; Leo and Aquarius should try to overreact. All of these are fixed signs like stability and control, but, like it or not, changes are in store for you.

For more about how this year's planets affect your sun sign, look to your annual forecast in the back of this book.

6

Your Star-Guide for Choosing the Best Partner

True astrology offers no "partnership insurance," but it does offer you enough clues to navigate even the stormiest relationship safely, whether it's an emotion-packed love affair or a pressurized business partnership.

The key is learning how to scout the trouble spots ahead of time and learn when you must expect to compromise and when you will have an easy flow of communication. Thus armed, you can work toward maintaining balance and harmony. Since we are all a configuration of planetary energies, there are no truly incompatible horoscopes. However, there are signs whose energy flows together easily. On the other hand, when communication is too easy, some couples become bored and look for stimulation elsewhere. In other combinations, there is so much excitement that the people involved have to split up or blow their circuits.

When we analyze a relationship astrologically, we are really dealing with the chemical interactions of the planets closest to the earth: the sun, moon, Mercury, Venus, and Mars. The sun sign can give us the basic character of the relationship, while the four other planets add specific dimensions, which can explain how two people who have a very difficult aspect between their sun signs can be very happy together. For instance, a Scorpio with a moon in Gemini might be much more compatible with a Gemini partner than another Scorpio with, say, a moon in Leo. So it is important to take those personal planets into account when speculating on whether a relationship will last.

The Basic Chemistry of Relationships

Successful partners often say, "We had great chemistry" to describe an instant compatibility, while others complain: "I don't know why we couldn't get together. We had everything going for us, but the chemistry was off." Astrology takes this comment quite literally. By now you know that each sign is described by an element (earth, air, fire, or water) and a quality (cardinal, fixed, mutable). Signs of the same element have a natural ease of communication. You've heard the saying "he's in his element" to describe someone who is able to use his energy easily and productively. When you are in your element with someone else, the same holds true.

You must also consider the quality of the signs, which really influences whether a couple will be on the same wavelength. If you remember, the quality of a sign is the way that sign operates. Signs of the same quality are of different elements (unless both partners are the same sign). For instance, Aries and Capricorn partners, both cardinal signs, will have very different, often competing points of view. Impatient Aries is idealistic and courageous, always in a hurry, while calculating Capricorn's emphasis will be on organization, purpose, and achievement. So these two signs may tend to grate on each other. Mutable Virgo's constant need to analyze and edit can thwart a freewheeling Sagittarius or Pisces. Two stubborn fixed signs such as Taurus and Scorpio might tune each other out or have a "Mexican standoff."

For quick reference, the general rules are:

1. Signs of the same *element* get along most easily.

    EARTH: Taurus, Virgo, Capricorn
    AIR: Gemini, Libra, Aquarius

FIRE: Aries, Leo, Sagittarius
WATER: Cancer, Scorpio, Pisces

2. Signs of the same *quality* will have to make compromises to resolve their differing points of veiw.

CARDINAL: Aries, Cancer, Libra, Capricorn
FIXED: Taurus, Leo, Scorpio, Aquarius
MUTABLE: Gemini, Virgo, Pisces, Sagittarius

3. Some elements mix more easily than others. If you go back to your very first chemistry lessons, remember what fire does to water. The analogy generally holds true for signs of these elements when the partnership is under stress. Fire sign energy will evaporate water. And an excess of water sign emotion will dampen fire's enthusiasm. Earth signs generally work well with water signs, and fire signs are more compatible with air.

If you are an air sign, does this mean that you should associate with only fire or other air signs who do not have the same quality? Not necessarily. Your horoscope is really a balance of many planets in different signs. And too much of *any* sign can easily tip the scales in a relationship.

The Compatibility Planets

The planets closest to the earth each play a different role in your relationships.

Mercury placements will show you how you each communicate and how your mind works. It will indicate your mental interests and your ability to concentrate. If you want constant mental stimulation, then your partner's Mercury in the same quality will give you a good debate, but you may have to constantly explain and justify your point of view. Mercury in the same sign will almost read your mind, but you may not have such lively dinner conversations.

Venus will indicate physical attraction and whether you have compatible tastes. Incompatible Venus placements can be very difficult in a long term relationship. A person who must have immaculate surroundings might not be happy with someone who must be surrounded with beloved objects and leaves clothes in the middle of the floor; or, in the same view, one partner who loves antiques and the other who craves high-tech gadgets.

Mars is sexual energy, your different tempers, your aggressive drive and ambition. A Mars in Aries, impatient and impulsive, might be driven to distraction by the picky critical Mars in Virgo.

The moon will show your emotional natures and what kind of atmosphere makes you happiest. The moon is such a strong factor that it can offset other, more stressful, forces between two people, especially if one person's moon is in the other person's sun sign.

In a business relationship, you might need a compatible Mercury and Mars. In a love affair, Mars and Venus would tell the tale. A long-lasting relationship especially should have good moon sign compatibility.

Sometimes, so-called stressful aspects will stimulate the relationship, providing sparks and excitement. Many passionate love affairs have Venus or Mars in the same quality. This can produce the "opposites attract" syndrome, where one partner provides what the other lacks. Again, the success depends on the matter of balance. Too much emphasis on any one element or quality usually tips the relationship to the extreme and unless there are other people in the scenario to provide what is missing, the relationship dissipates. A combination with no planets in earth signs would be very bad for business. One with no water might lack feeling or creativity.

Your Best Business Partner:
Should have a compatible Mars and Mercury in the same element or a complimentary element, so communications will flow easily and your ambitions are focused in the same direction. If your horoscope has few planets in earth, you should look for someone with a predominant planet in earth, to oversee the working operations. If your business depends on

sales, fire signs are most effective here. Creativity and emotional understanding are favored by the water signs.

Your Best Love Partner:

The most romantic affairs are those between partners whose Mars and Venus are in the same element or quality. The same element will produce soul mates; the same quality will produce sparks.

Long-term relationships fare well if the sun and moon are in the same element. It is better here if the moons are not in the same quality. You'll want emotional harmony, rather than stimulation, over the long haul.

Fill in this chart to check out potential partners, using the Venus, Mars tables in Chapter 2. The Mercury and moon placements can be estimated from information provided in Chapters 2 and 8.

Compatibility Chart

Partner A:	Partner B:
Sign/Quality/Element	Sign/Quality/Element
SUN_____	_____
MOON_____	_____
MARS_____	_____
VENUS_____	_____
MERCURY_____	_____

7

What and Why You Need To Know About the Moon

The moon is our most useful planet and the one that affects your daily life most strongly. It rules the tides and your body (which is mostly water), fertility and growth, and everyone's mood.

More than any other celestial body, the moon captures our imagination and fantasies. No other planet has such a hold on our emotions, both literally and figuratively. It's our closest neighbor, the only other object in the cosmos man has visited, yet this beautiful and fascinating friend still leaves many of our questions unanswered. We still wonder if it is a broken-off part of our own planet, a visitor from outer space that was trapped in the earth's force field, or a piece of the sun. And no astronomer has yet explained how this relatively tiny satellite happen to orbit at a distance which makes it appear to be the same *size* as the sun, from the earth's point of view. Was that just another of nature's intriguing coincidences? Because the moon's diameter is constant, astronomers have used it for centuries as a measuring device to confirm the size of the sun during solar eclipses.

Many scientists now believe that the moon plays an even more important role as a kind of cosmic bodyguard. Without its protective magnetic field, life here might not be possible. They echo the intuitive knowledge of many ancient peoples who worshipped the moon as the giver of life even before they turned to the sun.

For thousands of years, faithful moon-watchers have noted and compiled data on the effects of the different phases of the moon and its corresponding rhythms on our everyday happenings. In many astrological systems, the sign the moon falls in at birth is considered even more important than the sun sign when drawing up horoscopes. Because the moon changes signs so swiftly, it is necessary to know the exact time of your birth to get a truly accurate moon reading. However, since each moon nature is quite distinct, you can make a good estimate from the information in this chapter.

The moon can teach you about the inner side of yourself, your needs and secrets, as well as those of others. It is your most personal planet, the receptive, reflective female nurturing side of you, and it reflects who you were nurtured by—the Mother, or mother figure, in your chart. In a man's chart the moon position also describes his female receptive emotional side, and the woman in his life who will have the deepest effect. (Venus reveals the kind of woman who attracts him physically.)

The moon can also help you plan your daily activities, according to the prevailing moon sign of the day. By flowing with the natural rhythms of the moon cycle, you'll find that there are times when people are more receptive to certain activities. Then, in a day or two, the group mood will change. Following the emotional tides of the moon cycle is one of the great secrets of those who have profited most through astrology.

Use the moon to help your world run smoothly:

- As a way to understand your own instinctive emotional needs and those of others. It is often useful to monitor when the moon passes the sun sign of those close to you.
- As a way to forecast the day's emotional weather.
- To play your activities according to the sign the moon is passing through and what is favored by that sign.

The sign the moon was passing through at your birth reflects your instinctive emotional nature—what appeals to you subconsciously. Check through these descriptions to find the moon sign which feels most familiar.

Moon in Aries: You are an idealistic impetuous person who falls in and out of love easily. This placement makes you both independent and ardent. You love a challenge, but could cool once your quarry is captured. You should cultivate patience and tolerance—or you will tend to gravitate toward those who treat you roughly, just for the challenge and excitement.

Moon in Taurus: You are a sentimental soul who is fond of the good life and gravitates to solid, secure relationships. You like displays of affection, and creature comforts, all the tangible trappings of a cozy, safe, calm atmosphere. You are sensual and steady emotionally, but very stubborn and determined. You can't be pushed. You should make an effort to broaden your horizons. Take a risk sometimes!

Moon in Gemini: You are a born flirt who loves social life and needs constant stimulation. You enjoy a lively professional, or at least outgoing, life. You may marry more than once and have a rather chaotic emotional life due to your difficulty with commitment and settling down. Be sure to find a partner who is also outgoing. You will have to learn at some point to focus your energies and to keep on an even keel. You tend to be somewhat fragmented: you do two things at once—have two homes, two lovers. If you can find a creative way to express your many-faceted nature, you'll be ahead of the game.

Moon in Cancer: Your needs are very much associated with your reactions to the needs of others. You are sensitive and self-protective, though some of you may mask this with a hard shell. This placement also gives an excellent memory and an uncanny ability to psyche out the needs of others. The moon is very strong in Cancer, so all of the lunar phases will affect you, especially full moons and eclipses. You are happiest at home and may work at home or turn your office into a second home, where you can nuture and comfort people—you may tend to "mother the world." This is an extremely psychic, intuitive position, and you may feel drawn to occult work in some way. Or you may get professionally involved with providing food and shelter.

Moon in Leo: This is a warm passionate moon that takes everything to heart. You are attracted to the noble, generous, and aristocratic in life and may be a bit of a snob. You have an innate ability to take command emotionally, but you do need strong support, loyalty, and loud applause from those you love. You are possessive of your loved ones and your turf—and will roar if anyone threatens to take over your territory.

Moon in Virgo: You are rather cool until you decide if others measure up. But once someone or something meets your ideal standards, you hold up your end of the arrangement perfectly. You may, in fact, drive yourself too hard to attain some notion of perfection. Try to be a bit easier on yourself and others. Don't always act the censor! You love to be the teacher, and are drawn to situations where you can change others for the better. But sometimes you must learn to accept others for what they are and enjoy what you have.

Moon in Libra: This is a partnership-oriented placement—you may find it difficult to be alone or to do things alone. But you must learn to lean on yourself, first. When you have learned emotional balance, you can have excellent relationships. It is best for you to avoid extremes, or your love life can be precarious. You thrive in a rather conservative, traditional, romantic relationship where you receive attention and flattery from your partner, but not possessiveness.

You'll be your most charming in an elegant, harmonious atmosphere.

Moon in Scorpio: This is a moon that enjoys and responds to intense passionate feelings. You may go to extremes and have a very dramatic emotional life, full of ardor, suspicion, jealousy, and obsession. It would be much healthier to channel your need for power and control into meaningful work. This is a good position for anyone in the fields of medicine, police work, research, the occult, psychoanalysis, or intuitive work as life-and-death situations don't faze you. But you take disappointments very hard.

Moon in Sagittarius: You take life's ups and downs with good humor and the proverbial grain of salt. You'll love 'em and leave 'em, and take off on a great adventure at a moment's notice. "Born free" could be your slogan. You can't stand to be possessed emotionally by anyone. Attracted by the exotic, you have wanderlust mentally and physically, and you may be too much in search of a new mental and spiritual stimulation to ever settle down.

Moon in Capricorn: Are you ever accused of being too cool and calculating? You have an earthy side, but you take prestige and position very seriously. Your strong drive to succeed extends to your romantic life, where you will be devoted to improving your life-style, rising to the top. You may be attracted to someone older or very much younger or from a different social world. It may be difficult to look at the lighter side of emotional relationships. You are dutiful and responsible to those you care for.

Moon in Aquarius: You are a people collector with many friends of all backgrounds. You are happiest surrounded by people and are uneasy when left alone. You usually stay friends with those with whom you get involved. Though tolerant and understanding, you are unpredictable. You don't like anything to be too rigid. You may resist working on schedule or you may have a very unconventional love life. With plenty of space, you will be able to sustain relationships. But you'll shy away from possessive types.

Moon in Pisces: You are very responsive emotionally and empathetic to others, especially if they have problems. (You may have to be on guard against attracting too many people with sob stories.) You'll be happiest if you can find a way to express your creative imagination in the arts or in the spiritual or healing professions. You may tend to escape in to a fantasy world or be attracted to exotic places or people. You need an emotional anchor as you are very sensitive to the moods of others. You are happiest near water, working in a field that gives you emotional variety. But steer clear of too much escapism (especially in alcohol) and keep a firm foothold in reality.

The Moon-Favored Activities

As the moon changes signs, the emotional weather also changes. The mood of the day then becomes colored by the new sign and intensified by whatever planets are passing through that sign. You can keep up with the moon's travels by following the listings in the daily forecast in the back of the book. Here is the best time for each activity according to the moon.

Moon in Aries: Now, when energy and tempers run high, is a fine day to get things off and running. Everyone is impatient and ready to get off the mark. You can sell that exciting scheme now with enthusiasm. You won't take no for an answer. You can motivate others or get motivated yourself. But you'll have no patience for details, so leave them for later. Be careful to check facts before jumping into any commitment. Relax with competitive sports: Run races, or practice judo.

Moon in Taurus: It's time to tackle the work load. You'll get things done today, give your ideas a solid foundation. You can make headway when it comes to investments, doing appraisals, buying land, and balancing the budget. But don't push. People will be more stubborn and inflexible today, so appeal to their creature comforts. Reward yourself with a good dinner. You'll be inclined to indulge in pleasures of the senses in the evening.

Moon in Gemini: This is a day to get on the telephone. Make those calls, write those letters. News and gossip spread fast. You'll find shortcuts today, but you may try to do too many things at once. Others are restless, too, and hard to pin down. Don't look for emotional commitment today. Keep your flirtations light. You'll feel the urge to get out and socialize. You may talk too much, remember to be discreet, keep secrets.

Moon in Cancer: This is a moody, sensitive day. Others take things personally, may feel easily slighted. TLC, mothering, and chicken soup may be on the menu. It's a great time to do things around the house, cook a hearty meal, entertain at home, spend time with family and children. You could be feeling nostalgic and indulge in some fond memories or quiet time alone. Your intuition is sharp—you'll have good insight into unspoken needs.

Moon in Leo: Show off a bit, now. This is a sunny, noisy day when others will be tooting their own horns, too. Socializing, spending big, treating yourself royally are good ideas. Don't believe all you hear. It's a good day to ask for a raise, sell yourself in some way and go out on the town. You'll also be tempted to blow the budget, pick up the check. Show your warm feelings to loved ones.

Moon in Virgo: Time to get back to reality. Go over the details today and fix what isn't working. Take care of health, self-maintenance, diet, food shopping, cleaning and laundry chores, and editing. This is not a good time to ask for a raise, unless you're prepared to face a critique. Everyone's in a picky, fault-finding mood. It's a great time for bookkeeping, budgeting, bill-paying, and taking the dog to the vet. Work off minor irritations at exercise class.

Moon in Libra: After getting chores out of the way, everyone is now in a much more charming mood. This is a good time to socialize, get married, or at least have a romantic encounter. Do things in twos now. In business, it's time to attend to legal matters, contracts, or sales. You can smooth over difficulties, socialize, and beautify yourself or your surroundings. Not a good time for confrontations or debates—you'll be somewhat indecisive. It is a better day for evaluating than taking action.

Moon in Scorpio: A terrific day for problem-solving, detective work, psychic or psychological work, or making love. Whatever requires intense focused passionate action goes well now. Things can be a bit heavy, emotionally, however. When the moon passes over Pluto, people tend to go to extremes and may overreact. Be on guard against jealousy and power plays.

Moon in Sagittarius: It's time to lighten up, have fun, bust loose. You'll feel more expansive and expound more on your philosophy of life. Teaching, writing, any kind of higher education or spiritual work are good activities. But don't try to get organized yet. Better to let the mind wander and explore those big ideas. Look at the overall general picture. You can make headway in sales, publishing, and forecasting now. Ask for a raise! Relax outdoors, with sports, animals, horse racing. You may be tempted to take a gamble.

Moon in Capricorn: Now you can work on organization, analyze what is working in your life, and eliminate what is not. The moon passing over Neptune, Uranus, and Saturn this year in Capricorn will make this time of the month especially eventful. You'll see ways to make those dreams realities. And you'll have some lessons in store. Use this time to take stock of your life, do some serious thinking, take care of responsibilities, visit Grandma. Leave the fun and frivolity for later.

Moon in Aquarius: People will be wanting to meet, get together in clubs, teams, parties. Even better if it's all for a worthy cause. Not a day for intimate one-on-one discussions. People are too detached or impersonal now. But it's a good time for spontaneous fun, mental stimulation, and trying something completely new. Wear that trendy outfit, work on or buy a computer, speak before your group. The day may have some surprises in store—don't plan on a fixed schedule.

Moon in Pisces: Now you can relax, let your hair down, have in-depth discussions. It's a day to be alone, rest and reflect or to be with someone very close. Get some creative input at a film, theater, musical or ballet. You could have some inspiring insights with meditation, prayer, or psychoanalysis. You could overindulge in feeling sorry for yourself (or someone else) in alcohol. Watch those "true confessions"—others could be feeling vulnerable now. It's also a day when you could fall for a tall story or a sob story or give in to self-pity. Better read or write some poetry, go out dancing, or watch a film instead.

Moon Lore:

- Hindus of northern India believe that eating food exposed to the rays of the full moon will help them live longer.
- In Naples, Italy, women prayed to the waxing moon to increase the size of their breasts.
- Moon worship thrived in ancient Egypt, where one of the sacred animals, the cat, was dedicated to the moon.
- Italian Dictator Benito Mussolini was deathly afraid of having moonlight fall on him while he slept.

- In West Africa, people believe babies are delivered by the "moon bird."
- The ancient Greeks considered the full moon the best time for a marriage.
- In the Middle Ages, a poem about the waxing and waning of the moon became the immortal "Jack and Jill" nursery rhyme. "Jack" comes from a verb meaning "to increase" and "Jill" from a verb meaning "to break down."
- Men as well as women are affected by lunar cycles and have an increase in sexual desire at the full moon.
- Violent urges come out in the open at the full moon. The assassinations of Julius Caesar, Alexander II, Leon Trotsky, Dominican dictator Rafael Trujillo, and Jesus Christ, as well as the My Lai massacre during the Vietnam War, are a few examples.
- In our solar system only the earth and perhaps Pluto have moons which are as large in proportion to the size of the parent planet.
- The total eclipse of 1706 spread more fear through the French army attacking Barcelona than the upcoming battle.
- In ancient Phoenicia, Phrygia, Greece, and Rome, moon goddesses were patronesses of childbirth and fertility.

8

The Great Debates: Astrology vs. Science and Religion

A young scientist set out to prove that astrology is nothing more than ignorance and superstition—and now has his own cable television show teaching viewers about astrology. An attractive female psychotherapist checks the astrology chart of her Friday night date to see if they'll be compatible. An astrophysicist calls an astrologer friend to confer on the implications of an upcoming Saturn-Uranus conjunction. A devout Catholic businessman refuses to sign contracts until after a Mercury retrograde period. These are only a few examples of the new astrology consciousness happening at the start of the 1990s.

In the last decade, as it has become common knowledge that even in this age of computers and demographics, world leaders still consult astrologers, astrology has been the subject of controversial headlines, TV talk shows, and magazine articles. Nearly everyone, it seems, secretly or openly takes a peek at his or her daily horoscope. In New York, early morning news shows have added daily horoscopes to please their viewers.

For astrologers, the forecast has never been better. The astrology business has been thriving. Where once it was difficult to find an astrologer, practitioners now advertise in newspapers and yellow pages. Some are highly qualified professionals, with years of study and proven expertise. Others simply dispense canned horoscopes from one of the many computer programs available. Still others give readings which depend more on the psychic talents of the reader than astrological technique. You can find an astrologer from the growing lists of the American Federation of Astrologers or the National Council for Geocosmic Research, two organizations which are dedicated to the advancement of astrological studies.

As the prevailing attitude changes from viewing astrology as entertainment to using it as a tool to help us plan our daily lives, there has also emerged a new wave of attacks. These come from two main sources, science and traditional religion. Perhaps many readers who do have a serious interest in astrology have been or will have occasion to defend it from either viewpoint.

In general, astrology debunkers have one thing in common: very little knowledge of astrology. It is rare to find an attacker who has ever had his or her horoscope chart done professionally or one who knows any astrological terminology beyond basic sun sign information. It very often happens that once a skeptic undertakes a serious exploration of astrology, he or she becomes an ardent advocate. In fact, the profession is full of astrologers who came from scientific disciplines, studied astrology for the purpose of disproving it, and ended up with great respect for this ancient art.

One such would-be debunker was a French statistician, Michel Gauquelin, who set out back in 1955 to disprove astrology by correlating astrological data for thousands of doctors, politicians, athletes and soldiers, and concluded that, indeed, it rested upon verifiable premises. Among his findings, he showed that Mars and Saturn contacts held true throughout the horoscopes of military leaders, and Mars propelled the horoscopes of athletes. He also confirmed planetary links between parent and child.

Actually, astrology has never claimed to be a science, a religion, or a psychology—through it has links to all three in their mutual origin in man's search for the truth and for his real purpose in life.

We might say that astrology is the place where science, spirit, and psyche meet.

Astrology has deep roots in all religions and can be found embedded in the spiritual history of every race. However, when religions became linked to doctrine and dogma, astrology, which has been accessible to everyone who wishes to study the planets, parted company with religion. In the Christian tradition, astrology was perceived as a threat to the established church, and astrologers were driven underground or persecuted. But the study of the planets and their relationship to the affairs of men continued, though astrology gained an unsavory reputation as fortunetelling, a connection that still lingers in the minds of those who try to discredit it.

Astrology is actually the study of cycles, a linking of forces in our own lives with the forces of the universe at large. But it is not fate. *You* are more than your chart. *You* can use the forces at your disposal as you wish. Most astrologers have seen similar charts in which one person has used the aspects in a positive way and another, with similar aspects, has become a criminal.

In its fundamental assumption that a given moment in time embodies the forces going on at that instant in the solar system, astrology does link us to a divine plan. When man first looked toward the heavens, it was in a wish to communicate with God, whether from a Babylonian ziggurat or a Mayan pyramid. The character of each sign of the zodiac was developed in a very systematic way, linking elements, qualities and polarities, as we have seen in Chapter 1, and the influence of the planets was determined after much observation. It is interesting that Mars, in all the various systems of astrology around the world, still embodies the same aggressive force; Venus is still the same kind of benevolent energy; and, from the time of the lunar goddesses of Babylonia, Phrygia, and Greece to modern psychological interpretations, the moon has represented our instinctive emotional self.

Many religious people are threatened by astrologers, first because they confuse modern-day astrology with the charlatans of the past or because they feel that someone interested in astrology will turn away from religion. However, as anyone who has delved seriously into astrology can attest, the study of astrology brings one closer to a religious understanding of the dynamic interchange between the universal plan, the material world and man's place in it. Astrology can, in a very practical way, help man keep in balance with the forces of the universe.

Scientists, on the other hand, attack astrology as a "pseudoscience" for its supposed lack of factual evidence. We are forever hearing comparisons between astrology and astronomy, which is really more of a parent-child relationship since astronomy grew out of astrology. History has conveniently forgotten that five of the most famous astronomers of all time were astrologers: Copernicus, Galileo, Tycho Brahe, Johannes Kepler, and Sir Isaac Newton.

Again, most scientists have not studied astrology, nor do they approach it scientifically. They do not respect astrology as a discipline in its own right, thereby missing the point of astrology. It is not concerned with linear facts but with linking man to the cosmos, linking the universe without to the universe within.

The rise of quantum physics could bridge the gap between science and astrology, as scientists begin to explore a different reality beyond the mechanistic materialistic view. Scientists are realizing that their own theories of natural phenomena are creations of the mind itself, depending on the position of the observer and the observed, and by no means the last word. When science begins to look at the universe within, perhaps the parent-child respect can be renewed, and once again, science and astrology can be part of the same family.

The great psychologist Carl Jung is responsible for creating quite a different attitude, one of partnership between astrology and psychology. Jung had great respect for astrology and used it in his practice to clarify points which he said he would otherwise have been unable to understand. "Astrology represents the summation of all the psychological knowledge of antiquity," he explained. Today, there are many psychologists who use astrology to help them penetrate in depth into the authentic personality of their clients. In turn, astrologers have benefited by psychological counseling techniques, using them to guide their clients toward personal growth and finding positive ways to handle the trends evident in their birth chart.

In the nineties, when the Aquarian Age takes root, we'll all be looking for ways to expand our lives. Perhaps by then a new, positive relationship will have been forged between astrology and science, and astrology and religion, as we find these disciplines more complementary than competitive.

9

Loving Every Sign in the Zodiac
All the possible pairs!

Many people find astrology most effective in their emotional life. It can help explain and deal with the thorniest romantic problems—such as why that Aquarius man would rather spend nights out with the boys than cuddling by the fire with a lovely Cancer—and what she can do about the situation. Or should a Gemini social butterfly settle down with a sexy Scorpio?

Astrologers are fond of making romantic dictums, rating a Scorpio-Cancer couple high, while dismissing a Pisces-Leo pair. But truly, there is no magic formula for finding the perfect mate, as one eligible female New York astrologer found out. Using her skills to analyze every man she met, she finally found one man whose chart harmonized beautifully with hers. But after one date, it was obvious that they were totally incompatible. However, the man did learn of a vacant apartment next door to the young lady and they are now living very happily side by side, if not together.

Though there are many variables to consider when analyzing a partnership, the most important factor is your willingness to compromise. Will you be able to adjust to your partner's innermost needs? Sun sign astrology can give you a very good general idea of what those basic needs will be. Take an Aquarius-Cancer couple—it's not a pairing that would be recommended by most astrologers. However, if the

Cancer lady is willing to be a pal to the Aquarian, taking part in his career or political interests, the marriage can work. Mrs. Ronald Reagan took this strategy in her marriage to the Aquarius former President. A potentially troublesome Gemini-Scorpio combination might work if the Gemini could curb her flirtatious tendencies and the Scorpio could be less possessive.

Your Best Love Times

Since the moon rules our emotional life, it makes sense to play its phases to your romantic advantage. Look for a new love with the new moon, especially when the new moon is in your sign (near your birthday). Declare your feelings on the full moon. Break up a relationship on the waning moon.

When Venus is in your sign or in a sign of the same element, you'll feel most seductive and desirable. Look up this year's Venus schedule in Chapter 2 and put your charms to good use.

Mars rules your sex drive. When it is transiting your sign, you'll feel heightened sexual energy. It's a good time to be more assertive in your relationships and make the first move. You are less likely to take or get "No" for an answer.

Here are the pros and cons of all the pairings possible for every sign with celebrity examples so you can visualize the romantic chemistry. Some couples had real-life romances, some teamed up only on the screen and other pairings are pure speculation. (The celebrities are listed in the same pair-up order as the signs.)

Aries-Aries: Billy Dee Williams and Diana Ross
PROS: You've found one partner who can keep up with you, matching your enthusiasm and energy.
COMPROMISES: Someone has to take the lead but neither wants to give up the reins. You both like to give the orders—and both have hot tempers. Don't fight fire with fire, here.

Aries-Taurus: Dennis Quaid and Cher
PROS: Aries provides the get up and go. Taurus provides stability, sensuality, and the follow-through.
COMPROMISES: Aries must learn patience; Taurus cannot be rushed. Aries has a quick, hot temper, Taurus is a slow volcano. Learn to discuss grievances calmly.

Aries-Gemini: Richard Chamberlain and Joan Collins
PROS: Geminis give Aries the challenge they crave. Aries gives constant excitement to Gemini. You'll never bore each other. This match can be stimulating on many levels.
COMPROMISES: Aries likes to be number one at all times. Gemini feels the more, the merrier. Aries must give Gemini space. Gemini must give Aries full attention.

Aries-Cancer: William Hurt and Kathleen Turner
PROS: You'll either sizzle or fizzle. Cancer plays up to the Aries ego, providing TLC on all levels. Aries is the baby who needs all the mothering Cancer loves to give.
COMPROMISES: Aries has to learn to grow up in this relationship, and Cancer must learn to let go.

Aries-Leo: Bette Davis and Robert Mitchum
PROS: This can be a passionate bonfire, if you can learn to share the limelight. Aries can rise to the occasion and be the proud and regal partner Leo longs for.
COMPROMISES: Both must learn to costar, not compete. And to control their tempers.

Aries-Virgo: Omarr Shariff and Sophia Loren
PROS: Aries makes the aggressive moves, while Virgo takes care of the details. Aries fires light Virgo passions. Both *can* meet each others high standards.
COMPROMISES: Virgo criticism can dampen Aries enthusiasm and ardor. Aries impulsiveness and impatience can irritate careful, practical Virgo.

Aries-Libra: Joan Crawford and Charlton Heston
PROS: Libra's tact and diplomacy smoothes over Aries' rough spots. Opposites attract! You're both outgoing, flirtatious, and discriminating. Libra is happy to let Aries make the decisions.
COMPROMISES: Aries has a feisty streak, while Libra avoids confrontations. You may need a third party to handle your differences.

Aries-Scorpio: Spencer Tracy and Katharine Hepburn
PROS: You two Mars-ruled signs can generate a lot of heat. You enjoy challenging each other in and out of bed.
COMPROMISES: Watch out for power plays—neither of you likes to give in, ever! Find a way to air grievances without getting overheated.

Aries-Sagittarius: Max von Sydow and Liv Ullmann
PROS: You are both idealists who give each other enough space. You could be great pals and traveling companions as well as fiery lovers.
COMPROMISES: Both of you tend to put your own interests first. Give each other some quality time now and then. And both are more concerned with adventure than with finance. Find someone stable to handle the finances.

Aries-Capricorn: Warren Beatty and Faye Dunaway
PROS: You are both achievers who work hard to accomplish a goal. You'll enjoy each other's energy. Capricorn brings maturity to Aries, while Aries enthusiasm rejuvenates Capricorn.
COMPROMISES: Capricorn's insistence on organization and function could smother Aries, who hates to be tied to anything and isn't especially concerned with status or stability. Your differences in method should be worked out before you make a commitment.

Aries-Aquarius: Hugh Hefner and Barbi Benton
PROS: Both these idealistic, freedom-loving signs have adventures to share and find each other stimu-

lating, inventive, and innovative companions. This works especially well if you share an idealistic cause.
COMPROMISES: Aries likes a great deal of attention, while Aquarius is more involved with group activities. If Aries doesn't come first and foremost, he or she will look elsewhere. Aquarius does not like demands of any kind—if Aries gets bossy, Aquarius will take off.

Aries-Pisces: Jean-Paul Belmondo and Ursula Andress
PROS: Pisces knows how to please, Aries knows how to tease. Both can feed each other's egos. Aries energy can really get Pisces moving.
COMPROMISES: Aries finds it difficult to see another point of view, while Pisces soaks up the vibes of everyone he or she meets. When Pisces turns negative, they can dampen Aries spirit. While Aries can seem callous or rude to sensitive Pisces.

Taurus-Taurus: Jack Nicholson and Shirley MacLaine
PROS: You can be true soul mates who understand each other's moods and share similar tastes.
COMPROMISES: You can either get bored by too much sameness, or get trapped in a Mexican standoff if you disagree. Both of you are extremely stubborn and unrelenting when opposed.

Taurus-Gemini: Queen Elizabeth II and Prince Philip
PROS: Taurus provides the stability and focus than Gemini needs. Gemini brings laughter, mental stimulation, and social savvy to Taurus' life.
COMPROMISES: Taurus might find Gemini too flighty and flirtatious. Gemini could feel fenced in with Taurus and look for other pastures.

Taurus-Cancer: Fred Astaire and Ginger Rogers
PROS: You make beautiful music together. Taurus brings security to Cancer. And Cancer gives Taurus the affection and mothering this sign adores.
COMPROMISES: Cancer's fluctuating moods may be difficult for Taurus to fathom. You'll have to

work out any brooding and sulking, by bringing grievances into the open before they build up.

Taurus-Leo: Barbra Streisand and Robert Redford
PROS: Leo expands Taurus horizons to a grand scale. You both enjoy comfort, luxury, and sensual pleasures. And Taurus will benefit from Leo's optimistic, confident personality.
COMPROMISES: Taurus could put a damper on Leo's spending and resist Leo's orders. These two stubborn signs can create an earthquake if tempers are aroused.

Taurus-Virgo: Debra Winger and Richard Gere
PROS: Both these signs bring out each other's romantic sentimental side as well as their earthy fantasies. Virgo appreciates Taurus' stability, and Taurus enjoys Virgo's mental stimulation.
COMPROMISES: Virgo's nagging, hypochondria and irritable nerves could ruffle Taurus' placid feathers. While Taurus may seem too opinionated, stubborn, and domineering for Virgo.

Taurus-Libra: Pierce Brosnan and Stephanie Zimbalist
PROS: Taurus provides the steady backup for Libra and appreciates Libra's good looks and charm. You both share a love of beautiful objects and surroundings —the good life. Taurus is also very decisive and usually affluent, which Libra appreciates.
COMPROMISES: Watch out for jealousy here. Taurus is very possessive, while Libra is sociable and loves to flirt (though it is usually harmless). Taurus might prefer to stay at home while Libra wants to go out on the town. Libra extravagance could strain thrifty Taurus budgets.

Taurus/Scorpio: Jessica Lange and Sam Sheppard
PROS: This is an intense love match of polar opposites. You both share great sensuality and emotional depth. Taurus calms Scorpio's paranoia, while Scorpio provides insight.
COMPROMISES: Your problems usually arise over

the matter of control. You are both possessive and like to run the show. Divide the territory equally from the start.

Taurus-Capricorn: Priscilla Presley and Elvis Presley
PROS: You both have similar goals and can help each other get there. You have good communication on all levels and share the same values.
COMPROMISES: Taurus may bridle over Capricorn's devotion to career and status. Home and family are Taurus priorities.

Taurus-Sagittarius: Barbra Streisand and Don Johnson
Mike Tyson and Robin Givens
PROS: Taurus gives Sagittarius stability, a fixed income, and solid backup for realizing this sign's dreams. While Sagittarius takes Taurus into exciting new territory, expanding horizons.
COMPROMISES: Sagittarius takes too many risks, especially financially, for Taurus, and characteristic outspokeness can wound Taurus' feelings and sense of privacy. Sagittarius likes to wander and has a roving eye while Taurus is the possessive type who likes to stay near home turf.

Taurus-Aquarius: Ryan O'Neal and Farrah Fawcett
PROS: Aquarius responds to Taurus sensuality, while Taurus is challenged to have exciting adventures. Aquarius gets Taurus out of a rut, while Taurus brings Aquarius down to earth.
COMPROMISES: Taurus naturally wants to settle down, and finds Aquarius too spacey, while Aquarius naturally wants freedom and finds Taurus too possessive.

Taurus-Pisces: Margot Fonteyn and Rudolf Nureyev
PROS: Taurus gives stability and substance to Pisces. Pisces' creativity and sensuality turn on Taurus. Both love the good things in life, which Pisces can create and Taurus can finance.
COMPROMISES: Taurus can't control or possess the elusive Pisces. And Pisces can't stand to be corralled.

Gemini-Gemini: Marilyn Monroe and Tony Curtis
PROS: This double dual sign combination is really four people at once. At least two are bound to get along. And you'll never be bored.
COMPROMISES: This combination may be too lightweight to play any serious scenes. When the realities of life hit, Gemini may float off.

Gemini-Cancer: Wallis Simpson and the Duke of Windsor
PROS: Gemini's light touch helps Cancer laugh away those blue moods, while Cancer gives emotional substance to Gemini.
COMPROMISES: Cancer may not be able to laugh off Gemini's flirtations. Gemini may find Cancer moods and devotion to mommy too much of a downer.

Gemini-Leo: John F. and Jacqueline Kennedy
PROS: Leo's poise and Gemini's charm make a formidable pair. Leo demands the best and Gemini is excited by the challenge to deliver. In turn, Leo will help Gemini's talents shine brighter.
COMPROMISES: Leo wants to hold on tight while Gemini slips through the fingers. Jealousy and pride could take a toll on this pair.

Gemini-Virgo: Tristan Rogers and Emma Samms
John Wayne and Lauren Bacall
PROS: There is good communication between you two Mercury-ruled signs. Virgo helps Gemini get organized, while Gemini helps Virgo lighten up. Gemini can take Virgo criticism with detached interest.
COMPROMISES: Gemini may find that Virgo's perfectionism a drag. And all that planning kills spontaneity. Virgo may find that Gemini lacks staying power.

Gemini-Libra: Joan Collins and Anthony Newley
PROS: This is a social pair of party animals. Neither is possessive; both will give each other plenty of space and excite each other mentally as well as physically.

COMPROMISES: Both must learn to come down to earth when dealing with everyday realities, or this can be all talk and no action.

Gemini-Scorpio: Laurence Olivier and Vivien Leigh
PROS: Scorpio is fascinated by changeable Gemini, someone who can never quite be fathomed or controlled. Gemini gets a feeling of substance and power from Scorpio and loves playing head games.
COMPROMISES: Scorpio must learn to lighten up. Too much heaviness will drive Gemini away. Gemini must learn to curb natural flirtatiousness; Scorpio must feel like the one and only.

Gemini-Sagittarius: Barry Manilow and Bette Midler
PROS: Gemini writes the songs for Sagittarius to sing. This is a terrific partnership that takes life and love lightly. You can be pals as well as lovers.
COMPROMISES: These two changeable signs may never get together. You need to find a structure, such as common work, to keep you involved. And you'll both have to learn to manage finances, or hire a third party.

Gemini-Capricorn: Jane Russell and Howard Hughes
PROS: Capricorn gives much needed structure to Gemini's life (Howard Hughes invented the famous bra that supported Jane Russell's physical endowments). Gemini adds lightness and humor to Capricorn's serious outlook.
COMPROMISES: Capricorn must be willing to kick up his or her heels and spend a little money. Otherwise Gemini may brand him or her as boring and stingy. Gemini needs to learn to take responsibility and follow through on those brilliant ideas.

Gemini-Aquarius: Connie Sellica and Tom Selleck
PROS: You both feel most secure in an open relationship. You'll give each other freedom and friendship as well as love. Yours is a partnership that stays fresh as you both contribute new experiences.
COMPROMISES: There may not be enough sparks

to ignite a grand passion. Some commitment is necessary to keep you together. Strong shared business or intellectual interests will help.

Gemini-Pisces: Martha and George Washington
PROS: You are two dual personalities with many facets to fascinate each other. You both crave variety and can provide it for each other.
COMPROMISES: Pisces sensitive feelings and Gemini's mental gyrations can jangle and irritate each other. Both need a source of stability and won't find it in each other. You need to find a structure to hold this relationship together.

Cancer-Cancer: Sylvester Stallone and Brigitte Nielson
PROS: You are both very moody and sensitive; you could give each other all the mothering you need. This pairing can make beautiful music (like Rodgers and Hammerstein) under the right circumstances.
COMPROMISES: If you both get moody and broody at the same time, there's no one to drag you out of the dumps. At that point, even minor disagreements get blown out of proportion. You may have to get away from each other from time to time to get perspective.

Cancer-Leo: Senator Robert and Elizabeth Dole
Mick Jagger and Jerry Hall
PROS: Cancer pampers Leo, who in turn gives Cancer a bright outlook and new self-esteem.
COMPROMISES: Cancer must keep those blue moods under wraps. Leo must consider Cancer's sensitive feelings and tone down their domineering side.

Cancer-Virgo: Meryl Streep and Jeremy Irons
PROS: You love to take care of each other and create a beautiful nurturing, well-organized home.
COMPROMISES: Virgo's criticism can be very hurtful to Cancer. And Cancer's mood fluctuations can be very irritating to Virgo.

Cancer-Libra: Robin Williams and Pam Dawber
Harrison Ford and Karen Allen

PROS: Librans can thrive under Cancer's nurturing, and both appreciate each other's sense of style and beauty. Cancer's calm down under Libra's harmonious influence.

COMPROMISES: Neither of you enjoys confrontations, so learn to settle your differences with calm negotiations. Libra should learn what sets off Cancer moods and behave accordingly. Cancer should learn not to take Libran detachment personally.

Cancer-Scorpio: Diana, Princess of Wales, and Prince Charles

PROS: Scorpio possessiveness gives Cancer the security he or she craves. They both have strong emotions and devotion to those they love.

COMPROMISES: Scorpios can go into deep melancholy moods, which Cancer understands but can't really lighten. Cancers can cling, which challenges Scorpio to break the bond.

Cancer-Sagittarius: Donald Sutherland and Jane Fonda

PROS: Sagittarius can joke Cancer out of a blue mood and off an exciting adventure. While Cancer makes Sagittarius glow with attention and applause.

COMPROMISES: Cancer is home-loving, Sagittarius is a wanderer. Sagittarius must cut down on risk-taking ventures, and Cancer must learn to cultivate a spirit of adventure. This combination takes much mutual adjustment.

Cancer-Capricorn: Harrison Ford and Diane Keaton

PROS: Cancer is the zodiac mother. Capricorn is the father. You both have a strong sense of family duty and love to take care of others.

COMPROMISES: Capricorn may be too involved with work to provide the attention and affection Cancer needs. And you both have melancholy moods —which can strike at the same time.

Cancer-Aquarius: Nancy and Ronald Reagan
PROS: Cancer can provide the backup and shrewd business savvy for ambitious Aquarius. And Cancer is the perfect audience for Aquarius. If the two have similar basic values, this can be a lasting union.
COMPROMISES: Here is the most impersonal sign paired with the most personal! Cancers love intimate relationships; Aquarians can be rather cool and detached, in one-to-one situations. Cancer will have to learn to share Aquarius interests. Aquarius will have to be more personal and demonstrative.

Cancer-Pisces: Carly Simon and James Taylor
PROS: Here is a very passionate emotional relationship, that seems to transcend any boundaries. You'll respond to each other creatively, especially. Cancer will give Pisces organization and business savvy to boot. Pisces will give Cancer support and loving attention that builds confidence.
COMPROMISES: This couple could drown in too much emotion. You may have to get away and detach or maintain separate interests. Cancer must learn not to smother Pisces. And both should find healthy ways to release negative emotions.

Leo-Leo: Madonna and Sean Penn
PROS: This works well as long as both are equally successful and happy in their roles. Then this regal pair can shine together.
COMPROMISES: Both must learn to share the spotlight and support each other in tough times. Leos must also learn to stake out their own territory and respect each other's turf.

Leo-Virgo: Robert Taylor and Greta Garbo
PROS: Virgo basks in Leo's warmth and confidence which can make ordinarily shy Virgo radiant. Leos gets Virgo's solid support and flattering attention to every mood.
COMPROMISES: Virgo's well-meaning criticism can bring Leo down. And Virgo's frugal nature is contrary to Leo's extravagance. Both will have to work

to understand and live with each other's point of view.

Leo-Libra: Gene Kelly and Rita Hayworth
PROS: Libra's style and Leo's flair blend beautifully. Both love the good life and enjoy providing for each other. Leo's sunny disposition brings out the best in Libra.
COMPROMISES: You are both big spenders who dislike balancing the budget. Someone has to learn to keep the finances in balance or this pair could go for broke.

Leo-Scorpio: Arnold Schwarzenegger and Maria Shriver
PROS: You are both proud and possessive signs who go all out for the loved one. You respect and value each other's powerful sense of commitment and natural charisma.
COMPROMISES: You both want power and control. Hopefully you have separate but equal arenas. This pair can run hot or cold depending on whether they can share the reins. Leo may resent Scorpio's secretive streak, while Scorpio will put the brakes on Leo's extravagant spending.

Leo-Capricorn: Jacqueline Kennedy and Aristotle Onassis
PROS: Leo is a prize worthy of Capricorn's efforts to gain stratus, class, and social poise. Capricorn is the good provider who sets the brilliant stage for Leo. Both love to move in high places.
COMPROMISE: Capricorns must learn to give Leo the personal attention they need (not just presents and parties). Leos must learn to modify their spending habits. Finances are divisive here.

Leo-Aquarius: Lonnie Anderson and Burt Reynolds
PROS: These opposite signs often get together. Leo's steady warmth seems to balance Aquarius' cool detached quality. Both are interested in helping humanity and in big projects, and both are comfortable in the limelight.

COMPROMISES: Aquarius must learn to make time for Leo and give them the flattery and emotional support they need. While Leo must loosen the reins and control natural jealousy, Aquarius needs to keep a feeling of independence.

Leo-Pisces: Robert de Niro and Liza Minelli
PROS: Leo boosts Pisces' self-esteem and encourages creativity while Pisces reciprocates with adoring attention.
COMPROMISES: Pisces are not easy to pin down. Learn to give your Leo loyalty and star treatment. Leos should give Pisces free rein while pushing for productivity (not easy!).

Virgo-Virgo: Linda Gray and Larry Hagman
PROS: Two of a kind who often find each other irresistible. Your sharp minds stimulate each other, and you also communicate on an earthy level. You'll agree on habits, and have the cleanest house in town.
COMPROMISES: You can dish out the criticism, but can you take it? Try not to get bogged down in details. And learn to accentuate the positive.

Virgo-Libra: John Ritter and Suzanne Somers
PROS: Libra's fine mind and cool objectivity are admired by Virgo. While Virgo easily makes the most intelligent decisions for both. Charm, good looks, aesthetic interests, and social poise can make this a compatible couple.
COMPROMISES: Virgo can throw Libra off balance with too much focus on the negative. Learn to give praise, frequently.

Virgo-Scorpio: Louis XVI and Marie Antoinette
PROS: Scorpio brings out the passionate earthy side of Virgo. Both signs live out their fantasies, while Scorpio benefits from Virgo's fidelity and practical help.
COMPROMISES: Don't resort to using sex to manipulate each other. If both of you play it cool, this could go into the deep freeze.

Virgo-Sagittarius: Sophia Loren and Carlo Ponti
PROS: Sagittarius inspires Virgo to take risks and reach new heights. Sag's positive, optimistic disposition conquers Virgo's insecurities. Virgo keeps up with Sagittarius mentally and provides down-to-earth common sense.
COMPROMISES: Sagittarius must control romantic explorations. Virgo will not stand for infidelity. Sagittarius is naturally devil-may-care, while Virgo takes life and love seriously.

Virgo-Capricorn: Humphrey Bogart and Lauren Bacall
Shelley Long and Ted Danson
PROS: These two achievers are magnetically attracted to each other. You communicate with and without words. Common goals and mutual values reinforce togetherness.
COMPROMISES: It's difficult to fault this pair. You may get bored with too much of a good thing and search for excitement and challenge elsewhere.

Virgo-Aquarius: Jacqueline Bisset and Alexander Godunov
Clark Gable and Claudette Colbert
PROS: This attraction starts on a mental level, then gets physical. Virgo is the supportive pal and backup companion Aquarius needs. Innovative ideas, electric charisma, and unpredictable charm turn Virgo on to Aquarius.
COMPROMISES: Virgo must learn to give Aquarius plenty of space and tone down the criticism. Aquarius must spend some time at home, and get organized.

Virgo-Pisces: Joan and Ted Kennedy
PROS: This pair of opposites initially seem to balance each other out. Pisces gives emotional support. Virgo has the push and practicality Pisces needs.
COMPROMISES: You must both learn to focus on positive values. Virgo should eliminate nagging and negative criticism. Pisces should cultivate objectivity and self-discipline.

Libra-Libra: Catherine Deneuve and Marcello Mastroianni
Christopher Reeve and Margot Kidder

PROS: You look wonderful together: the epitome of charm, good looks, and style. Socially, you're a winning combination, and romantically, you're the couple that does everything together.
COMPROMISES: You are heavy on glamour and light on practical matters. You both vacillate maddeningly when making decisions. And neither likes to bring up problems. You'll learn to schedule regular times to discuss thorny issues calmly and objectively.

Libra-Scorpio: Bryant Gumbel and Jane Pauley
PROS: Differences make for strong chemistry between you. Scorpio's calm masks an inner intensity that Libra finds exciting. While Libra's powerful charm and winning smile intrigue Scorpio.
COMPROMISES: Libras must learn to curb flirtatiousness and rampant spending. Scorpios must cool their suspicious nature to give Libra some space.

Libra-Sagittarius: Rita Hayworth and Frank Sinatra
PROS: Libra fans Sagittarius' flame. You two idealists will have a meeting of minds and emotions. Libran diplomacy smoothes over Sagittarian bluntness. Sagittarian humor keeps Libra in balance.
COMPROMISES: Sagittarians are dreamers who believe in luck (or faith), while Librans need a secure launching pad for their fantasies. Both are flirtatious; however, Sagittarius is out for more than a few laughs. Learn to take your commitments seriously.

Libra-Capricorn: Catherine Deneuve and Cary Grant
PROS: Libran diplomacy is a social asset to Capricorn. Both of you love the elegant traditional life-style and help each other get it.
COMPROMISES: Capricorn is careful with cash, while Libra likes to spend on clothes and objets d'art. Capricorn needs lots of time alone, while Libra needs togetherness.

Libra-Aquarius: Sarah and Andrew, the Duke and Duchess of York

PROS: You are good pals, first, lovers later. This pair knows enough to give each other breathing space. If both share interests, this combination is a winner.
COMPROMISES: There is some tension because of Libra's need for attention, and Aquarius's need for freedom.

Libra-Pisces: Michael Douglas and Glenn Close

PROS: You turn each other on, creatively. You both know how to boost each other's egos. This works particularly well if you share business interests.
COMPROMISES: Both of you can drift away if you don't have solid support from your partner. And you may need someone to help you make decisions. With Libra's waffling and Pisces; self-doubts, you need outside reenforcement.

Scorpio-Scorpio: Roy Rogers and Dale Evans

PROS: There are happy trails for this couple who have a meeting of the minds as well as emotions. You'll match intensity and commitment, as well as charisma.
COMPROMISES: "Who's boss?" could be your theme as you both like to control. You are possessive, but heaven forbid someone tries to control you! Settle power struggles openly if possible.

Scorpio-Sagittarius: Marlo Thomas and Phil Donahue

PROS: This can be a powerful physical attraction, as Scorpio lights Sagittarius' fires for an erotic adventure. Sagittarius supplies the humor to lighten things up and the idealism to impress Scorpio.
COMPROMISES: Scorpio will insist that Sagittarius focus wandering energies and learn financial discipline. Sagittarius may feel closed in by Scorpio's power trip.

Scorpio-Capricorn: Mike Nichols and Diane Sawyer

PROS: Scorpio's intensity is just the thing to take Capricorn's mind away from business. You are two

achievers, who love power and position, yet can get engrossed in each other.
COMPROMISES: Capricorn is no one to trifle or play head games with. Scorpio may have taken on more than he or she bargained for. Watch for power struggles.

Scorpio-Aquarius: Linda Evans and John Forsythe
Tatum O'Neal and John MacEnroe
PROS: There is mutual respect here. You will both defend your beliefs, regardless of public opinion. You could have a very unconventional relationship. Both of you are open to experimentation and innovation.
COMPROMISES: Aquarius' need for freedom could run up against Scorpio's need to control. Scorpios will have to downplay their possessive side, while Aquarius will have to learn intimacy.

Scorpio-Pisces: Demi Moore and Bruce Willis,
Goldie Hawn and Kurt Russell,
Richard Burton and Elizabeth Taylor
PROS: This a zodiac love match that seems to be made in heaven. You'll stay in each other's life, married or not! You are emotional soul mates who commune on all levels.
COMPROMISES: Pisces resists control and needs creative and personal freedom. Too much togetherness could drown this relationship. Learn not to give into negative feelings and spend some time away from each other.

Sagittarius-Sagittarius: Jane Fonda and Tom Hayden
PROS: You are great pals and traveling companions who share each other's ideals and interests. This is a couple that is together even when far apart geographically.
COMPROMISES: Find someone to take care of the home fires (or alternate). You may be traveling so much that you'll miss each other. You will also need to find someone to keep finances in order.

Sagittarius-Capricorn: Maria Callas and Aristotle Onassis
PROS: Capricorn can focus and organize Sagittarians, while Sagittarius brings humor and challenge to Capricorn. You both have lofty goals and a fondness for high places.
COMPROMISES: This meeting of optimist-pessimist points of view could cancel each other out. Sagittarius should learn to plan ahead, Capricorn to be more spontaneous and not take life so seriously.

Sagittarius-Aquarius: Woody Allen and Mia Farrow
PROS: Aquarius is the perfect muse for Sagittarius. Both understand each other's need for freedom and neither is overly possessive. Sagittarius is fascinated by Aquarian unpredictability, while Aquarius is inspired by Sagittarian philosophy.
COMPROMISES: There could be more talk than action here. You both need to come down to earth from time to time and deal with everyday realities.

Sagittarius-Pisces: Frank and Barbara Sinatra
PROS: You are both restless questers who crave variety and stimulation. You inspire each other mentally and share many spiritual trips.
COMPROMISES: Sagittarius must be considerate of Pisces' sensitive feelings. They won't always laugh off rude remarks or make a quick recovery after temper tantrum. Pisces must keep a positive attitude and express enthusiasm for Sagittarian schemes and dreams.

Capricorn-Capricorn: Cary Grant and Dyan Cannon
PROS: You can build a strong foundation for the future together. You understand each other's goals and are willing to help each other climb to the top.
COMPROMISES: You may get so involved with work that there is no time for earthy pleasures. Take time out to kick up your heels. Otherwise this relationship could wilt of boredom.

Capricorn-Aquarius: Dolly Parton and Burt Reynolds
PROS: Capricorn is often called a "lone wolf" and Aquarius is often called an "oddball." When these two get together the happenings are unpredictable. But Capricorn has the know-how to make innovative Aquarian ideas materialize.
COMPROMISES: Capricorn's a traditionalist, while Aquarius is miles ahead of the crowd. You may not find a common meeting ground. Aquarius may feel held back by Capricorn's material goals. Capricorn must experiment with new ideas and Aquarius must learn to value structure and order.

Capricorn-Pisces: Victoria Principal and Patrick Duffy
PROS: A good exchange of talents. Capricorn gives Pisces security and acts as a buffer to the outside world. Pisces gives Capricorn glamour and soft sensuality.
COMPROMISES: Realize that you are radically different types and enjoy the differences. You may not always communicate, or share the same values, but you can stimulate each other. Pisces can learn discipline from Capricorn and contribute creative ideas.

Aquarius-Aquarius: Clark Gable and Lana Turner
PROS: This will be an equal partnership, where you both give each other unlimited freedom. But you'll also know when to be there for each other—together, in mind, if not in body.
COMPROMISES: Shared interests are the key to keeping you two wanderers together. Otherwise you may look for more challenge elsewhere—or someone who will cater to your ego and support *your* cause.

Aquarius-Pisces: Cybill Shepherd and Bruce Willis
Paul Newman and Joanne Woodward
PROS: You sun-sign neighbors are great pals who, even though you have differing points of view, give each other plenty of space! And you communicate very well on an intuitive level.
COMPROMISES: Aquarius should stay home once

in a while or Pisces may wander in search of more intense emotional involvements.

Pisces-Pisces: Elizabeth Taylor and Rex Harrison
PROS: You are psychic soul mates, who may have too much in common. But you can empathize with each other and work very well together creatively.
COMPROMISES: Avoid catering to each other's negative moods or overindulging in self-pity. You will be happiest if you both have a strong creative outlet that brings you recognition and material reward.

10

All About Libra

The Libra Man

The most debonair man of the zodiac, Libra is always appropriately attired and beautifully mannered, never flashy or overdone. He appears charming, cool, and well mannered at all times, but his delicately balanced nervous system is highly sensitive to disharmony of any sort. Whether the cause is blatantly rude behavior or simply a picture tilted out of alignment or a color mismatched, he will pick it up instantly. And when he is seriously offended, he will vanish into thin air, often without airing his grievances.

In his desire to have an orderly, harmonious world around him, the Libra man avoids emotional situations. Instead, he prefers more mental relationships where he can get involved with abstract concepts and idealistic issues, particularly those concerned with fairness or aesthetics. On that level, he is charming, witty, and intelligent. And, like Jesse Jackson, he can be extremely eloquent when speaking up for a cause.

Situations that demand quick decisions can be fraught with anxiety for the Libra man. He'll mull over both sides of the question endlessly, until he has reached a completely fair conclusion. Too many alternatives can leave him in a quandary. He is better off working with a partner or on a team where he does the evaluating and someone else makes the final decision. He also excells as a mediator, where his calm objectivity can balance both sides of an argument.

As a Husband

The Libra man is made for partnership, and spends much time and effort to find his perfect "other half." His mate should be someone who shares his aesthetic tastes and ideals, but who can also make the decisions. Therefore she should have a strong, but not competitive, point of view. He avoids confrontations, especially domestic ones, so a temperamental or demanding or overly emotional wife could throw him off balance. His partner should encourage calm discussions and objectivity, instead of tears and emotional scenes. When he does find the right woman, he can be a very romantic, flattering, thoughtful husband, who provides his wife with gracious living and perennial romance.

Famous Libra Men

Bruce Springsteen
Michael Douglas
Mark Hamill
Christopher Reeve
Julio Iglésias
Bryant Gumbel
Jerry Lee Lewis
Johnny Mathis
Sting
Armand Assante
Charleton Heston
Oliver North
John Lennon
Ralph Lauren
Jesse Jackson

The Libra Woman

The Libra woman is one of the most feminine in the zodiac, yet she is constantly balancing her femininity with a strong-willed masculine side, as England's Prime Minister Margaret Thatcher demonstrates. Though the Libra woman may come across as a delicate beauty rather than a liberated woman, she can fend for herself against strong competition. Usually she prefers the company of men, which allows her to exercise both sides of her nature, combining the feminine flirt and the equal partner. Many "love goddesses" such as Brigitte Bardot, Suzanne Somers, and Rita Hayworth, all born under this sign, have surprised others with the strong personality under their seductive physical appearance.

The Libra woman engages in a variety of activities to balance her life. She rarely focuses on one aspect of anything. She can be most successful at work which combines her artistic and social skills, and which involves either a partner or a team. She really needs other people to interact with and may get quite depressed when left totally alone. She is happiest when she can be a peacemaker or strategist, guiding others to the right course. Her looks and diplomacy are great social assets, making her popular with a wide scope of friends.

Libra as a Wife

Because Libra enjoys sharing her experiences and working with a partner, she is naturally geared for marriage. If her husband complements her and shares her interests, she can offer support and well-considered advice, as well as a beautiful home geared to entertaining. She can provide much-needed objectivity and social skills to a decisive man of action. But though her home will be in exquisite taste, she is not the stay-at-home type. She is more likely to balance home life with professional or social interests.

Famous Libra Women

Prime Minister Margaret Thatcher
Sarah, the Duchess of York
Heather Locklear
Marie Osmond
Barbara Walters
Olivia Newton-John
Catherine Deneuve

Madeline Kahn
Sigourney Weaver
Susan Sarandon
Angie Dickenson
Karen Allen
Pam Dawber
Martina Navratilova
Margot Kidder

11

Libra's Rising Signs

How the moment you were born influences your horoscope

At the moment you were born, when you assumed a physical body and became an independent person, an astrological sign—that is, a specific 30-degree portion of the zodiac—was passing over the eastern horizon. Called your "rising sign" or ascendant, this sign is very important, because it sets your horoscope (or "astrological life") in motion. In effect, it says "Here I am!" announcing your arrival in the world.

Rising signs change every two hours with the earth's rotation. If you were born early in the morning when the sun was on the horizon (which makes your sun sigh also your rising sign), then you will come across to others like the prototype of your sun sign. That is also why we call those born with their sun sign on the horizon a "double Aquarius" or a "double Virgo." You have twice as much input from that sign.

If you were born with another sign on the horizon, you will announce yourself more like that other sign. This other sign will mask slightly—or completely disguise—your basic sun sign character. If people have difficulty guessing your sun sign, this is probably the reason, particularly if you have a very outgoing ascendant, such a Leo ascendant and a rather shy sun sign, like Virgo.

On the other hand, a rather conservative Capricorn ascendant can tone down the intensity of a Scorpio or make a jovial Sagittarian seem far more serious than he really is. Your rising sign is your "cover" or mask. Often a person will project just one facet of a rising sign—for instance, one person with a Sagittarius rising would be a lover of horses and a world traveler, another with the same ascendant would be spiritual leader.

In your horoscope chart, the other signs follow the rising sign in sequence, rotating counterclockwise. Therefore, the rising sign sets up the tone of your chart. It rules the first house, which is the physical body—your appearance—and also influences your style, tastes, health, and physical environment (where you are most comfortable working and living).

You'll find your rising sign on the chart in Chapter 11. Since rising signs move rapidly, you should know your birth time as close to the minute as possible. If you are unsure about the exact time, but know within a few hours, check the following descriptions to see which is most like the personality you project.

Libra with Aries Rising— You Speak Your Mind

You appear so independent that others may not guess you really need a strong partner for balance. This placement gives the normally diplomatic Libra an assertive streak. You'll voice strong opinions when you feel justice is violated, which leads you into more debates and confrontations than others of your sign. But you love the stimulation of constant activity. Keep your balance by letting off steam in sports. You're a stylish dresser, the first to wear the newest trends!

Libra with Taurus Rising—Pleasures of the Senses

You have the strong influence of two Venus-ruled signs, giving you the inclination to indulge all your senses in both a physical and mental way. Your aesthetic Libra nature is overlayed with Taurean sensuality, giving you an earthier image combined with great charm, dimples, and a beautiful voice. A winning hand! You may gravitate toward Taurean fields such as gardening, real estate, design, food.

Libra with Gemini Rising—Charm Personified

You have a knack for saying the right thing at the right time. Your quick wit and very social nature communicates well via the written or spoken word. You do best in a situation where you mediate between constantly changing groups. The atmosphere must be stimulating, with lots of interesting people coming and going. Physically, you have fine features and probably have fair skin and hair. Guard your delicate nervous system by relaxing at home with a good book once in a while.

Libra with Cancer Rising—Emotional Ups and Downs

Concerns about security needs mask your Libran detachment. This sensitive ascendant makes your Libran scales sway with the phases of the moon. It can also give you a maternal, caring air. You'd be wonderful in a field that involves nurturing others—perhaps the hotel or restaurant business, which also has a social aspect. Physically, your body tends to hold water; you may have a rounded moon face, beautiful delicate skin, and a sensitive stomach.

Libra with Leo Rising—
Applause, Applause

You are an outgoing charmer who craves center stage and loud applause. Physically, you are very impressive, with a combination of balanced features, beautiful hair, very elegant but slightly flamboyant clothes, and, if female, beautiful jewelry. You may choose a career in the performing arts, or one which puts you before an audience, such as a courtroom lawyer. Guard against jealousy and be willing to share the spotlight occasionally.

Libra with Virgo Rising—
Critical Views

You have a sharp critical mind, more inclined to analyze and criticize than exercise the famous Libran diplomacy. You have very high standards and flawless taste. Your appearance and surroundings are a model of neatness and order but perfectionist tendencies could take a toll on your delicate sense of balance and your relationships with others. You could become a health and fitness devotee or be drawn to the health care industry or make an excellent editor. You're most fulfilled when doing truly useful work.

Libra with Libra Rising—
A Balancing Act

You have twice as much Libra charm and good looks, but also double trouble making up your mind. For that reason, you may prefer to do things in tandem with a decisive partner (or partners). You function best where there is social stimulation, where you are acting as a host or hostess, mediator or diplomat. Your forte is bringing people together in a tasteful harmonious situation. You avoid confrontations, unless in the role of impartial mediator. You may do especially well in the legal field.

Libra with Scorpio Rising— Air of Mystery

You have a tantalizing air of mystery that makes you seem more intense than other Librans. You give the impression of knowing just where you are going, though you may be vacillating underneath. Scorpio risings wear black often, have penetrating bedroom eyes and a magnetic presence that fascinates the opposite sex. You like to be around power and often get involved in intense all-or-nothing situations. This liking for extremes could put heavy demands on your Libran sense of balance.

Libra with Sagittarius Rising— Lucky Strike

You tend to be more impulsive and ready to take a gamble than other Librans. You'll speak your mind, getting right to the point in conversation, with less time spent on social niceties. You are very idealistic, with Sagittarius-type interests such as philosophy, religion, and higher education. This placement may also give you good athletic ability and strong legs. Your sense of humor is robust rather than witty. You like horses or horse-related activities. You may travel a great deal and be fascinated by the exotic.

Libra with Capricorn Rising— The Aristocrat

More serious and conservative than other Librans, you have a classy, old money look. Your taste runs to the traditional, and you tend to value things that are either useful or recognized status objects. Physically, your vulnerable areas are your joints and teeth. You may be more thrifty than the average Libra, less prone to break the budget on objects of art. You prefer a structured environment where you can easily measure your rise to the top.

Rising Signs—A.M. Births

	1 AM	2 AM	3 AM	4 AM	5 AM	6 AM	7 AM	8 AM	9 AM	10 AM	11 AM	12 NOON
Jan 1	Lib	Sc	Sc	Sc	Sag	Sag	Cap	Cap	Aq	Aq	Pis	Ar
Jan 9	Lib	Sc	Sc	Sag	Sag	Sag	Cap	Cap	Aq	Pis	Ar	Tau
Jan 17	Sc	Sc	Sc	Sag	Sag	Cap	Cap	Aq	Aq	Pis	Ar	Tau
Jan 25	Sc	Sc	Sag	Sag	Sag	Cap	Cap	Aq	Pis	Ar	Tau	Tau
Feb 2	Sc	Sc	Sag	Sag	Cap	Cap	Aq	Pis	Pis	Ar	Tau	Gem
Feb 10	Sc	Sag	Sag	Sag	Cap	Cap	Aq	Pis	Ar	Tau	Tau	Gem
Feb 18	Sc	Sag	Sag	Cap	Cap	Aq	Pis	Pis	Ar	Tau	Gem	Gem
Feb 26	Sag	Sag	Sag	Cap	Aq	Aq	Pis	Ar	Tau	Tau	Gem	Gem
Mar 6	Sag	Sag	Cap	Cap	Aq	Pis	Pis	Ar	Tau	Gem	Gem	Cap
Mar 14	Sag	Cap	Cap	Aq	Aq	Pis	Ar	Tau	Tau	Gem	Gem	Can
Mar 22	Sag	Cap	Cap	Aq	Pis	Ar	Ar	Tau	Gem	Gem	Can	Can
Mar 30	Cap	Cap	Aq	Pis	Pis	Ar	Tau	Tau	Gem	Can	Can	Can
Apr 7	Cap	Cap	Aq	Pis	Ar	Ar	Tau	Gem	Gem	Can	Can	Leo
Apr 14	Cap	Aq	Aq	Pis	Ar	Tau	Tau	Gem	Gem	Can	Can	Leo
Apr 22	Cap	Aq	Pis	Ar	Ar	Tau	Gem	Gem	Gem	Can	Leo	Leo
Apr 30	Aq	Aq	Pis	Ar	Tau	Tau	Gem	Can	Can	Can	Leo	Leo
May 8	Aq	Pis	Ar	Ar	Tau	Gem	Gem	Can	Can	Leo	Leo	Leo
May 16	Aq	Pis	Ar	Tau	Gem	Gem	Can	Can	Can	Leo	Leo	Vir
May 24	Pis	Ar	Ar	Tau	Gem	Gem	Can	Can	Leo	Leo	Leo	Vir
June 1	Pis	Ar	Tau	Gem	Gem	Can	Can	Can	Leo	Leo	Vir	Vir
June 9	Ar	Ar	Tau	Gem	Gem	Can	Can	Leo	Leo	Leo	Vir	Vir
June 17	Ar	Tau	Gem	Gem	Can	Can	Can	Leo	Leo	Vir	Vir	Vir
June 25	Tau	Tau	Gem	Gem	Can	Can	Leo	Leo	Leo	Vir	Vir	Lib
July 3	Tau	Gem	Gem	Can	Can	Can	Leo	Leo	Vir	Vir	Vir	Lib
July 11	Tau	Gem	Gem	Can	Can	Leo	Leo	Leo	Vir	Vir	Lib	Lib
July 18	Gem	Gem	Can	Can	Can	Leo	Leo	Vir	Vir	Vir	Lib	Lib
July 26	Gem	Gem	Can	Can	Leo	Leo	Vir	Vir	Vir	Lib	Lib	Lib
Aug 3	Gem	Can	Can	Can	Leo	Leo	Vir	Vir	Vir	Lib	Lib	Sc
Aug 11	Gem	Can	Can	Leo	Leo	Leo	Vir	Vir	Lib	Lib	Lib	Sc
Aug 18	Can	Can	Can	Leo	Leo	Vir	Vir	Vir	Lib	Lib	Sc	Sc
Aug 27	Can	Can	Leo	Leo	Leo	Vir	Vir	Lib	Lib	Lib	Sc	Sc
Sept 4	Can	Can	Leo	Leo	Leo	Vir	Vir	Vir	Lib	Lib	Sc	Sc
Sept 12	Can	Leo	Leo	Leo	Vir	Vir	Lib	Lib	Lib	Sc	Sc	Sag
Sept 30	Leo	Leo	Leo	Vir	Vir	Vir	Lib	Lib	Sc	Sc	Sc	Sag
Sept 28	Leo	Leo	Leo	Vir	Vir	Lib	Lib	Lib	Sc	Sc	Sag	Sag
Oct 6	Leo	Leo	Vir	Vir	Vir	Lib	Lib	Sc	Sc	Sc	Sag	Sag
Oct 14	Leo	Vir	Vir	Vir	Lib	Lib	Lib	Sc	Sc	Sag	Sag	Cap
Oct 22	Leo	Vir	Vir	Lib	Lib	Lib	Sc	Sc	Sc	Sag	Sag	Cap
Oct 30	Vir	Vir	Vir	Lib	Lib	Sc	Sc	Sc	Sag	Sag	Cap	Cap
Nov 7	Vir	Vir	Lib	Lib	Lib	Sc	Sc	Sc	Sag	Sag	Cap	Cap
Nov 15	Vir	Vir	Lib	Lib	Sc	Sc	Sc	Sag	Sag	Cap	Cap	Aq
Nov 23	Vir	Lib	Lib	Lib	Sc	Sc	Sag	Sag	Sag	Cap	Cap	Aq
Dec 1	Vir	Lib	Lib	Sc	Sc	Sc	Sag	Sag	Cap	Cap	Aq	Aq
Dec 9	Lib	Lib	Lib	Sc	Sc	Sag	Sag	Sag	Cap	Cap	Aq	Pis
Dec 18	Lib	Lib	Sc	Sc	Sc	Sag	Sag	Cap	Cap	Aq	Aq	Pis
Dec 28	Lib	Lib	Sc	Sc	Sag	Sag	Sag	Cap	Aq	Aq	Pis	Ar

Rising Signs—P.M. Births

	1 PM	2 PM	3 PM	4 PM	5 PM	6 PM	7 PM	8 PM	9 PM	10 PM	11 PM	12 MIDNIGHT
Jan 1	Tau	Gem	Gem	Can	Can	Can	Leo	Leo	Vir	Vir	Vir	Lib
Jan 9	Tau	Gem	Gem	Can	Can	Leo	Leo	Leo	Vir	Vir	Vir	Lib
Jan 17	Gem	Gem	Can	Can	Can	Leo	Leo	Vir	Vir	Vir	Lib	Lib
Jan 25	Gem	Gem	Can	Can	Leo	Leo	Leo	Vir	Vir	Lib	Lib	Lib
Feb 2	Gem	Can	Can	Can	Leo	Leo	Vir	Vir	Vir	Lib	Lib	Sc
Feb 10	Gem	Can	Can	Leo	Leo	Leo	Vir	Vir	Lib	Lib	Lib	Sc
Feb 18	Can	Can	Can	Leo	Leo	Vir	Vir	Vir	Lib	Lib	Sc	Sc
Feb 26	Can	Can	Leo	Leo	Leo	Vir	Vir	Lib	Lib	Lib	Sc	Sc
Mar 6	Can	Leo	Leo	Leo	Vir	Vir	Vir	Lib	Lib	Sc	Sc	Sc
Mar 14	Can	Leo	Leo	Vir	Vir	Vir	Lib	Lib	Lib	Sc	Sc	Sag
Mar 22	Leo	Leo	Leo	Vir	Vir	Lib	Lib	Lib	Sc	Sc	Sc	Sag
Mar 30	Leo	Leo	Vir	Vir	Vir	Lib	Lib	Sc	Sc	Sc	Sag	Sag
Apr 7	Leo	Leo	Vir	Vir	Lib	Lib	Lib	Sc	Sc	Sc	Sag	Sag
Apr 14	Leo	Vir	Vir	Vir	Lib	Lib	Sc	Sc	Sc	Sag	Sag	Cap
Apr 22	Leo	Vir	Vir	Lib	Lib	Lib	Sc	Sc	Sc	Sag	Sag	Cap
Apr 30	Vir	Vir	Vir	Lib	Lib	Sc	Sc	Sc	Sag	Sag	Cap	Cap
May 8	Vir	Vir	Lib	Lib	Lib	Sc	Sc	Sag	Sag	Sag	Cap	Cap
May 16	Vir	Vir	Lib	Lib	Sc	Sc	Sc	Sag	Sag	Cap	Cap	Aq
May 24	Vir	Lib	Lib	Lib	Sc	Sc	Sag	Sag	Sag	Cap	Cap	Aq
June 1	Vir	Lib	Lib	Sc	Sc	Sc	Sag	Sag	Cap	Cap	Aq	Aq
June 9	Lib	Lib	Lib	Sc	Sc	Sag	Sag	Sag	Cap	Cap	Aq	Pis
June 17	Lib	Lib	Sc	Sc	Sc	Sag	Sag	Cap	Cap	Aq	Aq	Pis
June 25	Lib	Lib	Sc	Sc	Sag	Sag	Sag	Cap	Cap	Aq	Pis	Ar
July 3	Lib	Sc	Sc	Sc	Sag	Sag	Cap	Cap	Aq	Aq	Pis	Ar
July 11	Lib	Sc	Sc	Sag	Sag	Sag	Cap	Cap	Aq	Pis	Ar	Tau
July 18	Sc	Sc	Sc	Sag	Sag	Cap	Cap	Aq	Aq	Pis	Ar	Tau
July 26	Sc	Sc	Sag	Sag	Sag	Cap	Cap	Aq	Pis	Ar	Tau	Tau
Aug 3	Sc	Sc	Sag	Sag	Cap	Cap	Aq	Aq	Pis	Ar	Tau	Gem
Aug 11	Sc	Sag	Sag	Sag	Cap	Cap	Aq	Pis	Ar	Tau	Tau	Gem
Aug 18	Sc	Sag	Sag	Cap	Cap	Aq	Pis	Pis	Ar	Tau	Gem	Gem
Aug 27	Sag	Sag	Sag	Cap	Cap	Aq	Pis	Ar	Tau	Tau	Gem	Gem
Sept 4	Sag	Sag	Cap	Cap	Aq	Pis	Pis	Ar	Tau	Gem	Gem	Can
Sept 12	Sag	Sag	Cap	Aq	Aq	Pis	Ar	Tau	Tau	Gem	Gem	Can
Sept 20	Sag	Cap	Cap	Aq	Pis	Pis	Ar	Tau	Gem	Gem	Can	Can
Sept 28	Cap	Cap	Aq	Aq	Pis	Ar	Tau	Tau	Gem	Gem	Can	Can
Oct 6	Cap	Cap	Aq	Pis	Ar	Ar	Tau	Gem	Gem	Can	Can	Leo
Oct 14	Cap	Aq	Aq	Pis	Ar	Tau	Tau	Gem	Gem	Can	Can	Leo
Oct 22	Cap	Aq	Pis	Ar	Ar	Tau	Gem	Gem	Can	Can	Leo	Leo
Oct 30	Aq	Aq	Pis	Ar	Tau	Tau	Gem	Can	Can	Can	Leo	Leo
Nov 7	Aq	Aq	Pis	Ar	Tau	Tau	Gem	Can	Can	Can	Leo	Leo
Nov 15	Aq	Pis	Ar	Tau	Gem	Gem	Can	Can	Can	Leo	Leo	Vir
Nov 23	Pis	Ar	Ar	Tau	Gem	Gem	Can	Can	Leo	Leo	Leo	Vir
Dec 1	Pis	Ar	Tau	Gem	Gem	Can	Can	Can	Leo	Leo	Vir	Vir
Dec 9	Ar	Tau	Tau	Gem	Gem	Can	Can	Leo	Leo	Leo	Vir	Vir
Dec 18	Ar	Tau	Gem	Gem	Can	Can	Can	Leo	Leo	Vir	Vir	Vir
Dec 28	Tau	Tau	Gem	Gem	Can	Can	Leo	Leo	Vir	Vir	Vir	Lib

Libra with Aquarius Rising— Unusual Tastes

You have highly original tastes—may be eccentric or unusual in looks or way of dressing. You like to surprise—even shock—others. You have an excellent mind, enjoy using it to deal with far-out issues, humanitarian or political causes. You may apply your flair for legalities in an unusual way. You like to be with people and in surroundings that are innovative, forward looking, and somewhat unpredictable. Your sense of color and style will also be more futuristic than other Librans. Physically, your circulation and ankles are vulnerable.

Libra with Pisces Rising— A Sympathetic Ear

Your vulnerable sympathetic manner draw those with sad stories to tell. You might choose work in hospitals or other charitable institutions for this reason. But your imaginative and theatrical tastes could also be at home in the film, theater or dance world, and in places near the water. Your emotional life is more colorful than other Librans, as you tend to fall for underdogs and could fall in love with love several times. Your vulnerable spots are the feet and the lymphatic system. Your body also tends to retain water. Watch a sensitivity to alcohol and drugs. Beautiful shoes could be your fashion fetish.

12

Libra Positives and Negatives

The Positive You

Love of fairness is your outstanding quality. Since your goal is harmony, you generally avoid unpleasantness or ugliness of any sort, preferring to resolve differences with calm discussion or diplomacy. Because you are able to detach yourself emotionally to examine both sides of a question, you make the most impartial judge. But Librans will stand up and fight when they perceive injustice, or use their persuasive powers to balance the situation.

Your sense of balance leads to a highly developed aesthetic taste. Librans are known for their elegance in dress and decor. Many world famous designers such as Ralph Lauren were born under this sign. Librans often choose artistic, creative, or literary careers.

Social skills come naturally to Libra. You have innate good manners, and a dislike of rudeness of any sort. You are a wonderful host or hostess, who has a talent for bringing people together in harmonious and beautiful surroundings.

You enjoy activities in the company of others and make an excellent partner for someone who balances your qualities.

Play Up: Sense of justice, high ideals, good taste, design talent, sense of balance, partnership qualifications, charm, and diplomacy.

The Negative You

You may be so interested in achieving harmony that you ignore the harsher realities of a situation. Some Librans escape into a fantasy world of intellectual or artistic interests and beautiful people.

Indecisiveness is the dark side of your positive ability to weigh the pros and cons of every situation. You can spend so much time waffling that nothing gets done.

Your infatuation with beauty could lead to superficial relationships based on romantic fantasies or physical attractions. Many Librans, who love to be in love, constantly change partners looking for the ideal mate.

Confrontations are so unsettling to you that you may avoid or postpone important issues rather than deal with unpleasantness. Others may dismiss you as all style, no substance.

Play Down: Indecisiveness, escapism, vanity, superficiality.

13

Your Libra Success Strategy

Choosing the right job involves much mental deliberation for Libra. A routine job won't do. Nor will work which involves quick decisions or too much detail. You look to satisfy your ideals in your work, in some way. Your job should be one that engages your mind, gives you social contacts and offers pleasant surroundings. You often work out abstract concepts of beauty and justice in careers in design, law, diplomacy, labor relations, art, fashion, strategic planning, or education. Your innate feeling for balance might lead you to a health-oriented field: you are especially good at diagnosis, massage, chiropractic, nutrition. You work very well with partners or on a team, thriving on the social contact and exchange of ideas. Though you are able to mediate between different groups, getting people to work together toward a common goal, you will be happiest if you avoid clashing egos and offices which continually assault your aesthetic tastes. Difficult working conditions can take a toll on your health in the long run.

Libra in Charge

You are a charming sociable boss who rarely raises his voice or handles anyone harshly. Even when annoyed, you are diplomatic. You bring together a winning team and keep everyone working in harmony. You are extremely fair with subordinates, delegating work so that no one assumes an excessive work load. You may have problems with confrontations —you are much better at smoothing over a difficult situation than coming to grips with it head on or making a quick turnaround. You may leave the face-off scenes to a partner and assume the role of mediator. Your office is always neat and harmonious since you are very conscious of appearances—you are careful to represent your company in the most elegant ways. You enjoy business entertaining and probably have a generous expense account.

Libra Teamwork

Libra thrives from working with others, though you avoid getting personal. You are usually the peacemaker, the one in the middle who brings opposing factions together. You have a charming telephone manner and work well in a spot where you meet the public directly or indirectly. Your workspace is always harmonious, well organized, and probably given some aesthetic touches, since Libra's work may suffer in an ugly or disorderly environment. You are a hard worker, but not a workaholic, sensing that you must balance your work life with play and exercise. Your good looks and natural diplomacy make you a good advertisement for your company in a public position.

To Get Ahead Fast:

Pick a job in an aesthetic environment where you deal with the public or with idealistic issues.

Play up your:

- Intelligence
- Balanced judgment
- Artistic talent
- Social skills
- Elegant taste

14

Libra's Place in the Family

The Libra Parent

The Libra parent adores intelligent, attractive, well-mannered children, and you'll do your very best to see that your own children fulfill that image. That means providing them with an excellent education and spending "quality time" with them. You would like to find a way to avoid the more mundane duties of parenthood, but you are happy to share interesting activities with your children, often planning special creative projects to share. When discipline is necessary, you'd prefer a calm, reasoned discussion better than an all-out show of power. In an extremely emotional scene, you will detach yourself completely. But when your scales are tipped, you'll be as irritable a parent as any. Or you may suddenly become cool and distant. Be sure to make up for this with a show of affection when your balance is restored, to keep the harmonious home life you love and need.

The Libra Child

The Libra child learns early about the power of charm and good looks. This is often a physically appealing child with an enchanting dimpled smile. This child is naturally sociable and enjoys the company of both children and adults. It is a rare Libra child who is a discipline problem. Because young Librans without a strong direction tend to drift with the mood of the group, they should be encouraged to develop their unique talents and powers of discrimination, to later stand on their own. In school, this child is usually popular and will often have to chose between social invitations and studies. In the teen years, the social pressures will mount, as the young Libra begins to look for a partner. This is the sign of "best friends," so Libras' choice of companions can have strong effects on their future direction. Beautiful Libra girls will be tempted to go steady or make an unwise early marriage. Chances are both sexes will fall in and out of love several times in their search for the perfect partner.

The Libra Stepparent

Libra can function well as a stepparent, realizing that in due time a family equilibrium can be restored. You will not demand instant acceptance, but will detach yourself until the children are ready to come to you, meanwhile providing a charming and hospitable atmosphere. You are very conscious of the children's rights and will treat them with fairness, allowing them the time they need with their parent. You will create activities and events where everyone can take part. However, if the children are too demanding or ill-mannered, you will not allow them to impose and will again detach yourself. Ultimately your fairness and charm should win them over.

The Libra Grandparent

Libran grandparents may not be the type to babysit or fuss over the grandchild, but they enjoy sharing their home and interests with the youngest generation, particularly if the children are attractive and well behaved. By this time, the Libran has achieved a degree of comfort and harmony in life and treats grandchildren as interesting companions rather than charges or responsibilities. You are not the type to take over for your daughter or daughter-in-law, nor will you offer unsolicited advice, but you will not tolerate too much disruption of your peace and quiet. If your grandchild shares your interests or is especially attentive and flattering, you may be happy to have found the ideal companion at last.

15

What Suits Libra Best

The Libra Environment

Because an off-colored wall or a tilted picture frame can upset your equilibrium, you should be sure to voice your preferences in the design of your environment. Your natural sense of harmony translates beautifully to interior design, where you have an eye for proportion, color harmony, and furniture arrangement. Libran rooms have a coordinated look, with furniture, colors, and fabrics either matching or relating beautifully. Effects that are too strong or dramatic are not for you. And you'll find vibrant colors difficult to live with. You'll place accessories in lovely still lifes, not to be disturbed, and will light the room to flatter the occupants. Because you love to entertain at home, you'll make provisions for receiving guests graciously.

Libra Music

Romantic music makes your heart sing. Libran artists Luciano Pavarotti, Julio Iglésias, and Yves Montand strike the right notes. Verdi, Liszt, and John Lennon wrote your kind of music.

Libra Flowers

Pink and lavender flowers are very Libra. Try a mix of lavender and open pale pink roses!

Libra Places

You'll take a favorite companion along on your trips. Libra loves to do things with people, remember? You'll love a vacation in elegant, cultured surroundings (no camping out, please), where you can dress up and socialize with nice people. With the most pleasant company, you'll unwind on a trip through the castles of the Loire valley, a weekend at an aristocratic English country house, waltzing in Vienna, floating through the vale of Kashmir, and breathing the clear clean air of the Swiss Alps—or Tibet, for the more adventurous.

Libra Colors

All shades of pink, but particularly the delicate pale shell colors. The pale cosmetic shades are flattering to everyone and promote a calm, harmonious feeling.

Libra Fashion Tips

Your natural sense of design and proportion makes you one of the most clothes-conscious signs. You are instinctively coordinated, with colors, accessories, and patterns chosen for perfect harmony and flattery to your special looks. Libra is at your most creative in "packaging" yourself beautifully. Your look is always complete from head to toe—you'd never wear the wrong shoes or carry an odd-looking bag. Many of you stick to one designer or design your own clothes to be put together perfectly. Your classic looks are never overwhelmed by garish colors, nor is your outfit dominated by one standout accessory. Rather than drama, you go for elegance. Hair and makeup are soft, just enough to give definition to your features.

16

Libra: Astro-Outlook for 1990

This is a highly significant year in your life, Libra. Many memorable events are likely to take place, particularly in your professional life, where a special triumph provides greater prestige, money, and security. Prepare to sign a contract that promises long-term benefits. But be ready for the extra responsibilities and demands of leadership that come with all this.

In your personal world, you are also about to make firmer commitments and long-range plans. If single, you could marry. If already married, you might expect an addition to the family. Married or single, you'll become more serious, settled, and prosperous.

There's much activity this year in your home or among family members, some of whom may be acting very oddly. You'll be anxious to conclude a property or rental agreement that breaks up old conditions and signals new ones. This is particularly likely *if you were born between September 29 and October 3*. If you do not change residence, you will alter your life-style in some significant way.

Check papers carefully before you purchase real estate. A clouded title or mysterious circumstances may have to be cleared up first, especially *if you were born between October 5 and 8*.

During the first half of the year, you'll gain through a generous executive, parent, or parent figure. Jupiter, the planet of good fortune, assures you extra prominence and recognition between January 1 and July 18. During the latter half of the year, Jupiter moves into your social realm, broadening opportunities and bringing prestigious friendships.

A romantic period occurs when Venus, planet of love and beauty, travels through Libra between October 1 and 25. This is a wonderful time to entertain—to bring out your best china and silver and impress social contacts. Personally, you'll feel radiant. It's a good time for beauty or grooming treatments, new clothes, and the purchase of luxury items for your own adornment.

Romance, excitement, and new starts are also favored during February, April, June, and November. September will be an important month for long-range plans. A move may take place in July. As always, you'll be most fortunate when the sun is in your own sign between September 23 and October 22. See the pages ahead for the full picture.

17

Fifteen Months of Day-by-Day Predictions

OCTOBER 1989

Sunday, October 1 (Moon in Libra to Scorpio 3:53 p.m.) An important month lies ahead. Your intuition tells you that you can reach a much larger audience. You'll be dynamic and enterprising. Complete a personal project today; be ready for the big events that lie ahead. Aries is on the scene. Watch number 9.

Monday, October 2 (Moon in Scorpio) It's time to evaluate a personal skill or talent. Have you been promoting it as boldly as you should? Greater confidence today can lead to more money in the bank as the real you is properly recognized. Treat yourself to some little luxury today, Libra.

Tuesday, October 3 (Moon in Scorpio) The accent is on security, savings, and a shopping trip that nets you an amazing bargain. Be willing to go from store to store to hunt down just what you want. A woman friend or associate could give you some valuable clues, if you ask. Cash in on number 2.

Wednesday, October 4 (Moon in Scorpio to Sagittarius 4:29 a.m.) Your zest for life will be very evident today. Even a trip around the block could be an exciting event because of your sincere interest and curiosity about everything you'll encounter. A new friend pops into the picture. Your mental vibes are in sync.

Thursday, October 5 (Moon in Sagittarius) Stick to routine. You'll recognize that patience is required today, but may be brimming with impulsive notions. Your best bet is to revise correspondence and other paperwork that was hastily written before. Stick with number 4.

Friday, October 6 (Moon in Sagittarius to Capricorn 3:45 p.m.) Dress in your best today, Libra. Romance could be as close as the corner store. Walking, running, jogging will be fine ways to meet new persons who are also out to enjoy the local neighborhood. A lively discussion with a Gemini is on the agenda.

Saturday, October 7 (Moon in Capricorn) Polish up your peacemaking skills; they'll be needed in a domestic situation. A stubborn Taurus type may be difficult to appease, especially if this person feels that the good things of life are being denied. Provide love, little luxuries. Pick number 6 today.

Sunday, October 8 (Moon in Capricorn) With such a busy week behind you, you'll feel the need to retreat into your own shell today. Soft music and quiet amusements are in order. Don't worry about inviting company; it's best to reach a deeper understanding of your own psyche. Pisces could show you how.

Monday, October 9 (Moon in Capricorn to Aquarius 12:07 a.m.) You'll feel responsibility strongly today, not only in work, but in a love situation. Nothing will occur halfway; you'll be asked to make commitments that will last! Someone who is equally serious appeals. Creativity flows. Your lucky number is 8.

Tuesday, October 10 (Moon in Aquarius) The accent is on young people, children, having fun. Be generous with your time; consider the needs of more than just your own kin. A recreational project could give you the chance to help many youths in a constructive way. Aries plays a key role.

Wednesday, October 11 (Moon in Aquarius to Pisces 4:38 a.m.) A new job opportunity is whispered in your ear. Since you may be tired of the same old routine, you'll be eager to hear more. Consider all the angles of a new project. Will you be allowed to work with up-to-date equipment? Look out for number 1.

Thursday, October 12 (Moon in Pisces) You'll welcome a slow pace, Libra. Take time to consider your health, diet, and nutrition. The domestic side of your nature will be aroused, causing you to play a nurturing role to someone who seems helpless or confused. Be especially helpful to a co-worker.

Friday, October 13 (Moon in Pisces to Aries 5:41 a.m.) Optimism prevails. If your mate, partner, or associate is in a down mood, try to lift that person's spirits. Your sense of humor will be delightful today. Laugh at troubles. You may have to refuse some invitations because of your popularity. Cash in on number 3.

Saturday, October 14 (Moon in Aries) You'll associate with solid citizens in a public project. A practical approach is best. Major obstacles can be overcome if you avoid extremes and accept the limitations imposed. This could be a testing time, so follow all the rules. An Aquarius appears.

Sunday, October 15 (Moon in Aries to Taurus 4:52 a.m.) A passionate undertone pervades this day. You could feel boxed in by the possessiveness of one you love. Your reaction is to escape to greater freedom. Before you do, discuss this matter in a heart-to-heart chat. Be understanding! The lucky number is 5.

Monday, October 16 (Moon in Taurus) Financial good fortune depends on your ability to weigh and balance a money opportunity today, Libra. Consider family needs, not just the essentials but the luxuries that make life worth living. If there is money left over, then invest conservatively.

Tuesday, October 17 (Moon in Taurus to Gemini 4:19 a.m.) Spiritual values will play a big role in your peace of mind. You've had your mind on worldly affairs, but need some time off to get away from it all. Even a few minutes of deep meditation will refresh you. Pisces shows you the way. Number 7 is a winner.

Wednesday, October 18 (Moon in Gemini) With renewed inspiration, you'll see how your business success can be increased. All methods that appeal to a widespread audience will be valuable. Consider mail order, publicity, advertising, or export/import techniques. A Capricorn has some answers you need.

Thursday, October 19 (Moon in Gemini to Cancer 6:09 a.m.) You move into high gear where your career is concerned. Someone who limited or resented your getting ahead is fading from the picture—or has already left. Dismiss resentment of this situation; look at the larger picture. Your lucky number is 9.

Friday, October 20 (Moon in Cancer) The accent is on your leadership ability, Libra. Don't be reluctant to blow your own horn today. You have a valuable idea and should not be reluctant because it is original and untried. Speak to someone on the executive level, possibly a Leo type.

Saturday, October 21 (Moon in Cancer to Leo 11:47 a.m.) Lessons you learned long ago will prove of value. The examples of parental figures prove to be influential. You might wish you could return to the good old days when life seemed less complicated. Don't force issues! Your lucky number is 2.

Sunday, October 22 (Moon in Leo) Involvement in a group provides fun and a sense of adventure. You'll promote your ideas with zeal and will be extra conscious of justice, right and wrong, and an urge to improve your character. Travel and education are accented. A Sagittarian plays a big role.

Monday, October 23 (Moon in Leo to Virgo 9:15 p.m.) Stick to the tried and true. Your desires today are actually within reach as long as you take the pains to complete a project. Self-discipline will be necessary; face that fact! Study details, and do the work yourself—don't delegate. Count on number 4.

Tuesday, October 24 (Moon in Virgo) Someone of the opposite sex with a probing mind will have many questions. You may feel that a secret matter regarding your affections could be revealed. A mental fencing match could be exciting, stimulating. Gemini and Virgo types play roles.

Wednesday, October 25 (Moon in Virgo) The accent is on family, home, and quiet entertainment. You'll feel you want to retreat from a public position today and enjoy your loved ones. Some confidential problems may be presented to you for solutions. Be understanding! The lucky number is 6.

Thursday, October 26 (Moon in Virgo to Libra 9:11 a.m.) Your imagination will be working overtime. Follow what seem to be valid hunches, but steer clear of wild schemes. You may be fooling yourself about a relationship; give matters a chance to settle down. Play a waiting game. A Pisces is in the picture.

Friday, October 27 (Moon in Libra) You'll pull out of a slump today and find yourself very much in the public eye. Past efforts beginning to pay off in a big way. You'll be placed in a position of leadership by someone who has observed you and decided you can do it! Stick with number 8.

Saturday, October 28 (Moon in Libra to Scorpio 9:11 p.m.) It's time to take stock of your appearance and personal habits. Libra. If you want to make changes, now is the time to rid yourself of outmoded clothes or negative ideas about yourself. A new self-image is in order. An Aries is encouraging.

Sunday, October 29 (Moon in Scorpio) You have a strong inclination to be extravagant today. You'll want to be noticed and to impress others, especially a

Leo type who is in the picture. You'll be most likely to spend on theatrical entertainment and romantic surroundings. Number 1 is your best bet.

Monday, October 30 (Moon in Scorpio) You'll take a second look at finances today, and wonder how you can build up your bank account again. Don't be impatient for results. Your basic security is not threatened. Highlight family interests; a loved one can seem very dependent now.

Tuesday, October 31 (Moon in Scorpio to Sagittarius 10:23 a.m.) As you tie up the events of this month, get in touch with those who have helped you and renew ties. Your local area is probably bustling with activity, making you restless to get involved in some highly social venture. Remember moderation! The lucky number is 3.

NOVEMBER 1989

Wednesday, November 1 (Moon in Sagittarius) You'll be more active and sports-minded. Running, walking, visiting with relatives and neighbors are favored. An original idea has you in its grip; you'll find it hard to talk about anything else. A fun-loving member of the opposite sex is dazzled.

Thursday, November 2 (Moon in Sagittarius to Capricorn 9:46 p.m.) Someone from your past appears on your doorstep. The talk will be nostalgic. Your yesterdays will seem more appealing than ever. Emotions run high; you could give way to moods where your family is concerned. Be patient! Play number 2 for luck.

Friday, November 3 (Moon in Capricorn) Your home will be the ideal place to entertain. You'll attract people who write, speak, teach, or travel. Plan light entertainment; no one will want to dwell on heavy issues. You'll see the funny side of a family situation, refusing to worry.

Saturday, November 4 (Moon in Capricorn) You'll attack chores today with gusto, pleased that you can accomplish so much. You've had many good times recently, so a routine job could seem a welcome relief. Settle down, follow rules, take one step at a time. Today your lucky number is 4.

Sunday, November 5 (Moon in Capricorn to Aquarius 7:09 a.m.) An outing today brings you in touch with one who has much conversational catching-up to do. A party, celebrating a birthday or anniversary may be on the agenda. Expect the unexpected; this could be a complete surprise to someone you admire.

Monday, November 6 (Moon in Aquarius) A gentle manner will be best in dealing with younger family members who are out of line. Adjustments in life-styles could be needed, and is probably the reason that disturbances are taking place. A touch of sentiment should help. Watch number 6.

Tuesday, November 7 (Moon in Aquarius to Pisces 1:25 p.m.) A Pisces type wants your assistance on a creative project. Your talent for art, design, or literature is accented. Let your imagination roam; many unique ideas will be forthcoming. You will prefer seclusion rather than a crowd. Give yourself room!

Wednesday, November 8 (Moon in Pisces) Today you'll see how to make more of your own enterprises. A serious tone pervades your workplace. Someone in power will be glad to share success secrets with you, provided you show the right attitude. Let your ambition shine. Try number 8 for luck.

Thursday, November 9 (Moon in Pisces to Aries 4:08 p.m.) You'll put the finishing touches on a large project. A sense of relief accompanies this action. The realization dawns that you've been too tied up with one facet of your talents; now it's time to reevaluate. A co-worker agrees. Aries plays a role.

Friday, November 10 (Moon in Aries) Your original ideas will be well received by a partner, mate, or associate. Don't be reluctant to explain recent discoveries or events. Your creative flair will spark an entirely fresh episode in this relationship. Your sex appeal is high. Today's number is 1.

Saturday, November 11 (Moon in Aries to Taurus 4:09 p.m.) A relative comes to visit, fulfilling your need for greater emotional security. There's great emphasis on food, shopping, and finding valuable or attractive purchases. You may feel somewhat hemmed in by the extra duties involved. Don't be moody!

Sunday, November 12 (Moon in Taurus) A lighthearted mood is more likely to appeal to a loved one than secrecy or brooding now. Traveling together can be a transforming experience if you investigate places of mutual deep interest. Sagittarius is in the picture. Luck rides with number 3.

Monday, November 13 (Moon in Taurus to Gemini 3:19 p.m.) You may be disturbed by some recent rise in price, especially in payments concerning taxes or insurance. Realize that it may be necessary to check these figures out. Some mistake may have been made. Don't take anything for granted. An Aquarius helps.

Tuesday, November 14 (Moon in Gemini) You'll feel freer to enjoy life, travel, and expand your mental horizons. A member of the opposite sex encourages you to rise above former limitations in some branch of your learning. Much amusing conversation shows off wit and wisdom. Watch number 5.

Wednesday, November 15 (Moon in Gemini to Cancer 3:51 p.m.) A break in your everyday routine involves a relative. You may have to go out of your way to settle a family dispute. Stick to conventional morals and ethics; you are providing a good example for a loved one. Taurus and Scorpio pay attention.

Thursday, November 16 (Moon in Cancer) You'll work behind the scenes, but will be recognized in spite of your background role. If you are puzzled by the actions of an authority figure, don't engage in wild speculation. Your imagination is working overtime. The lucky number today is 7.

Friday, November 17 (Moon in Cancer to Leo 7:45 p.m.) The accent is on success, money, prestige. You'll see things more clearly today; now's the time to let those at the top know about your long-range ambitions. Be conservative, not flashy. Your seriousness of purpose helps. A Capricorn encourages you.

Saturday, November 18 (Moon in Leo) Take a closer look at your friendships and acquaintances. Your current goals can be greatly helped or hindered depending upon your associations. One person, in particular, could be wasting your time and not contributing much. Play number 9 for luck.

Sunday, November 19 (Moon in Leo) A time of greater individuality is at hand. Don't just follow the crowd, no matter how close you have felt to a certain group of people in the past. Strike out for yourself in the area of creativity. A fiery Leo type is ready to applaud your efforts.

Monday, November 20 (Moon in Leo to Virgo 3:54 a.m.) It may be necessary to backtrack a bit in your bid for independence. An older woman or devoted relative issues a call for assistance. You cannot really turn this person down right now. A confidence is shared with you; respect it. Stick with number 2.

Tuesday, November 21 (Moon in Virgo) Your faith in the future reasserts itself. Although secret fears and doubts have to be battled, you'll emerge a winner. Your beliefs have undergone a trial, possibly one that only you will realize. Sagittarius and Gemini types raise your spirits.

Wednesday, November 22 (Moon in Virgo to Libra 3:25 p.m.) Practical details must be dealt with. Accept the need for a routine day; avoid those tempting side trips that beckon to you. You'll feel greater satisfaction by retreating within yourself and dealing with mundane personal matters. The lucky number is 4.

Thursday, November 23 (Moon in Libra) By now, you're ready to have some fun. The moon is in your sign today, Libra, and your romantic feelings are dominant. You'll attract someone of the opposite sex who will be very verbal about your appearance, your talents, and will praise you highly.

Friday, November 24 (Moon in Libra) Your sense of responsibility surges to the forefront. You become the peacemaker today in a family quarrel or disagreement. Something about your own good sense of balance and calmness influences others to listen to you, kiss and make up. Cash in on number 6.

Saturday, November 25 (Moon in Libra to Scorpio 4:13 a.m.) Money matters may seem confusing, outrageously so. You could be incensed about a bill that seems highly inflated. Wait until tomorrow before taking any action. If you're writing personal checks, be sure you have not made an error in calculation. Go slow.

Sunday, November 26 (Moon in Scorpio) You'll see facts and figures more clearly today. In buying or selling, you'll deal with quality goods, conservative stores or methods. Capricorn and Cancer people can help guide you to make the most of your assets. Number 8 will be significant.

Monday, November 27 (Moon in Scorpio to Sagittarius 4:30 p.m.) Accent your generosity and a spirit of giving. Something you considered valuable in the past can be of greater use to someone else now. Go through your personal possessions and rid yourself of anything that is a burden now. An Aries and another Libra play prominent roles.

Tuesday, November 28 (Moon in Sagittarius) A telephone call turns your life around today, leading you in a new direction. You'll see innovative ways to improve your daily routine. Romantic thoughts add a special thrill; you realize someone does care! Count on number 1.

Wednesday, November 29 (Moon in Sagittarius to Capricorn 3:26 a.m.) A period of waiting for the right moment may seem like game-playing, but it is not. You won't have to make the first move romantically if you are tactful, patient, and sensitive to the feelings of a loved one. Someone equally sensitive will appeal!

Thursday, November 30 (Moon in Capricorn) Your home could become the scene of much activity, involving a visitor from afar. You'll be discussing intellectual subjects; so keep abreast of daily conditions in the world. Your sense of justice will be accented, Libra. The lucky number is 3.

DECEMBER 1989

Friday, December 1 (Moon in Capricorn) You've gained greater self-understanding in recent months. Now you can begin to put some insights into action, but gently. Today, a discussion with a family member convinces you that those near and dear need more of your attention. Be aware!

Saturday, December 2 (Moon in Capricorn to Aquarius 12:42 p.m.) This could be a wonderful shopping day as long as you don't indulge in overextravagance or time-wasting activities. Your strong desire for amusement as the day progresses will keep you from accomplishing much. Your lucky number will be 3.

Sunday, December 3 (Moon in Aquarius) You'll be more disciplined and detail-minded today. Keep promises made to younger relatives. A recreational trip could turn into a responsible work project where you're concerned. Be grateful others involved are having fun. Aquarius is in the picture.

Monday, December 4 (Moon in Aquarius to Pisces 7:48 p.m.) A phone conversation with someone of the opposite sex turns inevitably to romance. You'll be able to talk your way into or out of favor or disfavor. Don't expect the status quo today; exciting changes are in the wind. Number 5 is a winner.

Tuesday, December 5 (Moon in Pisces) You'll be able to delineate your responsibilities more clearly in a work situation. Co-workers may have been trying to put too much on your shoulders; don't allow this to happen. You'll work best in a peaceful, artistic environment. Taurus is on hand.

Wednesday, December 6 (Moon in Pisces) A puzzling situation is ready to be solved. You'll be a supersleuth in discovering how a daily associate feels, but may not be able to do more than sympathize. Avoid crowds today; you'll be too sensitive to the vibes of others. Number 7 pays off.

Thursday, December 7 (Moon in Pisces to Aries 12:11 a.m.) The emphasis is on partnerships, particularly those involving business. You're ready to make a long-term commitment because you realize that another has been loyal and trustworthy. A romantic undertone is present. You'll really admire this person.

Friday, December 8 (Moon in Aries) Your relationships will thrive today as long as you remain generous and ready to rise above another's pettiness. Too possessive an attitude could be harmful; look at the big picture, including the growth potential of others. Your lucky number will be 9.

Saturday, December 9 (Moon in Aries to Taurus 1:59 a.m.) A physical attraction is accented. You'll be bolder than usual and ready to make the first move toward one who delights you. You'll reach an unusual rapport and deep understanding with a loved one. ESP could be involved. A Leo type is on your wavelength.

Sunday, December 10 (Moon in Taurus) Dig deep to solve a mystery. A relative who is moody and uncommunicative is possibly hiding something that you could help with. Money or joint funds may be involved. Be tactful; don't force issues or answers today. Stick with number 2.

Monday, December 11 (Moon in Taurus to Gemini 2:15 a.m.) A yen to travel or to contact someone far away drives you today. You'll be restless and unwilling to settle down to minor matters when such great activity is taking place elsewhere. Don't use up energy just spinning wheels; arrive at a firm decision about this.

Tuesday, December 12 (Moon in Gemini) The full moon highlights matters at a distance. This is no time to give way to impulse, even if those around you are excited or overly emotional. Your own cool head and good Libran sense of balance will help you to work this out. Try number 4 for luck.

Wednesday, December 13 (Moon in Gemini to Cancer 2:49 a.m.) New information arrives, encouraging you in career interests. Put aside doubts about your desire to write, speak, or communicate with a VIP. You'll be able to charm someone with your intelligence. Your sex appeal is high; just ask a Gemini type!

Thursday, December 14 (Moon in Cancer) The emphasis is on duties and obligations to parents or authority figures. You may feel weighted down by the extra duties of the season. If so, it's time to ask for help. You do not need to take on more than your share of burdens. The lucky number is 6.

Friday, December 15 (Moon in Cancer to Leo 5:41 a.m.) Just when you thought you'd have some time for yourself, a group or organization requires your presence. You may not feel particularly social today, but could prove to be an inspiration to someone because of your special artistic or musical talents.

Saturday, December 16 (Moon in Leo) Long-range goals and ambitions are accented. A social gathering puts you in touch with someone of great accomplishment. You can learn much from this person that will further your own success. Be especially observant of techniques. Your lucky number is 8.

Sunday, December 17 (Moon in Leo to Virgo 12:19 p.m.) The spotlight is on charity, altruism, and helping those who can't help themselves. You'll accomplish more as a member of a group bent on helping others. Your own creative powers can be put to use to further this cause. An Aries is in the lead.

Monday, December 18 (Moon in Virgo) You'd really like to shout a new idea from the housetops, but you'd be wise to develop it in private instead. Secrecy is vital in anything involving love or money. The attention will be turned in your direction soon enough. Ask Leo. For luck, play number 1.

Tuesday, December 19 (Moon in Virgo to Libra 10:45 p.m.) It's time for a planning session with your family. A surprise gift or occasion will bring great pleasure to a loved one—if you keep from spilling the beans. This person is very intuitive, and may guess very easily what's going on. A parent is involved.

Wednesday, December 20 (Moon in Libra) You go into a lunar high cycle, feeling very strongly about your personal views and enthusiasms. Keep the tone light; don't try to force your opinions upon others, even though you have the ability to do so. Exercise good judgment. The lucky number is 3.

Thursday, December 21 (Moon in Libra) Keep busy; you'll be able to accomplish a great deal of practical work even though others around you are wasting time. Self-discipline in changing some personal habit will be effective today. You'll be in the right place at the right time; keep going!

Friday, December 22 (Moon in Libra to Scorpio 11:18 a.m.) A sales pitch you make in the a.m. hours could result in greater financial gain later in the day. Your communication skills are especially favored. You could even talk your way into an intriguing romantic situation tonight. Your lucky number is 5.

Saturday, December 23 (Moon in Scorpio) A rearrangement of furniture or living space may be needed. Be willing to spend money to make your home seem more festive, warm and inviting. That person whose stubborn tactics frustrate you will be more docile if the environment is festive today.

Sunday, December 24 (Moon in Scorpio to Sagittarius 11:37 p.m.) Spiritual values will provide the most lasting contentment today. You'll be inspired by beauty, music, candlelight, and enduring truths. Mere material possessions seem less important than usual. A Pisces type shares your feeling. Take a chance on number 7.

Monday, December 25 (Moon in Sagittarius) Your leadership talents are accented. Relatives and neighbors will turn to you for advice and organization of the day's events. Today, a very special promise or commitment may be made to a loved one. You'll be in a serious mood with a Capricorn.

Tuesday, December 26 (Moon in Sagittarius) As the end of the year approaches, you see the need to put aside negative thinking. If a relative has limited you in some way, prepare for greater self-confidence in the year ahead. Wipe the slate clean and decide what's next. Number 9 is best.

Wednesday, December 27 (Moon in Sagittarius to Capricorn 10:10 a.m.) A new start in your relationships can be made today. You'll see where family traditions have benefitted you and where your conservative attitude has held you back. You'll prepare to get in on the ground floor of a new enterprise with a Leo.

Thursday, December 28 (Moon in Capricorn) A sense of insecurity might cause you to cling closer to a relative or familiar face today. It's only temporary, a symptom of the passing year. Enjoy old stories and customs; talk about the past. Cooking and comfort absorb you. Number 2 is a lucky choice.

Friday, December 29 (Moon in Capricorn to Aquarius 6:38 p.m.) An urge to socialize reasserts itself. Your interest turns to higher education, philosophy, or travel. You'll bring the world into your own home via TV, books, letters, or visitors. Focus on improving your mind. Sagittarius and Gemini inspire you.

Saturday, December 30 (Moon in Aquarius) There's much to do planning a celebration. You'll be given the detail work, the routine tasks. Accept them gratefully. This is where the greatest pleasure can be gained today. Romance takes on a practical tone, but the excitement will return. Number 4 is your best bet.

Sunday, December 31 (Moon in Aquarius) The aspects are excellent for a gala celebration. You'll be in a party mood—looking for love, stimulating conversation, and a variety of personalities about you. The year ends on a note of happiness and excitement. Be prepared for thrilling changes.

JANUARY 1990

Monday, January 1 (Moon in Aries to Pisces 1:10 a.m.) The first day of year for you is marked by urgent calls and messages. The holiday spirit continues to prevail, and the aspects favor your personal magnetism, creativity, sensuality, sex appeal. You'll get to the heart of matters. Be optimistic despite a slight twinge of conscience about last night's celebration.

Tuesday, January 2 (Moon in Pisces) You'll be reunited with one who seemed argumentative two nights ago. Focus on basic issues and communication. You can reach a mutual understanding with an older woman, possibly a family member. Your sense of purpose and direction is restored as resolutions are defined. Cancer and Capricorn play significant roles. The lucky number is 2.

Wednesday, January 3 (Moon in Pisces to Aries 5:57 a.m.) Diversify; get in touch with those who share your ideas, particularly Gemini, Cancer, and Sagittarius. A political or charitable activity causes you to become more aware of your wardrobe, appearance, diet, body image. You'll be invited to a social affair which could involve travel.

Thursday, January 4 (Moon in Aries) Hot number combinations: 9 and 1 and 8 and 5. The emphasis is on special agreements, contracts, financial obligations. An unorthodox relationship commands your attention and cries out for solution. Protect your possessions and reputation, and refuse to give up something of value for nothing. Taurus, Leo, and Aquarius are in the picture.

Friday, January 5 (Moon in Aries to Taurus 9:04 a.m.) Be ready for change, travel, variety, communication with one who would be a close associate or partner. Make inquiries, and test the waters. A mercurial Gemini makes promises—and passes. Get your ideas on paper, express yourself, but be sure to check your source material. A flirtation could become meaningful.

Saturday, January 6 (Moon in Taurus) You'll learn more about property, money, expenditures by one close to you, probably a relative. Money belonging to another figures prominently. A domestic adjustment is on the agenda—you could be serious about a change of residence or marital status. You'll receive a gift as part of a romantic gesture.

Sunday, January 7 (Moon in Taurus to Gemini 11:02 a.m.) The lunar position accents mystery, intrigue, secrets, the financial status of a close associate, partner, or mate. Today's emphasis falls on meditation, privacy, and communication with one confined to home or hospital. A secret meeting will be proposed—wait for more information from Pisces or Virgo. Today's number is 7.

Monday, January 8 (Moon in Gemini) A good lunar aspect coincides with philosophy, theology, communication, publishing, and travel. What had been a secret is now out in the open. A commitment is made, a relationship intensifies, while the responsibility of deadline looms large. You'll be dealing with older persons who are willing to reward for contributions.

Tuesday, January 9 (Moon in Gemini to Cancer 12:52 p.m.) You'll finish a project; a search is completed. You'll reach more people if you focus on communication, publishing, advertising. You meet with one who shares your ideals and is physically attractive, possibly an Aries, Leo, or another Libra. Count on number 9.

Wednesday, January 10 (Moon in Cancer) Stress independence, creativity, career, and business. The moon position highlights promotion, production, and ways of successfully dealing with higher-ups. A romantic involvement with a restless Leo requires serious attention. There's a chance for a constructive start in a new direction. Take the initiative in getting to the heart of matters. Watch number 1.

Thursday, January 11 (Moon in Cancer to Leo 4:03 p.m.) Hot number combination: 2 and 1 and 4. The full moon position coincides with an unusual relationship with one in authority. It's a good day for romance, creativity, a display of courage. What appears written in stone can actually be erased. You could successfully seek renegotiation of agreement.

Friday, January 12 (Moon in Leo) Diversify, display showmanship, exude confidence. You have a sudden surge of popularity. Those who previously resisted proposals will now be receptive. Focus on friends, aspirations, powers of persuasion. Your performance will be rated outstanding. The emphasis falls on gain through business or career, romance, style, design.

Saturday, January 13 (Moon in Leo to Virgo 9:58 p.m.) Lucky numbers: 1, 10, 4, 5, 13, 22. Your sense of direction is restored, confidence replaces ennui. You are on more solid ground, emotionally and financially. You're due, on this day, to win friends and influence people. A romantic involvement lends spice. Scorpio plays a significant role.

Sunday, January 14 (Moon in Virgo) Young persons provide pleasure, inspiration—your morale zooms upward as a result. A short trip could involve a creative endeavor. Gain is indicated through reading, writing, and exchange of ideas. Some very restless people will seek your counsel and approval. Gemini, Virgo, and Sagittarius people figure prominently.

Monday, January 15 (Moon in Virgo) An agreement made Sunday could be put into effect, involving changes in connection with your home, furniture, sales, or purchases. A promise made to a young person should be fulfilled. Someone who really cares will be extra cooperative. Trust a Taurus or another Libra. Stick with number 6.

Tuesday, January 16 (Moon in Virgo to Libra 7:18 a.m.) Hot number combinations: 7 and 5 and 3 and 4. Today's scenario involves clandestine operations, secret deals. You'll meet someone who talks about spies or betrayals. Be wary of a heavy drinker. You'll hear from one who had been out of sight. You could actually be dealing with a fugitive.

Wednesday, January 17 (Moon in Libra) Lucky numbers: 7, 17, 18, 6, 36, 49. Circumstances favor your actions, reactions, contacts, and plans. This is your power-play day! The number cycle and moon in your sign coincides with individuality, high finance, and a strong love relationship. Cancer and Capricorn are on your side.

Thursday, January 18 (Moon in Libra to Scorpio 7:16 p.m.) What had been considered a lost cause will be revived. Almost without explanation inquiries are received—you might even be asked to appear before the media. You'll have a rare opportunity to publicize and advertize your talents or products. Aries and another Libra play outstanding roles. The lucky number is 9.

Friday, January 19 (Moon in Scorpio) A verbal agreement will now be formalized. You'll get promises in writing. Protect your interests by being creatively selfish. Stress originality, independence, a pioneering spirit. You'll make money by making fresh start in a different direction. Leo has some good ideas.

Saturday, January 20 (Moon in Scorpio) Lucky numbers: 20, 8, 22, 7, 43, 18. A reunion with a relative is top priority today. It involves both money and emotions. A major domestic adjustment takes place—you'll feel more secure as a result. The emphasis falls on payments, collections, personal possessions. A Cancer is very much in the picture.

Sunday, January 21 (Moon in Scorpio to Sagittarius 7:44 a.m.) Show your versatility and sense of humor today. A short trip could involve children and a zoo, motion picture, or theatrical performance. The holiday spirit prevails; you become more aware of your appearance, clothing, weight, body image. A financial commitment will be itemized. Sagittarian plays a role. Try number 3.

Monday, January 22 (Moon in Sagittarius) A break from tradition proves beneficial. The lunar, numerical cycles highlight trips, visits, relatives, willingness to tear down in order to rebuild on a more suitable base. A relative talks about the possibility of relocating. Be aware of zoning ordinances. Taurus and Scorpio people play significant roles.

Tuesday, January 23 (Moon in Sagittarius to Capricorn 6:28 p.m.) It's a good day for writing, reading, publishing, communication with one at a distance. Ideas can be transformed into viable concepts. Make inquiries; give full rein to your curiosity. One who relies on your judgment will express appreciation, perhaps repay a loan. Gemini, Virgo, and Sagittarius are part of today's action.

Wednesday, January 24 (Moon in Capricorn) Lucky numbers: 10, 16, 8, 2, 14, 18. Focus on property, an older family member, basic procedures, rules and regulations. Check the fine print, legal rights, and permissions. Remove a safety hazard; check your automobile tires. A relative is serious about resolutions or purchasing a luxury item or art object.

Thursday, January 25 (Moon in Capricorn) Define terms, be openminded without being gullible. You'll meet some very practical people who may appear cold but who actually have your best interests at heart. You'll receive information about real estate or the living quarters of an older relative. Taurus, Leo, and Capricorn figure prominently.

Friday, January 26 (Moon in Capricorn to Aquarius 2:25 a.m.) The new moon position accents the conclusion of a transaction, end of a search, ability to locate an article that had been lost, missing, or stolen. An older person cooperates, lends the benefit of fund-raising experience. Enlightenment is gained through association with a Capricorn. Stick to the practical course.

Saturday, January 27 (Moon in Aquarius) Finish what you start; refuse to be influenced by a disruptive person. It's a good time for creativity, change, travel, variety. You'll make an exciting discovery. Your sex appeal will be very much in evidence. You'll benefit as result of written material. Aries or another Libra take notice. The lucky number is 9.

Sunday, January 28 (Moon in Aquarius to Pisces 7:51 a.m.) Stress independence and originality. Be willing to investigate subjects previously pushed aside. Pleasure is in store with pets and children. A Leo displays showmanship, helps you get the green light for a creative project. You'll get the proverbial second chance. A friendship could be transformed into a romance. Play number 1 today.

Monday, January 29 (Moon in Pisces) Your intuition rings true. A relative may appear eccentric but could actually be testing you. Keep an open mind, share knowledge, learn through the process of teaching. You'll actually be one step ahead of the competition. A reward is due; you could win a contest. Cancer, Capricorn, and Aquarius play key roles. Play number 4 today.

Tuesday, January 30 (Moon in Pisces to Aries 11:34 a.m.) Pay attention to your job, basic issues, pets, dependents, and health. Check your weight, review resolutions about diet and nutrition. You'll be invited to a social affair; your morale zooms upwards as result of a unique communication. Gemini and Sagittarius are good company. The lucky number is 3.

Wednesday, January 31 (Moon in Aries) Lucky numbers: 22, 31, 1, 9, 16, 25. You could be heaving a sigh of relief, "I survived January and if I could do that I know the rest of the year will be okay!" Today's agenda includes legal affairs, special documents, a partnership proposal, and your marital status. A clash of ideas will prove beneficial. Scorpio is stimulating.

FEBRUARY 1990

Thursday, February 1 (Moon in Aries to Taurus 2:27 p.m.) A tangle of red tape is overcome through help from a close associate, partner, or mate. You'll have the chance to get a more suitable display for your product. Special success is indicated in dealings with women and the public in general. Check legal documents; the spotlight will be on rights and permissions.

Friday, February 2 (Moon in Taurus) A clash of ideas is featured. Your intellectual curiosity sparkles. Your marital status is reviewed along with financial prospects. The key is diversification. Look beyond the immediate, check messages and calls, verify views via source material. Gemini and Sagittarius figure prominently. Your number is 3.

Saturday, February 3 (Moon in Taurus to Gemini 5:13 p.m.) What appears to be a roadblock could be transformed into a stepping-stone. Be thorough, dig deep, check references. A relationship that begins as bizarre will soon get back on track. Those who mean much to you will confide problems, mostly dealing with money. Taurus and Scorpio play roles.

Sunday, February 4 (Moon in Gemini) Spiritual values surface—you also hear from people at a distance. The accent falls on communications, revelation, correspondence, and unique requests. Someone of the opposite sex wants something more than mere flirtation. You'll be dealing with active, alert, vibrant Geminis, Virgos, and Sagittarians.

Monday, February 5 (Moon in Gemini to Cancer 8:27 p.m.) A relative talks about long-range plans. The emphasis falls on ideas and ideals, romance, extrasensory perception. Travel arrangements should now be seriously considered. A domestic adjustment comes after the sale or purchase of special equipment or luxury items. Another Libra plays a paramount role. Play it safe with number 6.

Tuesday, February 6 (Moon in Cancer) Hot number combinations: 1 and 7 and 2 and 5. Define terms; separate fact from fancy. You'll be tempted to see others in a romantic light. But for your own benefit, be realistic. The lunar position emphasizes responsibility and participation in a community, charitable or political project. Accept the leadership role.

Wednesday, February 7 (Moon in Cancer) Lucky numbers: 17, 18, 20, 33, 14, 2. A relationship intensifies; you might find yourself carrying burden not rightfully your own. Clarify your position and intentions. A promotion is due; you'll get credit which you should have had at least two months ago. Cancer and Capricorn people comprise today's cast of characters.

Thursday, February 8 (Moon in Cancer to Leo 12:52 a.m.) Circumstances swing suddenly in your favor —the lunar, numerical cycles highlight friendship, romance, speculation, an outstanding performance. You get almost anything requested by using your powers of persuasion. More people are drawn to you; your personal horizons broaden, and you could receive an invitation to travel. The lucky number is 9.

Friday, February 9 (Moon in Leo) The full moon position accents romance, publicity, chance to recover loss. Someone of the opposite sex confides feelings and seeks response. Think with your head as well as your heart. Highlight versatility, humor, speculation, and communication. Gemini and Sagittarius figure prominently. Count on number 3.

Saturday, February 10 (Moon in Leo to Virgo 7:13 a.m.) An opportunity recently missed is again presented, which means you have the proverbial second chance. The emphasis remains on your ability to win friends and influence people. Some who are envious, possibly resentful, will now be in your corner. Know it, proceed with vigor and confidence. A Cancer is involved.

Sunday, February 11 (Moon in Virgo) Give attention to one who is temporarily confined to home or hospital. Be discriminating, select quality. Show your humor; realize that a long-distance call could verify your views and possibly lead to a profitable assignment or enterprise. Focus on publishing, advertising, politics.

Monday, February 12 (Moon in Virgo to Libra 4:10 p.m.) A break from tradition is necessary—some persons have been weighing heavily on you with their sad stories. Be sympathetic but don't become inextricably involved. A devious person could target you as providing something valuable for nothing in return. For true information look behind the scenes. Stick with number 4.

Tuesday, February 13 (Moon in Libra) Today's scenario highlights initiative, curiosity, and ability to articulate ideas and feelings both verbally and through the written word. Optimism replaces a tendency towards boredom. Someone of the opposite sex, previously indifferent, will now look at you with new eyes. Gemini and Virgo are attractive now.

Wednesday, February 14 (Moon in Libra) You'll receive a gift representing a token of affection and more Valentine's Day cards than in previous years. The moon in your sign points to balance, design, romance, correct judgment, and timing. A family member seeks to prove love. Taurus and another Libra play significant roles. Pick number 6 today.

Thursday, February 15 (Moon in Libra to Scorpio 3:35 a.m.) Hot number combinations: 2 and 7 and 3 and 4. Your judgment and intuition are on target—be confident of your own capabilities. Lead rather than follow; be receptive to a Pisces or Virgo who expresses genuine interest in your welfare.

Friday, February 16 (Moon in Scorpio) Focus on payments, collections, and intensified relationships. Nothing occurs halfway—commitments are made, deadlines are set. It's a time of dedication, passion, secret yearnings. You could learn more about a trust fund, securities, bonds, the possibility of an inheritance. Scorpio plays a role.

Saturday, February 17 (Moon in Scorpio to Sagittarius 4:07 p.m.) What had been left hanging can now be resurrected, including an affair of the heart. An old flame communicates, attempting to rekindle a spark. Be aware, alert; protect yourself in emotional clinches. You'll hear news about payments, debts, royalties. What had been lost can now be recovered. Aries plays the title role. Your lucky number is 9.

Sunday, February 18 (Moon in Sagittarius) Show independence, creativity, and rapport with children. A short trip could involve relatives. Focus on versatility, entertainment, relief from recent tensions. Get to the heart of matters; discuss feelings with Leo and Aquarius. Be active, but avoid heavy lifting.

Monday, February 19 (Moon in Sagittarius) At a reunion gourmet dinner tonight, emotions tend to overrule logic. Forces are scattered; you may find yourself pulled in many directions simultaneously. Ride with the tide, keeping your sense of humor. A Gemini could provide the missing link. A Sagittarian also plays an important role.

Tuesday, February 20 (Moon in Sagittarius to Capricorn 3:30 a.m.) Read between the lines; be aware of the small print and hidden clauses. Check tax and lease requirements. A close relative, possibly a brother or sister, talks about holiday travel aimed at a family reunion. Be aware of practical aspects, including time and expenditures. Be aware of weather conditions, wardrobe, and basic expectations.

Wednesday, February 21 (Moon in Capricorn) You'll learn more about real estate, shelter, and tricks nature can play. Be sure insurance policies are up to date. Take special care while driving; avoid heavy drinkers. One who previously disappointed you may plead for another chance. Keep your distance; play the waiting game. A Scorpio is involved.

Thursday, February 22 (Moon in Capricorn to Aquarius 11:53 a.m.) Be ready for change, travel, variety. Start negotiations involving home or property. Gather information by making inquiries, satisfying your curiosity. Call and write, get varied estimates. If thorough, you'll win by finding a real bargain. A recent friendship formed with an attorney could now pay dividends. Count on number 5.

Friday, February 23 (Moon in Aquarius) A good lunar aspect coincides with speculation, sensuality, variety, personal magnetism, and sex appeal. Your sales ability is heightened; people are drawn to you; creative endeavor could receive favorable publicity. What had been hidden will be revealed—to your advantage. Play number 6 today.

Saturday, February 24 (Moon in Aquarius to Pisces 4:50 p.m.) Lucky numbers: 11, 24, 18, 33, 17, 22. Keep an aura of glamour and mystery. It will be necessary to be discreet. You are likely to be involved in a clandestine meeting or arrangement. You'll have a revelation about a Pisces or Virgo who seeks to wine and dine you.

Sunday, February 25 (Moon in Pisces) The new moon position highlights employment, pets, and people who rely upon your generosity, intuition, judgment. A new job opportunity is featured. You'll also be in contact with those who share your ideals and are willing to work to fulfill them. A strong romantic attachment is possible with Capricorn.

Monday, February 26 (Moon in Pisces to Aries 7:17 p.m.) You'll finish a project; a burden is lifted; a long-distance communication relates to your personal appearance or travel. Take special care in handling sharp objects, including kitchen knives. Control your tendency to act on impulse. Aries and another Libra play dominant roles.

Tuesday, February 27 (Moon in Aries) Hot daily number combinations: 3 and 1 and 4 and 5. Stress independence, style, creativity, and intellectual curiosity. You'll benefit by reading, writing, or special studies now. What had been an obstacle will be removed, funding can be obtained through an unorthodox procedure. Consult a Cancer.

Wednesday, February 28 (Moon in Aries to Taurus 8:43 p.m.) The lunar position accents your marital status, publicity, a clash of ideas or the completion of a legal transaction. A relative is sincere about a reconciliation. Be receptive, realize a financial dispute is due to be settled in your favor. You can afford to be a gracious winner. Taurus and Scorpio people figure prominently. Count on number 2.

MARCH 1990

Thursday, March 1 (Moon in Taurus) A boisterous person actually lacks a solid plan. Be aware of it, exercise caution in connection with your signature. You tend now to attract those who offer quick money schemes. Keep your balance and sense of humor. And refuse to give up something of value for nothing. The message will become clear.

Friday, March 2 (Moon in Taurus to Gemini 10:38 p.m.) Check details in connection with expenditures, savings plans, legal agreements affecting money that actually is under the aegis of another, either a close associate, partner, or mate. Interest in the unusual; perhaps the bizarre is highlighted during this cycle. Taurus and Scorpio figure prominently.

Saturday, March 3 (Moon in Gemini) Lucky numbers: 13, 2, 12, 25, 17, 44. Be ready for change, travel, variety—take notes, submit ideas, formats. Someone of the opposite sex may want nothing more than mere flirtation. Know it; protect yourself in emotional clinches; be discreet; protect sources and possessions. A Gemini is involved.

Sunday, March 4 (Moon in Gemini) It may be necessary to revise, review, rebuild, and to hold a serious discussion with a relative about a move. Emotions tend to rule logic, it will be necessary to be diplomatic. The emphasis falls on philosophy, theology, greater awareness of spiritual values. Another Libra plays a significant role.

Monday, March 5 (Moon in Gemini to Cancer 2:03 a.m.) Define terms, look beyond the immediate, realize that a long-distance communication could presage a journey. Focus on information, publishing, advertising, and distribution of pertinent data. A romance could involve what you might regard as your soul mate. Pisces and Virgo are important to you now. Play number 7 today.

Tuesday, March 6 (Moon in Cancer) Hot number combinations: 2 and 5 and 3 and 6. The emphasis falls on production, responsibility, opportunity for greater financial reward. As a relationship intensifies, commitment is made, you'll know where you stand, and there will be a clear outline of potential. The lunar position stresses achievement. A Cancer figures in today's scenario.

Wednesday, March 7 (Moon in Cancer to Leo 7:25 a.m.) The spotlight falls on career and business. Today you have the confidence to deal with very important people. You'll come out of your shell;

more people become aware of your capabilities and express interest in your views and actions. You'll be questioned and interviewed. Aries and another Libra share your day. Number 9 is a winner.

Thursday, March 8 (Moon in Leo) Today you can make dreams come true. Both astrological and numerical cycles highlight your charm, persuasiveness, romantic ideals, and sex appeal. You'll win friends and influence people. Financial gain is indicated through career or business activities. Your performance will be rated outstanding. Take a chance on number 1.

Friday, March 9 (Moon in Leo to Virgo 2:47 p.m.) There is special rapport with Leo today. A short journey is possible along with surprise visit with relatives. You'll have a chance to show your creativity and share your knowledge with a young person. Today's scenario features drama, popularity, publicity, humor through unorthodox plans, and actions. Cancer and Aquarius play dominant roles.

Saturday, March 10 (Moon in Virgo) Lucky numbers: 10, 19, 6, 23, 22, 5. Show humor, and versatility; keep plans flexible. You'll make valuable contacts. An important person is duly impressed and offers moral support. This Gemini or Sagittarius would make an excellent future reference.

Sunday, March 11 (Moon in Virgo) The full moon accents romance, creativity, restlessness, desire to meditate and to get to the source. The emphasis is on hospitals, institutions, private organizations, and contact with someone temporarily incapacitated. Be discerning; a motive will be discovered; you'll benefit if you are on the alert. A Virgo is involved.

Monday, March 12 (Moon in Virgo to Libra 12:09 a.m.) The lunar position highlights mystery, intrigue, glamour, secret fears and doubts. Get your ideas on paper; be discriminating; dispel rumors; protect your reputation. Someone behind the scenes may be telling stories. A recent visit by a relative resulted in an exchange of ideas. But a visitor may embellish, what began as an innocent idea could be transformed into a horror story.

Tuesday, March 13 (Moon in Libra) The moon in your sign accents a financial opportunity, personal magnetism, your ability to be at right place at a crucial moment. Circumstances turn in your favor; your judgment and intuition will be on target. Wear bright colors; be conspicuous by your presence. An important domestic adjustment will be to your advantage.

Wednesday, March 14 (Moon in Libra to Scorpio 11:25 a.m.) Strive for balance, be receptive without being gullible. It's a good day for artistic or romantic activities. Be discreet, play your cards close to the chest; turn on your charm while playing the waiting game. Someone who seeks your vulnerable spot talks about home and family and greater financial security. Watch out for Pisces. Number 7 is best.

Thursday, March 15 (Moon in Scorpio) What you have been seeking is close at hand and discovery is imminent. Focus on money, profit, and investments now. You'll find an article that had been lost, missing, or stolen. A love relationship is stronger than you think. You'll have more responsibility and deadline pressure. A Capricorn is involved.

Friday, March 16 (Moon in Scorpio to Sagittarius 11:57 p.m.) You'll be free to travel, payment for past work will be forthcoming. You'll get extra recognition; love is in the picture; more people will agree to your demands. Focus on movement, creativity, style, design, removal of previous limitations. Aries and another Libra figure prominently. Play number 9 today.

Saturday, March 17 (Moon in Sagittarius) Celebrate but remember resolutions about moderation. New contacts prove valuable; you'll get to heart of matters; romance could flourish if you are willing to make intelligent concessions. Today's events highlight stubborness, fresh starts, contacts with younger persons. But avoid heavy lifting!

Sunday, March 18 (Moon in Sagittarius) Plans for a family reunion could be postponed by a relative in transit. Be flexible and keep your sense of humor. Another dilemma involving property, money, family affairs will be resolved. A special note—the cycle points to gourmet dining this evening. The lucky number is 2.

Monday, March 19 (Moon in Sagittarius to Capricorn 12:02 p.m.) Check your wardrobe, legal papers, respond to a message from a relative in transit. Trips, visits, and literary activities are highlighted. Keep your resolution about diet and nutrition. You'll become more aware of your appearance, clothing, weight, and body image. Cancer and Capricorn also take notice. Choose number 5 today.

Tuesday, March 20 (Moon in Capricorn) It may be necessary to review notes, to check source material, to rebuild on a different base. The lunar position emphasizes security, home ownership, and long-range prospects. A transaction involving property could be completed. An older person might arrange a date with one you'll find intriguing. Taurus is involved.

Wednesday, March 21 (Moon in Capricorn to Aquarius 9:31 p.m.) Lucky numbers: 8, 17, 14, 10, 32, 35. You'll have more room; personal horizons grow larger; a journey becomes more than a mere wish. Get your papers in order; you'll be involved with a very romantic Gemini, Virgo, or Sagittarius.

Thursday, March 22 (Moon in Aquarius) All indicators point to domestic area, including a possible change of residence or marital status. Attention centers around gifts, harmony, music, purchase or sale of an art object or luxury item. You'll be concerned about money due, past favors, and romantic inclinations on the part of one who currently leaves you cool.

Friday, March 23 (Moon in Aquarius) A decision reached yesterday can now be put into action. Focus on change, travel, variety, creativity, and a spirit of adventure. It's a good day for speculation, movement, sensuality, sex appeal. But much that occurs will be of a clandestine nature. The need for discretion will become obvious. Play it safe with number 7.

Saturday, March 24 (Moon in Aquarius to Pisces 3:09 a.m.) The key word is "intensity." Nothing will happen halfway now. It is all or nothing. Emotional involvement combines with increased activity in the career and business arena. You'll meet a deadline, financial reward will be ample, and you could be madly in love. A Cancer is part of today's excitement.

Sunday, March 25 (Moon in Pisces) You'll finish what you start today. There will be direct dealings with those who rely on your intuition, judgment, good will. Someone who has had a run of poor luck will seek counsel and is sincere. Share your knowledge; recognize spiritual values and do lend a helping hand.

Monday, March 26 (Moon in Pisces to Aries 5:16 a.m.) Get ready for a fresh start, permit optimism to replace brooding, yearning, ennui. A new task will actually result in inspiration and bring you in contact with those who share your basic ideals. Cancer, Leo, and Capricorn will play outstanding roles. A health report will be encouraging.

Tuesday, March 27 (Moon in Aries) Fight a tendency to brood due to revelations by a family member. Money is involved along with home, property, security. Legal documents require attention; also be aware of public relations, image, rights, and permissions. Attention will also center around cooperative efforts, a possible partnership, and your marital status.

Wednesday, March 28 (Moon in Aries to Taurus 5:27 a.m.) Realize a clash of ideas could prove stimulating and constructive. You might actually join forces with one whose political views may be opposite your own. Keep an open mind; search for the truth; realize rules are not written in stone. There will be changes, you'll have a chance to renegotiate your contract.

Thursday, March 29 (Moon in Taurus) Focus on determination, discrimination the ability to select quality instead of quantity. Stick to your principles; it is not necessary to radically modify plans. Money owed you will be paid following a minor disagreement. The law is on your side, and the opposition realizes it. A Scorpio is involved. Stick with number 4.

Friday, March 30 (Moon in Taurus to Gemini 5:42 a.m.) Be ready for variety, inquiries, speculation, and flirtation. Dig deep for information; check references; take nothing for granted in connection with a financial agreement. A Virgo wants to control your spending habits. Be diplomatic, but refuse to give up the reins of your own destiny.

Saturday, March 31 (Moon in Gemini) An agreement made earlier this month will now pay dividends. Attention centers around publishing, communication, education, a journey. A domestic adjustment is made after a relative takes you into confidence. Money, life-style, residence, and romance are involved. Taurus, Leo, and Scorpio are important to you now. The lucky number is 6.

APRIL 1990

Sunday, April 1 (Moon in Gemini to Cancer 7:50 a.m.) Realize this is April 1—a message, telephone call, long-distance communication requires analysis, not instant acceptance. What had been apparently settled is actually subject to change. Keep your options open, realize a member of opposite sex is restless and may be irritable. Don't press issues!

Monday, April 2 (Moon in Cancer) Exchange ideas; realize the emphasis is on your ability to deal with those in authority. Self-expression is important. Read and write, stress communication. Some persons, previously indifferent, will now show interest in your format, concept. Gemini, Virgo, and Sagittarius take notice.

Tuesday, April 3 (Moon in Cancer to Leo 12:50 p.m.) Hot number combinations: 2 and 4 and 1 and 3. Pay attention to home security and a family relationship. Money that had been withheld will be released. You'll also get credit long overdue. A professional superior says, "Stop hiding your light under bushel!" Regard this as a sound compliment. Taurus plays a paramount role.

Wednesday, April 4 (Moon in Leo) Lucky numbers: 10, 4, 14, 33, 22, 44. Almost as if a sudden windstorm, circumstances swing in your favor. What had been resistance will be transformed into a welcome mat. It's a good time to socialize, speculate, use your personal magnetism and powers of persuasion. Pisces and Virgo will be impressed.

Thursday, April 5 (Moon in Leo to Virgo 8:42 p.m.) Make this your power play day! Both astrological and numerical cycles highlight intensity, reward, meeting deadlines. Now you can hit the financial jackpot. You hold the trump card; you are in the driver's seat, you can actually "pick and choose." An older person helps obtain greater audience and funding. Cancer and Capricorn figure prominently.

Friday, April 6 (Moon in Virgo) What appears to be a setback is merely a temporary delay. You've made quite an impact these past few days—people will not soon forget. Reach beyond your previous limitations; realize that a "lost love" is due to be revised. The lunar emphasis falls on hospitals, institutions, groups, secrets, glamour, and mystery. Play number 9 to win.

Saturday, April 7 (Moon in Virgo) You've asked for greater knowledge, inspiration, and now your request is granted, shedding light on areas previously censored. A romantic secret meeting stimulates your creative juices. You'll make a fresh start in a new direction. Be discreet, avoid heavy lifting. Leo, Aries, and Aquarius are important to you now.

Sunday, April 8 (Moon in Virgo to Libra 6:45 a.m.) You'll know what to do at a crucial moment. The moon in your sign helps you take the initiative, win friends, and act as arbiter in settling family disputes. Focus on diplomacy and use new techniques to deal with a young person whose ego is easily bruised. The subject of an allowance is on the agenda.

Monday, April 9 (Moon in Libra) You'll have a reason to celebrate after you get news about a brighter financial picture. Focus on communication, publishing, royalties. The cycle continues high; your judgment and intuition are on target. Now is the time to expand horizons and check legal papers, including your passport. An insurance policy payment is likely due. The lucky number is 3.

Tuesday, April 10 (Moon in Libra to Scorpio 6:18 p.m.) A problem is solved through an unorthodox procedure. The full moon in your sign highlights romance, creativity, and a special ability to deal with public. What had been held in reserve will now be released. Your personal magnetism soars, physical attraction, and sex appeal draw an Aquarian to your side. Count on number 4.

Wednesday, April 11 (Moon in Scorpio) The current cycle highlights investments and personal possessions. You can find an article that had been lost, missing, or stolen. The spotlight falls on money, payments, and collections—any chance to increase your income. Check sales figures; be positive about accounting procedures. Be aware of tax and license requirements. Your best number is 5.

Thursday, April 12 (Moon in Scorpio) You get what you want through powers of persuasion. Don't force issues. Diplomacy now is your lethal weapon.

The lunar position continues to accent rights and permissions, property value, definition of who owns what. A major domestic adjustment occurs, which could involve the purchase of a luxury item. Taurus is in the picture.

Friday, April 13 (Moon in Scorpio to Sagittarius 6:48 a.m.) This is not a bad luck day! You hear some good news about a relative; you'll get a payment or reward for an idea recently submitted to a publication or employer. The focus falls on trips, visits, concepts, the possibility of a short journey. Define youir terms; stress reality as contrasted to wishful thinking. A Pisces is involved. Number 7 is a winner.

Saturday, April 14 (Moon in Sagittarius) What had been considered a loss could actually prove to be a stepping-stone toward your ultimate goal. An older person, possibly a parent, expresses faith and willingness to cooperate. You'll have deadlines, more responsibility, and an intensified relationship. You'll become more familiar with rules and regulations.

Sunday, April 15 (Moon in Sagittarius to Capricorn 7:15 p.m.) Finish what you start, avoid a temptation to skip essentials. Some source material could be outdated; know it, and bring methods up to state of the art. A message, previously a puzzle, will become crystal-clear if you look beyond the immediate; know that your search is going to prove fruitful. Aries is involved. Stick with number 9.

Monday, April 16 (Moon in Capricorn) Stress independence and creativity. Be willing to negotiate regarding property ownership. You'll be surprised because those who had been stubborn will now be willing to make intelligent concessions. Take special care while in an automobile—avoid driving with a heavy drinker. Take a chance on number 3.

Tuesday, April 17 (Moon in Capricorn) Many contacts, dealings, transactions will relate to women today. You'll be concerned with quality, security, long-range prospects. The emphasis also falls on public auctions, antiques, furniture, food. A decision will be reached which will affect your ultimate direction. Cancer is in the picture.

Wednesday, April 18 (Moon in Capricorn to Aquarius 5:53 a.m.) Today's scenario highlights greater freedom of thought and action. Information obtained less than a week ago can now be put to constructive, perhaps profitable, use. Review notes; check your source material. Emphasize self-expression. Gemini and Sagittarius are helpful. The lucky number is 3.

Thursday, April 19 (Moon in Aquarius) A good lunar aspect coincides with creative endeavors, significant changes, and communication from a relative who was a recent visitor. A break from the past will prove constructive. Be aware of tax, license, and lease requirements. A Scorpio will have much to do with the budget. Number 6 is best.

Friday, April 20 (Moon in Aquarius to Pisces 12:57 p.m.) Benefits accrue due to recently signed agreements. You'll gain the advantage in connection with interest rates. A relationship grows more serious. Make inquiries; satisfy your intellectual curiosity. A pet or dependent commands more than usual attention. Virgo and Sagittarius are important to you today. Your best bet is number 5.

Saturday, April 21 (Moon in Pisces) Lucky numbers: 12, 7, 17, 27, 33, 18. A relative talks about employment, work methods, diet, and general health. You have an unusual chance to attract those who share your political beliefs. Emphasize diplomacy; be aware of costs; use your powers of persuasion. Another Libra is involved.

Sunday, April 22 (Moon in Pisces to Aries 3:59 p.m.) The scenario relates to mystery, intrigue, and clandestine arrangements. Be discreet; play your cards close to your chest; don't reveal all. Backstage maneuvers are featured; you'll have access to privileged information. Perfect your techniques, be open-minded but avoid being gullible. Pisces plays a significant role.

Monday, April 23 (Moon in Aries) A waiting period is over—an agreement can be signed, a commitment is made. A love relationship intensifies, with today's emphasis on partnership, cooperation, balance, and marital status. You are in a position to execute a power play. Don't settle for second best, get quality and your money's worth. Ask a Cancer.

Tuesday, April 24 (Moon in Aries to Taurus 4:03 p.m.) Take the initiative, stress originality, agree to an innovative procedure. It's a day for public relations, when your image and reputation count. A dynamic person is drawn to you, could become a valuable ally. Look beyond the immediate; realize many people are fascinated by your views and want to know more about your future intentions.

Wednesday, April 25 (Moon in Taurus) The new moon accents tax requirements, regulations, and money relating to your partner or mate. Dig deep for information; you could make a discovery which presently saves money and could elevate profits in future. Reading material is more important than usual. Taurus, Leo and Scorpio figure prominently.

Thursday, April 26 (Moon in Taurus to Gemini 3:12 p.m.) A robust person talks about the occult, the mantic arts, and sciences. Give full play to your curiosity but maintain your standards. Demand proof, not mere anecdotal material. You'll receive guidance from one who helped in the past. Today's spotlight falls on your direction, purpose, and ultimate goals. Aquarian plays a role.

Friday, April 27 (Moon in Gemini) Today's emphasis falls on movement, ideas, enthusiasm, experiment, contact with a relative recently estranged. Take notes; submit concepts and formats. A short trip could be part of today's exciting scenario. As the puzzle pieces fall into place, you gain an overall view which has been missing. Gemini is in picture. The lucky number is 3.

Saturday, April 28 (Moon in Gemini to Cancer 3:40 p.m.) The current cycle coincides with education, publishing, communication, travel. Inquiries will be answered. The focus also falls on spiritual values, speculation, romance. You'll find many travel folders in the mail today, and you may find your soul mate tonight.

Sunday, April 29 (Moon in Cancer) Future prospects relate to your business and career. Someone of the opposite sex expresses feelings in a frank manner. You'll learn where you stand in connection with relatives and personal relationships. The spotlight falls on communication, reading, and writing, a unique tour. Gemini, Virgo, and Sagittarius keep you company.

Monday, April 30 (Moon in Cancer to Leo 7:09 p.m.) A domestic adjustment featured, which could include beautifying your home surroundings. A loved one makes a major concession; harmony is restored as a result. Your popularity increases, especially where dealings with women are concerned. You'll discover a unique dining place decorated in antiques. The owner is likely to be a Cancer. Choose number 6.

MAY 1990

Tuesday, May 1 (Moon in Leo) Almost as if there is a sudden brisk wind, events transpire to work in your favor. It's a good time for creativity, style, variety, listing restrictions. Wishes are fulfilled, romance replaces gloom. Get your thoughts on paper; spotlight self-expression. You'll be dealing with lively, dynamic people who appreciate your special abilities.

Wednesday, May 2 (Moon in Leo) Ask for what you need; be diplomatic but firm. A relative discusses a possible purchase, sale or visit in connection with your family. You'll have luck in matters of speculation; you'll also gain allies and win major points. Taurus, Scorpio and another Libra are on your side.

Thursday, May 3 (Moon in Leo to Virgo 2:18 a.m.) Hot number combinations: 5 and 2 and 3 and 1. Look behind the scenes, realize that someone has been keeping a secret. Check references, bring your source material up to date. Be sure you are using techniques that represent a state of the art. Pisces and Virgo play dynamic roles.

Friday, May 4 (Moon in Virgo) Be discriminating; choose quality; realize this can be your power-play day. What had been a secret will now be out in the open. Your responsibilities increase and a relationship intensifies. You'll have success dealing with older people, especially Taurus, Cancer, and Capricorn men.

Saturday, May 5 (Moon in Virgo to Libra 12:29 p.m.) Lucky numbers: 12, 3, 23, 5, 27, 15. What had been held back will be released—to your advantage. Someone of the opposite sex has not been sure of feelings, will express doubt, will actually seek your counsel. Strive for a complete assignment, open lines of communication, give serious consideration to a journey.

Sunday, May 6 (Moon in Libra) A love relationship is tested; wisdom and discipline will be required if you are to do the right thing. The spotlight falls on affection; a major domestic adjustment brings more popularity and recognition. Be direct, get to the heart of matters with a Leo. Count on number 1.

Monday, May 7 (Moon in Libra) Someone who borrowed an object will now recant and will seek your forgiveness. Be generous, especially if a relative is involved. Your intuition is a reliable guide. Be discreet, but also be in touch with one who is connected with a hospital or institution. Cancer, Capricorn, and Aquarius are on the scene.

Tuesday, May 8 (Moon in Libra to Scorpio 12:23 a.m.) Hot number combinations: 8 and 2 and 1 and 4. Diversify; give full play to your intellectual curiosity. Read and write; dig deep for information;

analyze your true feelings. Long-range prospects will be clarified. A social invitation could include travel. Gemini and Sagittarius play significant roles.

Wednesday, May 9 (Moon in Scorpio) The full moon coincides with your inner drive, romance, and creativity. You can locate what had been lost, missing or stolen. You'll earn more money; you'll have success dealing with the public and this will apply especially to contacts with women. Taurus, Scorpio, and another Libra play dynamic roles.

Thursday, May 10 (Moon in Scorpio to Sagittarius 12:26 p.m.) Hot number combinations: 5 and 5 and 3 and 7. Be ready for change, travel, variety, a strong love relationship. The tendency is to act on impulse, but try to give logic equal time. Protect yourself in emotional clinches, ferret out information which had been zealously guarded. A Virgo is involved.

Friday, May 11 (Moon in Sagittarius) Forces are scattered but the pieces eventually fall into place. The key is to recognize a completed picture when it is available. This means see places, people as they exist, not merely as you would have them be. A short trip may be necessary in connection with a relative.

Saturday, May 12 (Moon in Sagittarius) Lucky numbers: 9, 18, 25, 34, 22, 33. Be open-minded; satisfy your curiosity; be generous but refuse to be gullible. Someone close to you, perhaps a relative, does want something for nothing. Know it and proceed accordingly. Today's action features idealism and romance. You express your feelings in an entertaining way.

Sunday, May 13 (Moon in Sagittarius to Capricorn 1:21 a.m.) What had been "settled" could now be revised. Be aware, alert; keep your options open. You'll have more responsibility, a chance for promotion and opportunity to increase your income. The spotlight falls on property; now you can successfully conclude a long-standing transaction. A judge could be involved in a property dispute.

Monday, May 14 (Moon in Capricorn) Stress independence and creativity. Be willing to be open-minded where suggestions are concerned. Steer away from committees, but review information—especially proposals by young person. Be aggressive, express yourself, make a fresh start in a new direction. Leo and Aquarius figure prominently. The lucky number is 1.

Tuesday, May 15 (Moon in Capricorn to Aquarius 12:31 p.m.) Take special care in traffic; avoid a tendency to disregard the rules. Your presence will be sought; popularity zooms upward; a new love will be on the horizon. A special warning—avoid heavy lifting! The lunar position emphasizes some restrictions and dealings with authority figure, perhaps a parent. Number 4 is best.

Wednesday, May 16 (Moon in Aquarius) Intuition rings true; the lunar aspect coincides with sensuality, creativity, variety, and sex appeal. Emphasize showmanship; advertize and publicize, fight for a better display for your talents, product. You'll be dealing with vigorous, dynamic people who have young ideas, especially Cancer, Capricorn, and Aquarius.

Thursday, May 17 (Moon in Aquarius to Pisces 8:54 p.m.) Diversify, communicate with someone connected with the travel bureau. Examine various possibilities, and be keenly aware of your own potential. The spotlight falls on your appearance, wardrobe, legal papers, and body image. Dig deep for information; but realize you get most by showing your versatility and sense of humor. Number 3 is best.

Friday, May 18 (Moon in Pisces) A career or business advance is indicated—you'll be on more solid ground; you'll learn more about rules and regulations; you'll also be made aware of tax and license requirements. Focus on strength, conviction, courage. You can tear down for the ultimate purpose of rebuilding on a more suitable structure.

Saturday, May 19 (Moon in Pisces) You'll have an unusual opportunity to communicate your thoughts, ideas, feelings to co-workers and family members. Exchange concepts; realize a clash of ideas can be more exciting than a clash of guns. Certain lessons will be driven home; you'll benefit as a result. A very nervous person will try to disrupt your equilibrium.

Sunday, May 20(Moon in Pisces to Aries 1:32 a.m.) You'll say, "At last a chance to relax and be with harmonious people!" To a great degree, you are right. Today's scenario spotlights family, diplomacy, art, music, and pleasant domestic relationships. The moon position accents cooperative efforts, balance, harmony, and constructive discussion about fashion, literature, style.

Monday, May 21 (Moon in Aries) Locate legal papers; have proof at hand. Today's scenario highlights partnership, publicity, public relations, and marital status. Define terms, see others in a realistic light. Welcome romance, but protect your vulnerable spots. This means don't lead with your chin! A Pisces figures prominently. Play number 7 to win.

Tuesday, May 22 (Moon in Aries to Taurus 2:43 a.m.) Some financial wrangling is part of today's action. It becomes a question of who owns what. Real estate might be involved, a will might be contested, money belonging to an estate could be the subject of controversy. Read between the lines; realize the opposition will attempt to use the element of surprise. Stick with number 8.

Wednesday, May 23 (Moon in Taurus) The lunar position accents the occult, mystery, and motivations. Have the courage of your own convictions. You'll be involved in a financial transaction; you'll be asked to make a decision regarding money that belongs to another person. A royalty could be received; a recent investment could pay dividends. Aries is involved.

Thursday, May 24 (Moon in Taurus to Gemini 2 a.m.) The new moon position accents communication, travel, philosophy, long-range prospects. Focus on romance, love, idealism, spirituality, and ability to perceive cycles and trends. A search for your soul mate could be concluded. Aries, Leo, and Sagittarius people figure in today's events. Play number 1 today.

Friday, May 25 (Moon in Gemini) Learn by teaching; share knowledge; be willing to participate in a political, charitable or publishing project. Publicize and advertise to disseminate pertinent information. You'll be asked to participate in a panel discussion that could involve the media. Talent as a book reviewer could surface. Stick with number 2.

Saturday, May 26 (Moon in Gemini to Cancer 1:34 a.m.) Social activities accelerate, and popularity increases; focus on business and career, standing in the community, and ability to deal successfully with powerful people. Don't hide your light under the bushel; ask questions; wear bright colors; volunteer for the entertainment committee. Have fun with Gemini and Sagittarius. Number 5 is your best bet.

Sunday, May 27 (Moon in Cancer) You're on solid ground despite misgivings expressed by an older person, possibly a family member. Stick to your principles, use lessons recently learned. Emphasize home, property, real estate, long-range prospects. A message or telephone call helps verify your views. Scorpio plays a role. Play number 4.

Monday, May 28 (Moon in Cancer to Leo 3:30 a.m.) Be ready for change, travel, variety, speculation, a possible romantic involvement. Money comes from business or career activity; popularity zooms upwards; your performance rating will be spectacular. Your creative drive comes to the surface, showmanship is evident, and some will be envious but others express admiration sincerely.

Tuesday, May 29 (Moon in Leo) A domestic adjustment is featured when a very stubborn person finally makes an intelligent concession. Though there is a clash of ideas, you will win friends and influence important people if you take the initiative and express your feelings in a dynamic entertaining way. A Leo takes notice. The lucky number is 7.

Wednesday, May 30 (Moon in Leo to Virgo 9:08 a.m.) A long-distance call stimulates your ego, causes your creative juices to move. Shake off any tendency towards lethargy. Set the pace; be a self-starter. You'll gain access to privileged information. It will be necessary to do some spying. If this means eavesdropping, so be it. Pisces and Virgo figure prominently.

Thursday, May 31 (Moon in Virgo) Be analytical; discern motives; look behind the scenes for answers. Today's scenario features a business opportunity, intensified romance, and deadlines. A chance exists to hit the financial jackpot—if you accept a challenge. An older person who lends the benefit of their experience could actually help obtain funding. A Capricorn is involved. Play number 8 to win.

JUNE 1990

Friday, June 1 (Moon in Virgo to Libra 6:31 p.m.) You're given privileged information by a Taurus who is close to your family. This could involve a sale or purchase, basic needs, romance that is blossoming and has been kept from you. The key now is diplomacy and discretion. Be willing to listen without being judgmental.

Saturday, June 2 (Moon in Libra) A decision is reached based on information received 24 hours ago. The moon is in your sign; the cycle moves up; your judgment and intuition will be on target. Define your terms, perfect your techniques, avoid a tendency to brood. Today's scenario highlights intrigue and mystery. A Pisces has the answers. The lucky number is 7.

Sunday, June 3 (Moon in Libra) The emphasis falls on power, authority, initiative, originality. Love plays a prominent role; the creative urges surface.

Accept the challenge of added responsibility. You'll meet a deadline with time to spare. A Cancer native helps you gain added recognition from Capricorn. Number 1 is a winner.

Monday, June 4 (Moon in Libra to Scorpio 6:22 a.m.) You'll finish what had been left hanging—a close associate could be envious, but you must look out for your own interests. Focus on payments, collections, and your credit rating and reputation. You'll reach more people; your personal horizons will be enlarged. Aries, Leo, and another Libra figure prominently. Watch number 4.

Tuesday, June 5 (Moon in Scorpio) Through a new process you make significant personal and career gains. You'll get to the heart of matters by being direct, by expressing feelings in a dynamic, original way. A member of the opposite sex is apt to proclaim, "You're like a new person!" Leo and Aquarius will be part of the action. Your number is 7 today.

Wednesday, June 6 (Moon in Scorpio to Sagittarius 7 p.m.) The emphasis falls on favorable publicity, a possible partnership, rapprochement with a family member. The financial dispute will be settled in your favor. You'll also add to your personal possessions. Cancer, Capricorn, and Aquarius play outstanding roles. The spotlight also falls on public relations, legal documents, marriage.

Thursday, June 7 (Moon in Sagittarius) Hot number combinations: 3 and 9 and 1 and 4. The emphasis falls on trips, visits, ideas, notes, and unusual gifts relating to time—this could be a sun dial, calendar, clock, or watch. Focus on versatility, humor, self-esteem, fitness, and your body image. Gemini and Sagittarius figure prominently. A long-distance call provides key data.

Friday, June 8 (Moon in Sagittarius) The full moon activates your creative juices and a yearning for one who is absent. Focus on idealism, travel, communication, publishing. You can express your feelings in a meaningful way. You'll learn more about a basic issue, which puts you on more solid emotional-financial ground. Scorpio is in the picture.

Saturday, June 9 (Moon in Sagittarius to Capricorn 7:12 a.m.) You'll meet a dynamic duo. What starts out as a blind date could result in a serious relationship. A clash of ideas only provides an extra spark of initiative and perhaps controversy. But you'll be stimulated and happier after breaking your routine. Your lucky number is 5.

Sunday, June 10 (Moon in Capricorn) It's an excellent time for a family gathering, for listening, for being diplomatic, for communicating with one who is confined to your home or hospital. Today's scenario accents flowers, music, visits, breaking bread with one close to you. Someone who owes you money will pay in more than one way. Taurus is featured.

Monday, June 11 (Moon in Capricorn to Aquarius 6:09 p.m.) Be open-minded, but avoid self-deception. This means express curiosity without being gullible. A sales person will want to show you around; an automobile or luxury item could be involved. Pay attention to details, small print, tax and lease requirements. Pisces and Virgo are involved.

Tuesday, June 12 (Moon in Aquarius) The good lunar aspect highlights creativity, variety, and success in dealing with children. Your personal magnetism will draw people to you; the cycle highlights sensuality and sex appeal. The emphasis also falls on strong love relationships, more responsibility, a chance to hit the financial jackpot. Capricorn plays an outstanding role.

Wednesday, June 13 (Moon in Aquarius) Lucky numbers: 2, 17,11, 22, 23, 33. A search is concluded, an assignment can be completed; a burden is lifted and happiness replaces fear, suspicion, doubt. Love plays a major role, you might even feel as if, "At last I have found my soul mate!" Aries and another Libra are on the scene.

Thursday, June 14 (Moon in Aquarius to Pisces 3 a.m.) Take the initiative, imprint your style, avoid heavy lifting, and assert your views in a confident way. The spotlight falls on employment, pets, dependents, a health report. You'll be given a new position and you'll have more to say about your own destiny. Leo and Aquarius are important to you now. The lucky number is 1.

Friday, June 15 (Moon in Pisces) Your intuition rings true; your sense of direction and purpose will be restored. You could receive two job offers. Stick to familiar ground, stay close to home, avoid driving with a heavy drinker. A quarrelsome person attempts to upset your emotional equilibrium. Keep your poise and balance with an Aquarian.

Saturday, June 16 (Moon in Pisces to Aries 8:55 a.m.) Today's aspects focus on entertainment, versatility, humor, your wardrobe, and sense of fitness. Social activities accelerate; a long-distance brings a party invitation that could also include travel. You'll receive a gift representing a token of appreciation from one you helped over a rough spot. Number 3 is best.

Sunday, June 17 (Moon in Aries) A person or situation that practically held you in bondage will no longer have the power to do so. This calls for a celebration, as your views are vindicated, justice prevails, and you could even receive a partnership or marriage proposal. Taurus, Leo, and Scorpio are on your side. Number 4 is a winner.

Monday, June 18 (Moon in Aries to Taurus 11:43 a.m.) Be ready for change, travel, variety, flirtation, a unique communication relating to your legal rights and permissions. Someone of the opposite sex is serious and wants more than a mere flirtation. You actually are in the driver's seat and could insist on changes or the renegotiation of an agreement. Gemini figures prominently. Number 5 is best.

Tuesday, June 19 (Moon in Taurus) Hot number combinations: 1 and 7 and 2 and 6. You'll be involved in a financial transaction involving the money of your partner or mate. A domestic adjustment could settle a dispute. In any case, it's time for a serious discussion about a possible change or residence or marital status. Your personal surroundings will be beautified.

Wednesday, June 20 (Moon in Taurus to Gemini 12:15 p.m.) You'll learn more about the true feelings of a special person. The lunar position highlights mystery, the occult, sensuality, and money possibly held in escrow. Dig deep for information, get rid of extra material, check your luggage, be positive about your weight requirements. Pisces can be helpful.

Thursday, June 21 (Moon in Gemini) What appears to be off key could actually be perfectly tuned. What needs to be done is being done but temporarily is out of reach. Focus on philosophy, theology, spiritual values, publishing, a journey. A relationship is strong but complicated. The age difference will be discussed with a Capricorn. Your lucky number is 8.

Friday, June 22 (Moon in Gemini to Cancer 12:10 p.m.) The new moon position highlights revelation, communication, distribution. You can now overcome distance and language barriers. You'll contact a foreign-born person who can help you with pertinent data. Reach beyond your previous limitations. Love is very much in the picture. An Aries is involved.

Saturday, June 23 (Moon in Cancer) Highlight your career, independence, creativity, and standing in the community. A break from tradition proves constructive. Create your own tradition by expressing yourself in an innovative way. A new love could be part of today's exciting scenario. A Leo brightens the day. Watch number 1.

Sunday, June 24 (Moon in Cancer to Leo 1:25 p.m.) The spotlight falls on family, food, security, life-style, and residence. You'll learn more about what your family wants and needs. Stick close to home if possible. A relative has a request that you can fulfill. Consult a Cancer. The lucky number is 2.

Monday, June 25 (Moon in Leo) Circumstances take a sudden turn in your favor. Elements of timing and luck ride with you. What seemed out of reach is now practically in your own backyard. Turn on your charm; use your powers of persuasion. You're going to win a contest either in a personal or professional area. A Sagittarian is good company.

Tuesday, June 26 (Moon in Leo to Virgo 5:42 p.m.) Read between the lines, be sure to check the rules. The moon highlights friends, hopes, wishes, romance, and speculation. You win favor with the public; your performance is considered outstanding. Money is gained from a career or business activity. A prominent person pays you a special compliment.

Wednesday, June 27 (Moon in Virgo) Be ready for change, travel, variety, a secret meeting. The key is to be analytical, to do some private detective work first. Discover motives, realize someone of the opposite sex is not entirely guileless. Focus also on reading and writing, on sharing knowledge, on learning through the process of teaching others.

Thursday, June 28 (Moon in Virgo) A domestic adjustment figures prominently. A restless person talks about an advertising or publicity scheme. Be diplomatic, but wait for more information. You'll receive a call or message which helps you reach a final decision. References must be checked. A Virgo is helpful now. Your best number is 6.

Friday, June 29 (Moon in Virgo to Libra 1:47 a.m.) What appeared to be a setback will boomerang in your favor. As the cycle moves up, you'll be at the right place at a crucial moment. A secret meeting relates to romance and lends spice. You'll be asked to keep a secret; the necessity for being discreet will be obvious. Pisces and Virgo play key roles. The lucky number is 7.

Saturday, June 30 (Moon in Libra) The moon in your sign coincides with your personality, appearance, powers of persuasion, and excellent timing. A love relationship intensifies; responsibilities increase but so do chances for greater financial reward. You'll be dealing with someone who possesses plenty of charm, is affluent and could help promote your welfare. Play number 8 to win.

JULY 1990

Sunday, July 1 (Moon in Libra to Scorpio 1:01 p.m.) Spiritual values surface, self-esteem soars upward, you know where you stand, and pleasure will be received from words by someone you hold in high regard. A family member talks about bright financial prospects. You'll be more secure, contentment will replace uncertainty. A Pisces is inspiring. The lucky number is 7.

Monday, July 2 (Moon in Scorpio) This can be your money and power play day! The emphasis falls on production, promotion, deadline pressure, a chance for greater financial reward. You'll also be lucky in love. Relationship grows strong, and more emotionally secure. An older person possibly a parent, will now take you seriously and could be of immeasurable help in connection with investments.

Tuesday, July 3 (Moon in Scorpio) Your timing is on target; you'll reach the right people. The focus also continues on achievement, style, design, and intensified love relationship. What had been lost can now be recovered. The emphasis is on valuables, personal possessions, payments, debts, your credit rating. Aries and another Libra play key roles. The lucky number is 9.

Wednesday, July 4 (Moon in Scorpio to Sagittarius 1:36 a.m.) Lucky numbers: 4, 7, 17, 18, 27, 9. The holiday spirit prevails, young people are part of the scenario. A get-together with a very romantic admirer lends spice. Have fun, but observe safety rules. Sparks will fly, not all of them the result of firecrackers. Leo or Aquarius are attracted now.

Thursday, July 5 (Moon in Sagittarius) Check foot-wear, take special care in connection with proper fit, avoid bumping into things with your knees and shins. A meeting with a relative leads to exotic dining. Cancer, Capricorn, and Aquarius join the party. Your intuition rings true; a short trip could be featured. The lucky number is 2.

Friday, July 6 (Moon in Sagittarius to Capricorn 1:40 p.m.) Hot number combinations: 3 and 6 and 1 and 8. Emphasize versatility; and realize plans are subject to change. Look beyond the immediate to see the potential. Keep recent resolutions about your diet, wardrobe, body image, nutrition. The lunar emphasis falls on snap judgment, messages, calls, and ideas which prove productive.

Saturday, July 7 (Moon in Capricorn) Check details, be positive about dates relating to delivery routes, policy payments, interest rates. The moon has moved into the sector of your horoscope relating to home, security, older people. A transaction with Taurus, Leo, or Scorpio is completed now. Number 4 is best for you.

Sunday, July 8 (Moon in Capricorn) The full moon position emphasizes a reunion with a loved one which stirs your creative talents. Be ready for an exciting discovery, change, travel, variety. You have an ability to communicate concepts in an entertaining, dramatic fashion. What appeared to be a setback is suddenly reversed—in your direction and favor.

Monday, July 9 (Moon in Capricorn to Aquarius 12:07 a.m.) An assignment can now be completed when the lunar aspect coincides with an ability to express yourself. Today brings adventure, creativity, children, sensuality, sex appeal. A major domestic adjustment occurs which ultimately proves beneficial. You'll receive a luxurious gift. Taurus, Scorpio, and another Libra are involved.

Tuesday, July 10 (Moon in Aquarius) Your tendency is to act on impulse, to leave yourself vulnerable. Be wary, protect yourself in the emotional clinches. Perfect techniques, define terms, be open-minded but not gullible. By looking behind the scenes, you learn secrets. A clandestine arrangement is part of today's intriguing scenario. Watch Virgo! The lucky number is 7.

Wednesday, July 11 (Moon in Aquarius to Pisces 8:30 a.m.) Intensity is today's key word—which relates to responsibility, challenge, deadlines, money, and love. You'll make changes; you'll shake off lethargy; tradition will be discarded, at least temporarily. Older persons work with you, you relate to a Capricorn father figure, one in a position of authority.

Thursday, July 12 (Moon in Pisces) Finish what you start, realize many look to you as an example or inspiration. Reach beyond your previous limitations, extend your sphere of influence. Note: Take special care in handling sharp objects, including kitchen knives. Aries and another Libra play significant roles. Number 9 brings good luck.

Friday, July 13 (Moon in Pisces to Aries 2:37 p.m.) You might be involved with one who wears a 20-gallon hat. This could actually be your lucky day. You'll be relieved of a burden which was not your own in the first place. Stress creativity, style, and independence. Be willing to make a fresh start. Display showmanship; investigate a possible advertising or publicity campaign.

Saturday, July 14 (Moon in Aries) Lucky numbers: 1, 9, 18, 10, 22, 33. Focus on cooperative efforts, timing, publicity, partnership, and marital status. There will be an agreement with a family member who questioned your expenditures. Today's scenario also highlights entertainment, relatives, gourmet dining, a significant domestic adjustment.

Sunday, July 15 (Moon in Aries to Taurus 6:29 p.m.) Talks, plans, creations will be ubiquitous. Realize it; communicate; put your own stamp or style on what you produce. Today's emphasis falls on communication, publishing, writing, and oral reports. There will be reason to celebrate, after a legal matter is resolved and you are relieved of tensions. Take a chance on number 3.

Monday, July 16 (Moon in Taurus) Someone who attempts to divert your attention from essentials should be ignored. You'll be handed money belonging to others—check interest rates, credit ratings, financial obligations. Know what is being held in escrow and realize there is one possibility of an inheritance. Scorpio plays a role.

Tuesday, July 17 (Moon in Taurus to Gemini 8:32 p.m.) Recent inquiries bring responses about the value of an estate, percentage of gains or losses. You could also learn more about a trust fund. Someone of the opposite sex is involved and so is a social activity that could include travel. Today's scenario also highlights trips, visits, gain through the written word. A Sagittarian is involved.

Wednesday, July 18 (Moon in Gemini) Today's emphasis is on a journey, philosophy, a domestic adjustment, communication, and clarification of long-range prospects. You'll be concerned with education, personal possessions and the financial status of a relative. Purchase or sale of an art object or luxury item could also be featured. Pick number 6 today.

Thursday, July 19 (Moon in Gemini to Cancer 9:44 p.m.) You'll be provided with privileged information. Focus on clandestine arrangements, secrets, institutions, hospitals, and communication with one who is temporarily incapacitated. What begins as a blind date could develop into a meaningful relationship. Pisces, Virgo, and another Libra figure prominently.

Friday, July 20 (Moon in Cancer) Pay attention to your career and prestige now. A production or promotion that had been held in abeyance will now surface. Creative sparks fly; a professional superior recognizes your worth and will do something about it. An older Cancer does care and you'll be aware of it.

Saturday, July 21 (Moon in Cancer to Leo 11:29 p.m.) You'll gain recognition; more people will be aware of your talents, intentions, and potential. A search for love could be successfully concluded. You won't be alone, fulfillment will replace emptiness. You'll gain access to valuable data; an invitation to travel will be extended. Leo figures prominently.

Sunday, July 22 (Moon in Leo) The new moon position accents a dynamic approach to problems, friends, aspirations, romance, and sensuality. You'll get to the heart of matters; you'll make fresh start. A young person confides feelings, seeks your counsel and approval. Remember not to "cast the first stone!" Cancer, Leo, and Virgo play key roles. Your best number is 1.

Monday, July 23 (Moon in Leo) Your intuition rings true; you learn by teaching, seek rapprochement with a family member who recently said, "I am sorry but it is done and there is nothing I can do about it!" You'll have the chance to recoup a loss, you'll deal with the public, good news will be related by a woman. Cancer, Leo and Aquarius are on hand.

Tuesday, July 24 (Moon in Leo to Virgo 3:18 a.m.) What appeared to be a trap will turn out to be a blessing in disguise. You'll have more room, but you'll also be protected. A legal advisor relays news which provides reason for optimism. Your popularity rises, social activities accelerate, you'll receive an addition to your wardrobe. Gemini and Sagittarius brighten your day.

Wednesday, July 25 (Moon in Virgo) Dig deep for information; be discriminating; select quality; be willing to tear down for ultimate purpose of rebuilding on a more suitable structure. An Aquarian associate talks about the possibility of relocating. Money comes from a source relating to your career, business activities. Follow through on your first impressions!

Thursday, July 26 (Moon in Virgo to Libra 10:19 a.m.) Examine motives, get your ideas on paper, dig deep for information. Be positive that your source material provides information representing a state of the art. This means don't settle for second best or play second fiddle. The spotlight falls on seclusion, meditation, contact with hospitals, institutions, charitable organizations.

Friday, July 27 (Moon in Libra) The moon in your sign accents initiative, personality, charm, and beauty. You'll make some concessions, but a domestic adjustment works in your favor and a financial dispute will be amicably settled. Your judgment and intuition will prove correct. Your feelings are on target. Taurus, Libra, and Scorpio figure prominently. Play number 6 to win.

Saturday, July 28 (Moon in Libra to Scorpio 8:40 p.m.) What had been discarded will be recovered. Focus on your appearance, fashion, personal magnetism, originality. You'll learn some important facts in a secret meeting with Leo. Remember that flattery can be your most valuable tool. Be clear about your wants and needs. Avoid any tendency towards self-deception. Be realistic!

Sunday, July 29 (Moon in Scorpio) Strive for substance rather than shadow. Stress realism, know there is a deadline and that money is involved. A relationship intensifies; responsibilities increase. The lunar position accents basic issues involving a financial transaction. Taurus, Cancer, and Capricorn persons play dynamic roles. The lucky number is 8.

Monday, July 30 (Moon in Scorpio) Finish what you start; leave no loose ends; be aware of your financial obligations. Check unpaid bills, demand compensation for service recently performed in connection with your professional duties. Your demands will stand up in court if necessary. A long-distance call verifies your views and plants seeds which could blossom into productive activity that includes education, travel.

Tuesday, July 31 (Moon in Scorpio to Sagittarius 9 a.m.) A fresh start provides encouragement, could result in profit. Show your inner feelings, desires, sensuality. A lost love will return and you'll get the proverbial second chance. The money picture is brighter than you thought possible. Be direct; take the initiative; stress individuality. You can count on number 1.

AUGUST 1990

Wednesday, August 1 (Moon in Sagittarius) News arrives concerning a unique mission or trip. A relative is involved, investment or basic security is also featured. Focus on intensity, deadlines, insurance policies, payments and collections. A relationship intensifies; responsibilities increase. Cancer and Capricorn figure prominently. Play number 8 today.

Thursday, August 2 (Moon in Sagittarius to Capricorn 9:09 p.m.) You are capable of perceiving your potential, of knowing what to do and when to do it. The emphasis also continues on versatility, a sense of fitness, a chance to receive valid information about an investment. Romance plays a key role; you learn more about yourself and a loved one. Your lucky number is 2.

Friday, August 3 (Moon in Capricorn) Stress independence, creativity, and self-expression. You'll make a fresh start; you'll receive information concerning security, home, and family. Be aware of restrictions, tax, and license requirements. Rules and regulations will ultimately prove beneficial. Leo plays a top role. Play number 1 to win.

Saturday, August 4 (Moon in Capricorn) Your intuition is on target. Family relationships are accented. What had been an estrangement could be transformed into a reconciliation. You'll have success in dealing with people, especially women. You'll detect trends and cycles; timing will improve; you could hit the financial jackpot as result. Get together with a Cancer.

Sunday, August 5 (Moon in Capricorn to Aquarius 7:19 a.m.) A request for more space is granted, bringing you greater freedom of thought and action. Your popularity increases as social activities accelerate. A long-distance call brings verification of your views and information that will prove valuable. Check legal papers, including your passport. Gemini is on hand. The lucky number is 3.

Monday, August 6 (Moon in Aquarius) The full moon coincides with emotional responses, impulsiveness, variety, a change of scene, sensuality, and sex appeal. As you break from tradition, a family member could object to your views, plans, intentions. Be kind and diplomatic, but don't desert your heart's desire. Play it safe with number 4.

Tuesday, August 7 (Moon in Aquarius to Pisces 2:55 p.m.) Today's scenario highlights variety, increased activity, a creative endeavor. Someone of the opposite sex plays a meaningful role, could have a direct effect on plans and actions. Focus on reading and writing, communication, travel, and flirtation that could become more serious than originally anticipated. Count on number 7.

Wednesday, August 8 (Moon in Pisces) Lucky numbers: 12, 3, 7, 16, 18, 49. What appeared impractical could now prove essential. Focus on work procedures, basic issues, general health, employment, and people who rely upon your generosity and judgment. Someone you helped in the past returns, is more self-reliant, and could actually repay a favor.

Thursday, August 9 (Moon in Pisces to Aries 8:13 p.m.) Focus on your intuition or extrasensory perception. A psychic discovery can help you avoid a pitfall. A close associate admits a past error and is willing to rectify a mistake. Look beyond the immediate, be open-minded, but avoid self-deception. See places and people as they actually are, not merely as you wish they might exist.

Friday, August 10 (Moon in Aries) What appears foreboding is likely to boomerang in your favor. Focus on losses, legal requirements, and special rights and permissions. The emphasis today falls on restrictions, your public image, and a possible partnership. You'll be told you've made a commitment even if you are unaware of it. Cancer and Capricorn figure prominently.

Saturday, August 11 (Moon in Aries to Taurus 11:55 p.m.) Stress independence and creativity today. Be willing to face the consequences of beliefs or actions. You can now reach more people, make financial gains in connection with communication or show business. More people will become aware of you; the powers that be could proclaim you box office material.

Sunday, August 12 (Moon in Taurus) Light is shed on a mystery now. Focus on your marital status, the earning capacity of one close to you. Pay attention to trust funds, savings accounts, and interest rates. Consult a Leo or Aquarius about the investment plans of your partner or mate. You need that extra expertise. Today's number is 1.

Monday, August 13 (Moon in Taurus) Dig deep for information; knowledge can be gained through a review of arcane literature. You need guidance to restore your sense of direction. The dilemma of where to go, with whom to be allied will be resolved. Dealings with the public increase; you'll successfully use your powers of persuasion.

Tuesday, August 14 (Moon in Taurus to Gemini 2:42 a.m.) Hot number combinations: 3 and 5 and 2 and 4. Diversify, communicate, add to your wardrobe, accept a social invitation that might include travel. You'll be more aware of your appearance, and body image. Keep recent resolutions about diet and nutrition. Another Libra plays a significant role.

Wednesday, August 15 (Moon in Gemini) Restrictions are removed; the key is to communicate, to advertise and publish, to express yourself, and to gain greater recognition of spiritual values. Focus on travel, language, distance, customs of other peoples' and nations. Although there are doubts, possibly fears, you actually are on more solid emotional-financial ground.

Thursday, August 16 (Moon in Gemini to Cancer 5:13 a.m.) Be ready for change, travel, variety, and a boost to your business. As your prestige swings upwards, a community leader could visit and impart valuable data. You'll be asked to cooperate in a unique project that borders on charitable or political activity. Gemini, Virgo, and Sagittarius figure prominently.

Friday, August 17 (Moon in Cancer) A domestic adjustment figures prominently. A conflict about your home and career will be amicably resolved with a third party as arbitor. Be diplomatic without abandoning your principles. You have a chance to increase your income—be receptive, and dress for the occasion. This evening favors entertainment and public relations.

Saturday, August 18 (Moon in Cancer to Leo 8:12 a.m.) An aura of mystery and glamour exists. Focus on romance, creativity, and valid psychic impressions. You'll choose the right numbers and could win a contest. Someone who previously was regarded as a mere acquaintance could now be seriously considered as a love partner. Pisces is in the picture. Pick number 7 now.

Sunday, August 19 (Moon in Leo) Today's aspects promise intensity and deadline pressure. But you can win your way through charm and persuasion. Suddenly, circumstances will turn in your favor, and what had been evasive becomes available. You'll profit through recent contacts, business, or career activities. The lucky number is 8.

Monday, August 20 (Moon in Leo to Virgo 12:33 p.m.) The new moon position emphasizes your ability to influence important people, to make headway in new career or business opportunities. Focus also on speculation, romance, creativity. You'll gain knowledge previously prohibited. A love relationship intensifies; you'll learn where you stand with an Aries.

Tuesday, August 21 (Moon in Virgo) The lunar position accents secrets, restrictions, contacts with those associated with hospitals, unique organizations, institutions. Stress style, creativity, originality, a pioneering spirit. An admirer will confide feelings and your spirits will be buoyed as result. The lucky number is 1.

Wednesday, August 22 (Moon in Virgo to Libra 7:17 p.m.) Your intuition is on target; you'll gain information about confidential activities. Open lines of communication; contact someone confined to home or hospital. But for the good of your own health, avoid heavy lifting. Favorable publicity will attend your efforts. A Cancer can be helpful.

Thursday, August 23 (Moon in Libra) The moon in your sign emphasizes appearance, personality, and self-confidence. Be willing to state your views in a frank, dynamic manner. Show that you do have sense of humor by laughing at your own foibles. You are going to attract allies, admiration and romance. Gemini and Sagittarius are the signs to watch. Count on number 3.

Friday, August 24 (Moon in Libra) Be willing to tear down in order to rebuild on a more secure base. Be familiar with rules and regulations, with special requirements, with rights and permissions. Heed your own counsel, realize that your judgment, intuition, and timing are likely to be on target. Taurus and Scorpio play key roles. Number 6 is your best bet.

Saturday, August 25 (Moon in Libra to Scorpio 4:57 a.m.) Synthesize information, discern motives, put together puzzle pieces. You'll receive a revelation about a money matter. You could be a winner if you are analytical. People are drawn to you; you'll be provided with inside information from a Sagittarian. The lucky number is 5.

Sunday, August 26 (Moon in Scorpio) You'll add to your possessions, possibly obtain a luxury item. Attention centers around the home and family, resolution of debate concerning investment procedures, finances. There will be talk about life-style, residence, possibility of a change of marital status. A special note—guard valuables, especially delicate crystal.

Monday, August 27 (Moon in Scorpio to Sagittarius 4:58 p.m.) The lunar position emphasizes payments, collections, your earning capacity. Define terms, clarify meanings, and perfect techniques. A burden could be lifted which involves expenses incurred by another. You've recently been close to someone who wants or expects something for nothing. Stop being a prime target!

Tuesday, August 28 (Moon in Sagittarius) A path is cleared, obstacles are removed. A relationship grows stronger, and the financial picture is brighter. Today's scenario highlights ideas which can be transformed into viable, valuable concepts. The emphasis is also on trips, visits, relatives, and your ability to consolidate recent gains. Capricorn plays a paramount role.

Wednesday, August 29 (Moon in Sagittarius) You get the proverbial second chance. Strive for greater independence; show the courage of convictions. Be direct, take the initiative, accent originality, innovation, and style. A lost love will communicate and could return. Aries, Leo, and Aquarius people figure prominently. You best bet is number 1.

Thursday, August 30 (Moon in Sagittarius to Capricorn 5:23 a.m.) Follow through on a hunch, trust your first impressions, check with someone who presented an idea or concept approximately three days ago. Favorable advantages accrue faster than you might have thought possible. A search is ended; a burden is lifted. Cancer, Capricorn, and Aquarius people play dynamic roles. The lucky number is 9.

Friday, August 31 (Moon in Capricorn) The spotlight falls on security, home, structure, design, and architecture. You'll be more aware of your surroundings, plans involving a special person. Your sense of direction and purpose can now be restored. Gourmet dining is on tap for tonight. Someone who served as a teacher is again ready and willing to cooperate. Number 2 is best.

SEPTEMBER 1990

Saturday, September 1 (Moon in Capricorn to Aquarius 3:51 p.m.) A revelation takes place in connection with a young family member. Plans change, property values are considered. This evening favors relaxation from tensions. Focus on romance, entertainment, creativity, vulnerability. Leo and Aquarius are good company. Lucky numbers: 1, 10, 28, 18, 17, 26.

Sunday, September 2 (Moon in Aquarius) What you learned yesterday will be used today. The spotlight continues on youth, rebelliousness, style, sensuality, sex appeal. Show your pioneering spirit and step out boldly. A relative talks about speculation, travel, and a romantic involvement. What is being sought is approval, not counsel.

Monday, September 3 (Moon in Aquarius to Pisces 11:06 a.m.) The lunar aspect highlights sensitivity, sensuality, a secret affair of the heart. It's a day for following your intuition about family relationships, security, and property. You're being pulled in two directions—choose the course that keeps you close to a loved one. Cancer and Aquarius play significant roles.

Tuesday, September 4 (Moon in Pisces) Attention centers around your weight, appearance, wardrobe, diet, nutrition, and body image. The lunar emphasis is on employment, basic issues, work procedures. You can attract people who share your ideals. A long-distance call relates to social activity, invitation to travel. A Sagittarian plays a significant role.

Wednesday, September 5 (Moon in Pisces) The full moon position coincides with creativity, romance, and ability to settle a financial dispute with someone close to you, possibly a very young person. Details require the kind of attention needed to push aside red tape. Papers must be signed; it will be necessary to study small print. Taurus and Scorpio are important now.

Thursday, September 6 (Moon in Pisces to Aries 3:23 a.m.) Hot number combinations: 1 and 9 and 3 and 6. The emphasis is on balance, creativity, design, and protection of your reputation and image. You'll contact a Virgo whose ideas may be opposite your own. There will be stimulation and inspiration. Later, attention will center around your partnership or marital status.

Friday, September 7 (Moon in Aries) Money comes from an unusual source—a formerly estranged family member. The cycle highlights domestic adjustment, marriage, contracts, and legal commitments. Check your source material, be sure of your rights and permissions. A break from tradition is indicated, which will ultimately prove beneficial. Scorpio is featured.

Saturday, September 8 (Moon in Aries to Taurus 5:56 a.m.) Define your terms; be wary about cosigning. Protect your credit rating, check an insurance policy, review tax and license requirements. Focus on the financial status of one close to you, including your partner or mate. Psychic impressions prove accurate, you'll discern the motives of others, and you'll learn exactly where you stand.

Sunday, September 9 (Moon in Taurus) Today's emphasis falls on power, authority, interest in the occult, and a solution to a mystery. A relationship intensifies; you're asked to assume added responsibility. Today's scenario involves deadline pressure. You'll be harassed, bothered, possibly bewildered, but you'll also have a rare chance to hit the financial jackpot. Stick with number 8.

Monday, September 10 (Moon in Taurus to Gemini 8:05 a.m.) You'll reach more people after an assignment is finished. Now you can go beyond previous limitations to romance and creativity. You'll also reach the end of a search. You'll meet an idealistic person who stimulates your interest in charity, politics, and homeless persons. Aries and another Libra are influential. The lucky number is 9.

Tuesday, September 11 (Moon in Gemini) Hot number combinations: 5 and 5 and 3 and 2. You'll make a fresh start in a new direction. It's a fine time for communication, romance, creativity, making travel plans. Spiritual values surge to the forefront. You'll be concerned with direction, language, purpose, and motivation. Get in touch with Leo and Aquarius.

Wednesday, September 12 (Moon in Gemini to Cancer 10:53 a.m.) Lucky numbers: 41, 3, 18, 5, 27, 14. A good lunar aspect coincides with idealism, soul-searching: "Why am I here?" Your intuition is on target; your ability to analyze character is highlighted. Focus on the possibility of a sea journey, publishing, communication, fulfillment of long-standing objectives.

Thursday, September 13 (Moon in Cancer) Diversify, look beyond the immediate, realize someone who appeared indifferent is actually going to boost your career and business activities. Focus on potential, versatility, humor, wardrobe, and body image. You'll become more aware of fitness, intellectual curiosity, education, and unique publications.

Friday, September 14 (Moon in Cancer to Leo 2:52 p.m.) What you sent for is due to arrive. This could be a government publication involving self-help, which adds up to vocational guidance. Pay attention to details, red tape, dealings with officials. One who seemed to discourage you will, in the long run, be an ally. Taurus, Leo, and Scorpio figure prominently. Lucky number is 4.

Saturday, September 15 (Moon in Leo) Let go of a losing proposition. The cycle turns around, circumstances move in your favor; a wish will be fulfilled. Focus on your persuasiveness, charm, popularity. You'll benefit from any career or business activity where you can win friends and influence important people. Romance and speculation are also featured.

Sunday, September 16 (Moon in Leo to Virgo 8:19 p.m.) A family gathering restores domestic harmony. Today's emphasis falls on music, balance, design, entertainment, and emotional fulfillment. Luck and timing ride with you—you could win a contest, especially by sticking with number 6. A communication received regarding accounting means you're going to get additional funds.

Monday, September 17 (Moon in Virgo) Clarify meanings, have a frank talk with one close to your heart. Today's scenario highlights illusion, possible self-deception, romance, creativity. Be open-minded, but avoid being gullible. Money and love continue to be featured—good fortune replaces pessimism. Today's emphasis falls on showmanship, charm, enthusiasm, and interest in a speculative venture. Your number is 7.

Tuesday, September 18 (Moon in Virgo) Be discriminating; choose quality over quantity. Focus on responsibility, secrets, a clandestine arrangement. Get in touch with someone confined to home or hospital. You'll be asked to participate in fund-raising for an institution or public radio or television station. Number 1 is best for you.

Wednesday, September 19 (Moon in Virgo to Libra 3:34 a.m.) A fresh start featured, you'll gain added independence as a result. An area previously dark or censored will receive the benefit of greater light. Today's emphasis falls on mystery, intrigue, glamour, and seduction. Strive for initiative; show leadership qualities even though you'll do your best work behind scenes. A Leo takes notice.

Thursday, September 20 (Moon in Libra) A contact made yesterday could now prove valuable. The moon in your sign coincides with correct judgment, timing. Lead rather than follow; set the pace; realize circumstances will turn swiftly and suddenly in your favor. You could win a judgment or arbitration. Wear bright colors; show confidence. Number 4 is best.

Friday, September 21 (Moon in Libra to Scorpio 1:06 p.m.) You'll attract allies, especially a former instructor who is within calling distance. The cycle continues high; your judgment and intuition will be on target. You'll be concerned with home, family, security, partnership, martial status. What had been moribund will again be alive and kicking. Business interest in your product is revived.

Saturday, September 22 (Moon in Scorpio) The emphasis falls on payments, collections, investments, ownership rights. Refuse to be a silent partner. Have your say and be specific—loud and clear. The cycle continues high, especially where finances are concerned. You'll locate an article that had been lost, missing, or stolen. Gemini and Sagittarius play roles.

Sunday, September 23 (Moon in Scorpio) Refuse to be encumbered by property belonging to another, to one who seldom shows appreciation for your efforts. Be aware of details, fine print, special requirements. It will be necessary to revamp, review, revise, possibly to rebuild at another location. This foreknowledge will help smooth the way. The lucky number is 3.

Monday, September 24 (Moon in Scorpio to Sagittarius 12:53 a.m.) Financial gain is indicated if you communicate, if you call and write, if you make pertinent inquiries. Reject the superficial, get promises in writing, get to heart of matters. The key is to be analytical, to discern motives, to perceive potential. Someone of the opposite sex does care and will become your strong ally.

Tuesday, September 25 (Moon in Sagittarius) The spotlight falls on trips, visits, relatives, and ideas which require further development. Be kind to a family member who admits a mistake and is willing to rectify an error. This means diplomacy is necessary, harmony can be restored if you are patient and reasonable. You'll receive compensation for broken material. Count on number 6.

Wednesday, September 26 (Moon in Sagittarius to Capricorn 1:37 p.m.) Don't be ashamed of being idealistic! Express your thoughts, stress romance, look to the future, and reject one who lacks faith and talent and is trying to pull you to a lower level. A short trip may involve a relative, could be necessary for the completion of a mission. Pisces and Virgo figure in today's exciting events. Play number 7 today.

Thursday, September 27 (Moon in Capricorn) The emphasis is on practicality and practical use of lessons learned within the past few weeks. You'll meet a hard-boiled person who talks about percentages, prices, odds, property value, long-range prospects. Aim high; deal with executives; assume greater responsibility for your own actions. A relationship intensifies!

Friday, September 28 (Moon in Capricorn) You'll finish an assignment, a burden will be lifted, and you'll receive answers to your proposals. Purchase or sale of property, including your home, could be part of the scenario. A lost love could return—be aware, alert, sensitive, and protect yourself in the emotional clinches. Aries and another Libra play significant roles. The lucky number is 9.

Saturday, September 29 (Moon in Capricorn to Aquarius 12:54 a.m.) Facts and figures, previously hidden, will come to light. You'll be surprised, but you'll actually gain as result. Check safety measures in your automobile, residence. Be especially wary about electrical outlets. A problem with refrigeration is possible unless you take proper precautions. Consult an Aquarian.

Sunday, September 30 (Moon in Aquarius) A reunion is indicated with a young person. Today's scenario highlights the excitement of discovery, creativity, style, romance. Be ready for change, travel, variety, a possible challenge to your integrity. Stick to your principles, avoid snap decisions despite urgings by a Cancer, Capricorn, or Aquarius.

OCTOBER 1990

Monday, October 1 (Moon in Aquarius to Pisces 8:43 a.m.) You could be amazed at the liveliness of this Monday! Today features physical attraction, creative skills, compliments from people you respect. You'll have a chance for a fresh start and you'll be on target in connection with money and love. Stress independence, style, initiative, and determination. The lucky number is 1.

Tuesday, October 2 (Moon in Pisces) Attention centers around basic issues, employment, home, security, money relating to young persons. A relative seeks to make amends for a recent error. Be gracious, generous, and don't cast the first stone. Cancer and Capricorn figure prominently. Gourmet dining is on tap for tonight.

Wednesday, October 3 (Moon in Pisces to Aries 12:42 p.m.) What had been settled could now appear to fall apart. This involves work procedures, dependents, promises relating to trips and relatives. Keep your sense of fitness and humor. Highlight versatility; look beyond the immediate; open lines of communication. Gemini and Sagittarius figure prominently.

Thursday, October 4 (Moon in Aries) The full moon position coincides with a creative urge, romance, and mental and physical stimulation. The lunar emphasis falls on an area relating to your partnership, public relations, contracts, marriage. Stand tall for your principles. Protect your reputation and credit rating. Taurus, Leo, and Scorpio play roles. Today's number is 4.

Friday, October 5 (Moon in Aries to Taurus 2:06 p.m.) A dialogue is featured with one whose ideas may conflict with your own. Focus on creativity, reading and writing, change and travel. You'll have a variety of experiences, some involving members of the opposite sex. What begins as a flirtation could culminate in something serious. Gemini and Virgo play dynamic roles.

Saturday, October 6 (Moon in Taurus) Lucky numbers: 6, 16, 2, 4, 13, 33. You'll learn more about the financial status of someone who recently made bizarre claims. The key is to dig deep to check your source material, to realize that money is involved and someone wants something for nothing with you being the prime target. Check accounting methods.

Sunday, October 7 (Moon in Taurus to Gemini 2:47 p.m.) Define terms, recognize spiritual values, realize that a mystery will soon be solved and this will be to your advantage. Today's emphasis also falls on beauty, music, sculpture, a reunion with a loved one. Plans made last May could now bear fruit. A clandestine maneuver could directly involve you and a Pisces.

Monday, October 8 (Moon in Gemini) A good lunar aspect coincides with philosophy, theology, or dissemination of pertinent information. Today's scenario also features creativity, communication, publishing, higher education. There's a possible journey on the agenda. You'll be asked to meet deadline. And as a relationship intensifies you'll also learn exactly where you stand in the arena of love.

Tuesday, October 9 (Moon in Gemini to Cancer 4:30 p.m.) A promise made yesterday can now be fulfilled. Limitations are removed; you'll have a chance to regain your sense of purpose and direction. You'll reach more people; a search will be concluded; love will be highlighted. You'll meet a lively person who stimulates your intellect and provides inspiration. A Gemini is featured.

Wednesday, October 10 (Moon in Cancer) Hot daily double numbers: 1 and 4 and 2 and 3. Focus on career, business, prestige, the possibility of a promotion. A superior is now willing to make a concession; it turns out your views have been verified and you'll get credit that had been withheld. Stress independence without being arrogant. A Leo is involved.

Thursday, October 11 (Moon in Cancer to Leo 8:17 p.m.) Follow through on a hunch; teach and learn; agree to a reunion with a family member. Focus on moods, psychic impressions, and your ability to sense trends and cycles. You'll be dealing with someone who is protective and does have your best interests at heart. Cancer, Taurus, and Capricorn figure prominently.

Friday, October 12 (Moon in Leo) Today's emphasis is on versatility, humor, and your ability to win friends and influence important people. Tensions are removed; your performance will be rated outstanding. You'll have luck in matters of speculation. A romantic interlude lends spice. Financial gain comes as result of business or career activity. Contact a Sagittarian.

Saturday, October 13 (Moon in Leo) Be willing to revise, review and seriously consider the possibility of relocating. Horizons broaden, new friendships are featured, and a relationship which had been mild could now turn hot. Check your basic requirements, especially those involving license and taxes. Study the fine print and read between the lines.

Sunday, October 14 (Moon in Leo to Virgo 2:21 a.m.) Be discriminating, analytical, and willing to discern motives. Go after the truth, and let the chips fall where they may. You'll make significant discoveries by doing some private detective work. As the cycle moves up, you'll learn secrets, you'll have access to information previously prohibited. The lucky number is 5.

Monday, October 15 (Moon in Virgo) A major domestic adjustment could include an actual change of residence or marital status. Much that occurs is behind the scenes. Be discreet; play cards close to your chest; don't tell all. Be diplomatic, and realize a very special person needs encouragement and affection. Number 8 is best for you.

Tuesday, October 16 (Moon in Virgo to Libra 10:27 a.m.) Define terms, keep an open mind but avoid being gullible. A sly person feels you are vulnerable in connection with flattery. Know it; steer away from this obsequious person. Focus on glamour, mystery, intrigue, a tendency toward deception. Pisces and Virgo play significant roles. Count on number 7.

Wednesday, October 17 (Moon in Libra) Lucky numbers: 4, 8, 37, 45, 19, 12. Today features added responsibility and pressure coinciding with an intensified love relationship. You'll be dealing with older persons, mainly men. You'll be in a position of authority and many will rely upon you to call the signals, especially Cancer and Capricorn.

Thursday, October 18 (Moon in Libra to Scorpio 8:24 p.m.) The new moon in your sign coincides with personality, originality, innovation, and ability to reach beyond your previous limitations. You get a fresh start; your appeals are granted, and your search for the ideal person could be successfully concluded. As a burden is lifted, you'll be rid of a losing proposition. The lucky number today is 9.

Friday, October 19 (Moon in Scorpio) Someone you recently met provided reliable data and as result you earn more money. Focus on payments, collections, and increased income. A special note—you will locate an article recently lost, missing, or stolen. Today's scenario also highlights physical attraction, soul-searching, questions about a long-standing relationship.

Saturday, October 20 (Moon in Scorpio) Pay attention to your family and take security measures now. You'll have a serious discussion about your life-style and budget. You'll receive favorable notices in the form of reviews or publicity. You'll also receive good news about a domestic adjustment or possible purchase of a furniture or automobile. A Cancer is involved.

Sunday, October 21 (Moon in Scorpio to Sagittarius 8:10 a.m.) Review resolutions about diet, nutrition and general health. As your popularity increases, social activities accelerate. You'll be more aware of your appearance, wardrobe, weight, and body image. A social invitation could involve a journey. Check legal papers, including your passport. Gemini and Sagittarius persons figure prominently. The lucky number is 3.

Monday, October 22 (Moon in Sagittarius) You could be the master of all you survey! Today's emphasis is on determination. Be willing to create your own traditions. You will take greater charge of your own fate. The scenario features money, romance, creativity, style, sensuality, sex appeal. Taurus, Leo, and Scorpio figure prominently. Stick with number 6.

Tuesday, October 23 (Moon in Sagittarius to Capricorn 9:03 p.m.) A close relative, possibly a brother or sister, decides to cooperate and helps you analyze your current situation. Focus on motivation, hidden meanings, subtle moves. Someone wants to tell you something. Be aware, alert, and sensitive to trends and cycles. Gemini, Virgo, and Sagittarius people play key roles.

Wednesday, October 24 (Moon in Capricorn) What had been regarded as moribund is again alive and kicking. This includes a real estate transaction, domestic adjustment, and personal possessions, or the possible purchase or sale of an art object, luxury item, or major household appliance. A relative makes a major concession which includes a gift. Taurus is involved. Try number 6 again.

Thursday, October 25 (Moon in Capricorn) A dichotomy exists—two persons are involved. One advocates a practical course. Another, whom you also respect, talks about fantasy and illusion, an unorthodox procedure that leaves no room for the middle ground. The key is to clarify meanings, to be sure terms are legal, to be positive about rights and permissions.

Friday, October 26 (Moon in Capricorn to Aquarius 9:14 a.m.) Deal with practical matters, household items, design and structure, architectural plans. Reject any superficial explanation. Go after the truth, realizing that justice is on your side. The emphasis falls on reality, an intensified relationship, a test of your ability to meet a deadline. A Capricorn is involved. The lucky number is 8.

Saturday, October 27 (Moon in Aquarius) You have a rare opportunity to put your ideas across in a creative, dynamic, and entertaining way. Focus on your charisma, personality, and sex appeal. The emphasis also falls on romance, variety, travel, increased social activity. A young person has a change of heart and will become an important ally. Aries and another Libra figure prominently.

Sunday, October 28 (Moon in Aquarius to Pisces 6:22 p.m.) Be direct, take the initiative, insist on getting to the heart of matters. A special note—avoid heavy lifting. You'll be dealing with young, vigorous people who are stubborn, dedicated and seek your guidance. Take greater charge of your own destiny, protect your possessions, give logic equal time with impulse. You can count on number 1.

Monday, October 29 (Moon in Pisces) What had been misplaced will be recovered. It's another day for taking care of practical matters, health, pets. People rely upon your generosity. Additional funds come as the result of a recent creative project. You'll have special success in communicating to the public, especially women. A Cancer plays a paramount role. The lucky number is 4.

Tuesday, October 30 (Moon in Pisces to Aries 11:15 p.m.) Hot number combinations: 1 and 2 and 4 and 3. Look beyond the immediate; expand your horizons; insist on more working room. You are going places following an initial delay. You'll receive a gift representing an addition to your wardrobe. The emphasis falls on humor, versatility, curiosity, and awareness of your body image. A Gemini is involved.

Wednesday, October 31 (Moon in Aries) The lunar position accents public appearances and ability to get on more solid financial-emotional ground. Some spirited people will act as if this indeed is a major holiday. You'll be offered, among other things, an abundance of pumpkin pie and whipped cream. Taurus, Leo, and Scorpio are on hand. Your best bet is number 4.

NOVEMBER 1990

Thursday, November 1 (Moon in Aries) Attention centers around a reunion, partnership, family structure, your marital status. You'll receive favorable notices. What had been missing will be recovered; this includes a legal document. Success is indicated in dealings with the public, especially women. Contact Cancer and Capricorn. The lucky number is 2.

Friday, November 2 (Moon in Aries to Taurus 12:32 a.m.) Examine various possibilities, realize money is at stake. Someone may want to get more than a fair share. The full moon position relates to the financial status of your partner or mate. The emphasis also falls on the creative urge, sensuality, a secret affair of the heart. Gemini has much to say. Number 3 is best for you.

Saturday, November 3 (Moon in Taurus) Be willing to tear down for the ultimate purpose of rebuilding on a different structure. The emphasis falls on popularity, financial status, ability to deal with one who is sensual, stubborn, attractive, and somewhat selfish. Guard your possessions, check insurance policies. Taurus, Cancer, and Scorpio figure prominently. Pick number 4 today.

Sunday, November 4 (Moon in Taurus to Gemini 12:06 a.m.) Open lines of communication; realize a young person could become a valuable ally. The emphasis falls on spiritual values, language, and distance. You have a serious discussion about a possible overseas journey on a publishing assignment. The day also favors change, variety, flirtation, and gain through creative endeavors.

Monday, November 5 (Moon in Gemini) You are not satisfied with the status quo and now you'll do something about it. The Mars position emphasizes contracts and special agreements. You'll profit through reading, writing, education, communication with one at a distance. A significant domestic adjustment relates to your life-style and personal surroundings.

Tuesday, November 6 (Moon in Gemini to Cancer 12:08 a.m.) Define meanings, get rid of superfluous material, streamline techniques, and realize that business or career advancement is strongly indicated. A mysterious ally is in the picture, will help open doors and introduce you to very important people. A romantic clandestine meeting could involve a Pisces.

Wednesday, November 7 (Moon in Cancer) Lucky numbers: 48, 49, 2, 11, 32, 33. You'll have more responsibility and a chance for greater financial reward. As a relationship intensifies, you'll learn where you stand and how far you can go. You'll be asked to meet a deadline, responsibilities increase, a professional superior recognizes your capabilities and puts it in writing.

Thursday, November 8 (Moon in Cancer to Leo 2:24 a.m.) Finish what you start, broaden horizons, accept an invitation that could include travel. Take notes, realize your own diary or memoirs can prove very important in the future. Focus now on reaching more persons, realizing you are capable of winning friends and successfully using your powers of persuasion. Your best number is 9.

Friday, November 9 (Moon in Leo) You recently complained about a lack of spice, zest, enthusiasm. Today you get more than your share! The emphasis falls on sensuality, and popularity. You can realize some fond hopes and wishes. Money comes from a surprise source which helps boost your morale. Leo, Aquarius, and another Libra figure prominently. The lucky number is 1.

Saturday, November 10 (Moon in Leo to Virgo 7:49 a.m.) You may be dealing with someone who is double-dealing. Check your references; be positive about your credit rating, source material, legal rights and permissions. The cycle remains high, and popularity continues on the rise. You could also be involved in a delightful flirtation or romance with a Cancer.

Sunday, November 11 (Moon in Virgo) Be analytical, discriminating, ready to choose quality. Focus on secrets, backstage maneuvers, a visit to a hospital or home. Give full rein to your curiosity, make inquiries, accept a social invitation that could include a fashion show. You'll be more aware of your own wardrobe, appearance, body image. Stick with number 3.

Monday, November 12 (Moon in Virgo to Libra 4:09 p.m.) You may feel tied up, but apparent red tape representing rules and regulations will actually work in your favor. Read between the lines; be aware of subtle nuances. Someone is attempting to tell you something of value about your personal possessions, and finances. Scorpio plays a role.

Tuesday, November 13 (Moon in Libra) The moon in your sign accents your ability to be at the right place at the crucial moment. Today's scenario highlights excitement, variety, discovery, and a strong love relationship. Curb any tendency to act strictly on impulse. Protect yourself in the emotional clinches; realize your own worth; let others know you are not without allies.

Wednesday, November 14 (Moon in Libra) The emphasis falls on personality, charm, appearance, and ability to win your way. Heed your own counsel, realize that your judgment and intuition will prove accurate. Someone who previously was indifferent will not show intense interest. You'll receive a gift from a relative on a peace-making mission. A Taurus is involved.

Thursday, November 15 (Moon in Libra to Scorpio 2:40 a.m.) Look beyond the immediate, realize you have much to learn about money and love. But you not only will learn, you'll definitely profit from recent lessons and experiences. What had been lost, missing, or stolen can be recovered. Your income potential is brighter than you anticipated. Play number 7, today.

Friday, November 16 (Moon in Scorpio) Hot number combinations: 8 and 2 and 4 and 1. Dig deep for information; realize someone of the opposite sex is attracted but there are some legal implications which make sudden, impulsive moves very unwise. Be positive about restrictions, rules, regulations, and tax and license requirements. Capricorn is in the picture.

Saturday, November 17 (Moon in Scorpio to Sagittarius 2:40 p.m.) The new moon position represents an opportunity to renew acquaintances, to review financial procedures, to reunite with one who inspired you intellectually and physically. The focus also falls on payments, collections, and fresh credit rating. You have a rare chance to begin again, to make amends to those who have faith in your plans, theories, and operations.

Sunday, November 18 (Moon in Sagittarius) You'll be on the move, pursuing an idea that could develop into a viable concept. A short trip is featured; you'll make a discovery; you'll also make a fresh start in a different direction. A new love could be on horizon. A Leo attempts to show you the light. Number 1 is a winner.

Monday, November 19 (Moon in Sagittarius)
Gather information, put puzzle pieces together, realize a relative who is sincere could also be confused. Keep your sense of humor. A long-distance call verifies your views and could ultimately result in a journey. A family gathering could feature ethnic food. Cancer and Capricorn play significant roles.

Tuesday, November 20 (Moon in Sagittarius to Capricorn 3:32 a.m.) You'll be with someone who has your best interests at heart. A frank discussion about family, home, and security will be featured. Long-range prospects will be clarified; you'll learn where you stand and what to do about it. Your present concept lacks solidity—review and rebuild. A Sagittarian offers good advice.

Wednesday, November 21 (Moon in Capricorn)
Check sources, be aware of design and structure, select durability. You'll consider buying a major household product. A real bargain is available if you insist on proper display, test, guarantee. You'll meet someone who at first appears disagreeable but could actually become an enthusiastic supporter.

Thursday, November 22 (Moon in Capricorn to Aquarius 4:07 p.m.) You'll have plenty to be thankful for; a family member whose health had been in question is well on the road to recovery. Be ready for change, travel, variety. A communication could involve a future journey. Realize also that a clash of ideas can be stimulating and not necessarily the cause of an argument.

Friday, November 23 (Moon in Aquarius) Give full play to your intellectual curiosity; strive to please a relative who recently helped you during a time of stress. The spotlight falls on children, variety, sensuality, and sex appeal. Imprint style, combine security with adventure. Today's scenario highlights music, flowers, and beauty. Realize that your relationship is back on track.

Saturday, November 24 (Moon in Aquarius) A good lunar aspect coincides with speculation, physical attraction, personal magnetism, and ability to be where the action is. A secret meeting takes place, lends spice and helps confirm ideas. You'll have access to inside information, and you'll learn just where the strings are attached. Virgo will figure prominently.

Sunday, November 25 (Moon in Aquarius to Pisces 2:32 a.m.) What seemed a lost opportunity will rebound in your favor. You'll be presented with facts and figures and asked to meet a deadline. A relationship that appeared to be finished receives a spark of life. This is to be a day of discovery, rediscovery, revamping, reviving, causing the apparently lifeless to again be alive and kicking. Play number 8 to win.

Monday, November 26 (Moon in Pisces) Someone attempts to stretch your credulity. Keep an open mind but avoid being gullible. Check legal papers, including your passport. Be aware of the location of your driver's license and birth certificate. The emphasis is on employment, basic issues, dependents, and people who rely upon your intuition and judgment. The health report is good.

Tuesday, November 27 (Moon in Pisces to Aries 9:07 a.m.) A pet, recently ill or injured, will recover. Your own psychic impressions are on target; you'll discover chicanery and be commended for it. A fresh light is thrown on a problem that had been vexing and annoying, creating an aura of tension. You'll know what to do, how to do it, you'll also make contact with someone who knows plenty about repairs, safety, and security.

Wednesday, November 28 (Moon in Aries) The current cycle emphasizes cooperation, joint efforts, partnership, legal agreement, and marital status. You'll be more aware of public relations, popularity, your image and appearance. You could be asked to attend an autograph party. A woman celebrity actually pays you a meaningful compliment. Cancer is the sign to watch.

Thursday, November 29 (Moon in Aries to Taurus 11:38 a.m.) Dig deep for information, make inquiries and double-check your legal rights and limits. You'll be concerned about one close to you in the matter of marriage. Call and write; open lines of communication; add to your wardrobe; prepare for a journey. Gemini and Sagittarius are in your life now. The lucky number is 3.

Friday, November 30 (Moon in Taurus) Hot number combinations: 2 and 6 and 4 and 3. Look for underlying motives; analyze character. Be sure about the facts before you make any promises in writing, sign deeds, or notarize public documents. Someone who seemed indifferent may know more than you are currently aware. A Taurus figures prominently.

DECEMBER 1990

Saturday, December 1 (Moon in Taurus to Gemini 11:23 a.m.) You could meet a sour cynic who, after a furtive glance over his shoulder, confides that he would appreciate a loan. Protect your own credit rating; overcome any impulse to co-sign. Open lines of communication; maintain a sense of fitness and humor. Gemini and Sagittarius play outstanding roles. Number 3 is best now.

Sunday, December 2 (Moon in Gemini) The full moon position accents your creative urge, idealism, romance, and recognition of spiritual values. The emphasis also falls on communication, travel, publishing, and understanding of long-range prospects. You'll break from tradition and feel a strong spirit of adventure. A Cancer makes waves now.

Monday, December 3 (Moon in Gemini to Cancer 10:28 a.m.) Lessons learned during the past 48 hours can now be put to practical use. Focus on speculation, added understanding of what you want and where to find it. You'll profit by writing, articulating your feelings, and trying your luck in number-choosing contests with 5.

Tuesday, December 4 (Moon in Cancer) Hot number combinations: 2 and 4 and 2 and 6. Funding is obtained, your career gets a boost, you'll receive a unique honor in recognition of recent participation in a political or charitable project. A domestic adjustment takes place, a family member seeks rapprochement. Taurus, Scorpio, and another Libra figure prominently.

Wednesday, December 5 (Moon in Cancer to Leo 11:01 a.m.) Play your cards close to your chest; trust your first impressions. You gain access, almost inadvertently, to inside information. Be discreet; keep an aura of mystery and glamour. A clandestine operation is featured where you'll gain recognition from an unusual source. Pisces and Virgo play roles. Stick with number 7.

Thursday, December 6 (Moon in Leo) You'll see through a ruse. An obsequious person wants something for nothing, possibly at your expense. But the cycle is such that you come out on top, you gain valuable allies, and you are capable now of transforming wishes into realities. A love relationship heats up, which boosts your confidence and provides an opportunity to hit the financial jackpot.

Friday, December 7 (Moon in Leo to Virgo 2:39 p.m.) The powerful influence continues to help you reach beyond previous limitations to win friends and influence important people. The spotlight also falls on romance, speculation, communication, an invitation to travel. Money comes as result of your career, business contacts, and activities. Aries will play a paramount role.

Saturday, December 8 (Moon in Virgo) Lucky numbers: 5, 26, 48, 8, 22, 18. You'll make a fresh start; light replaces darkness; you gain added knowledge; you'll realize a relationship that began as flirtation is being transformed into something serious.

Emphasize originality, independence, determination, the courage of your convictions.

Sunday, December 9 (Moon in Virgo to Libra 2:38 p.m.) You are likely to wax philosophical as you learn of the hospitalization of one close to you. Focus on meditation, a family reunion, intuition, regaining of confidence in connection with purpose, direction. Attention centers around your family, home, security, ability to deal with an older Capricorn woman.

Monday, December 10 (Moon in Libra) You'll have more working room now. Your popularity zooms upwards, which coincides with the moon in your sign. Your judgment, intuition is on target—circumstances take a sudden swing in your favor. Today's emphasis falls on communication, social activity, charm, grace, humor, more awareness of your appearance and body image. Gemini takes notice.

Tuesday, December 11 (Moon in Libra) You'll break from tradition; you'll learn more about practical issues, including tax and license requirements. A special note—verify legal rights and permissions. Study source material; read between the lines. Taurus, Leo, and Scorpio have much to offer. The lucky number is 4.

Wednesday, December 12 (Moon in Libra to Scorpio 8:28 a.m.) Be ready for change, travel, variety, and involvement with a Gemini or Virgo who is attractive but also restless and uncertain about inner feelings. Be analytical; protect yourself in the emotional clinches. Read and write, express feelings, communicate with a Sagittarius at a distance.

Thursday, December 13 (Moon in Scorpio) You have a valid opportunity to increase your income. Today's emphasis falls on payments, collections, music, flowers, charm, ability to attract someone who previously appeared indifferent. A special note—the odds are that you will recover an article recently lost, missing, or stolen. You'll receive a gift which represents a genuine token of affection.

Friday, December 14 (Moon in Scorpio to Sagittarius 8:44 p.m.) Clarify meanings, realize that delay does not necessarily equal loss. Money will be obtained, there will be an initial disappointment but you'll make up for this by finding something better. The cycle continues high; you'll be at the right place at a crucial moment. Pisces is in the picture. Number 7 is best.

Saturday, December 15 (Moon in Sagittarius) Contact made through a relative proves fruitful and profitable. You are likely to be involved in an intense relationship where you are given an ultimatum. It's time to make a decision about the future. You'll be dealing with older persons, especially men. A business venture could require a short trip.

Sunday, December 16 (Moon in Sagittarius) All stops are out where feelings, affection, and love enter the picture. Focus on relatives, communication, and ability to enlarge your horizons. A long-distance call could involve a social activity, possible travel. Check legal documents, including your passport. A recent family photograph could be the subject of conversation.

Monday, December 17 (Moon in Sagittarius to Capricorn 9:35 a.m.) Today's discussion centers around relatives, food, security, trips, visits, surprises. Focus on versatility and ability to make a fresh start in a different direction. The new moon coincides with reading, writing, travel, ability to put across ideas in a meaningful manner. A Sagittarian will play a paramount role.

Tuesday, December 18 (Moon in Capricorn) Your sense of prophesy surges to the forefront—you'll know the outcome of a transaction before it actually is finished. This applies especially to home, property, family, long-term agreements. Be aware of rules and regulations; realize there is no free lunch and you will get nothing for nothing. An Aquarian is involved. Play number 2 today.

Wednesday, December 19 (Moon in Capricorn)
Your bargaining position is strong, but don't force issues. Remain flexible, keep options open, combine social events with business. You can win your way; additional funds will be forthcoming; you'll have every right to celebrate tonight. Meantime, review resolutions about diet, nutrition, and general health.

Thursday, December 20 (Moon in Capricorn to Aquarius 9:59 p.m.) Hot number combinations: 2 and 1 and 4 and 3. A good lunar aspect coincides with speculation, sensuality, physical attraction, sex appeal. You achieve goal via unorthodox procedure. Someone who lacks faith attempts to discourage you. Be kind, but stand firm on principles. Scorpio plays a dynamic role.

Friday, December 21 (Moon in Aquarius) Discern motives; realize a relationship, although temporarily rocky, will right itself. Focus on change, travel, variety, flirtation, speculation, self-expression. You'll be enthusiastic, creative, confident, and full of joie de vivre. Enjoy yourself with Gemini, Virgo, and Sagittarius this evening. Take a chance on number 5.

Saturday, December 22 (Moon in Aquarius to Pisces 8:48 a.m.) Focus on pleasure, feeling that you no longer are alone. A family gathering could be on today's agenda. You'll enjoy dancing, music, entertainment, and the company of children. Your charm and personal magnetism will be appreciated by Taurus, Leo, and Scorpio. Feel free to speculate on number 6.

Sunday, December 23 (Moon in Pisces) Spiritual values are emphasized, you learn more about the health of a relative, your own psychic impressions will prove accurate. Look behind the scenes, realize that what had been hidden will be revealed—much to your advantage. A lost love could communicate, creating mixed feelings. Number 9 is your best bet.

Monday, December 24 (Moon in Pisces to Aries 9:45 p.m.) The holiday spirit prevails, but also is mingled with commercialism. You could become self-critical and you might be worrying over nothing in connection with gifts, wardrobe, appearance, sensitivity of friends, relatives. Tensions created as a result of the holiday rush should not be permitted to create dissention with a loved one.

Tuesday, December 25 (Moon in Aries) Focus on promises, gifts, a spirit of cooperation, a clash of ideas, your marital status. A burden is removed; travel plans are clarified and a long-distance call brings excitement and apprehension. Love will be the dominant theme. You'll review a contract offer that could involve a partnership with an Aries.

Wednesday, December 26 (Moon in Aries to Taurus 9:09 p.m.) Children, initiative, and intellectual curiosity combine to make this a meaningful, memorable day. Stress determination, courage, your pioneering spirit. A path will be cleared for you to make a fresh start. For you, love will actually be many-splendored. Leo and Aquarius are supportive now.

Thursday, December 27 (Moon in Taurus) A visitor from out of town wants to share a New Year's Eve celebration. Be aware of your budget, but also realize that entertainment and fun need not depend on money alone. Plan ahead; be innovative; know that a Taurus will cooperate and that what appears to be a failure will boomerang in your favor.

Friday, December 28 (Moon in Taurus to Gemini 10:26 p.m.) A burden is lifted; a long-distance call verifies your views and puts you in the mood to celebrate. Attention centers around distance, purpose, wardrobe, general appearance, social activity, and body image. Some very lively, active, bright, alert people will be part of this stimulating scenario, including a Gemini.

Saturday, December 29 (Moon in Gemini) Restrictions are removed, you'll be free to speculate, to travel, to perceive your own potential. On this dramatic day, you'll reach more people; many will say,

"Where have you been all my life!" It's a time to express imagination, creativity, speculation, romance. Scorpio is involved.

Sunday, December 30 (Moon in Gemini to Cancer 10:03 p.m.) A long-distance call helps reunite the family. You'll speculate on the upcoming year; your own traditions are likely to be valid. Realize that one who had been distant will now be close. Be receptive without being maudlin. The meaning will be clear; a burden will be lifted, you'll feel mature but not old.

Monday, December 31 (Moon in Cancer) New Year's Eve coincides with confidence, communication with a professional superior, plans for business or career advancement. Stick to familiar ground, be moderate and wary of those who drink to excess. Focus on music, harmony, family relationships, receipt of a late gift. Another Libra figures prominently. The lucky number is 6.

About the Author

Born on August 5, 1926, in Philadelphia, Omarr was the only astrologer ever given full-time duty in the U.S. Army as an astrologer. He also is regarded as the most erudite astrologer of our time and the best-known, through his syndicated column (300 newspapers) and his radio and television programs (he is Merv Griffin's "resident astrologer"). Omarr has been called the most "knowledgeable astrologer since Evangeline Adams." His forecasts of Nixon's downfall, the end of World War II in mid-August of 1945, the assassination of John F. Kennedy, Roosevelt's election to a fourth term and his death in office . . . these and many others are on record and quoted enough to be considered "legendary."

About This Series

This is one of a series of
twelve Day-by-Day Astrological Guides
for the signs in 1990
by Sydney Omarr